# The American Revolution

CORE DOCUMENTS

# The American Revolution

~ CORE DOCUMENTS ~

*Selected and Introduced by*

Robert M. S. McDonald

ASHBROOK PRESS

Copyright © 2019 Ashbrook Center, Ashland University

Library of Congress Cataloging-in-Publication Data

The American Revolution: Core Documents
Selected and Introduced by Robert M. S. McDonald

1. United States—Politics and government.
ISBN 978-1-878802-51-4 (pbk.)

Cover images, above the title, left to right:
Gilbert Stuart, *John Adams*, c. 1821. National Gallery of Art, Alisa Mellon Bruce Fund, 1979.4.1.
Gilbert Stuart, *Abigail Smith Adams* (Mrs. John Adams), 1800/1815. National Gallery of Art, Gift of Mrs. Robert Homans, 1954.7.2.
Gilbert Stuart, *George Washington* (Vaughan Portrait), 1795. National Gallery of Art, Andrew W. Mellon Collection, 1942.8.27.
Joseph Siffred Duplessis, *Benjamin Franklin*, c. 1785. National Portrait Gallery, Smithsonian Institution; gift of the Morris and Gwendolyn Cafritz Foundation, NPG.87.43.
Gilbert Stuart, *Thomas Jefferson: The Edgehill Portrait*, c. 1805/1821. National Portrait Gallery, Smithsonian Institution; owned jointly with Monticello, Thomas Jefferson Foundation, Incorporated, Charlottesville, Virginia; purchase funds provided by the Regents of the Smithsonian Institution, the Trustees of the Thomas Jefferson Foundation, Incorporated, and the Enid and Crosby Kemper Foundation. NPG.82.97.

Cover image, below the title:
John Trumbull, *Surrender of Lord Cornwallis*, 1820. Rotunda of the US Capitol, Washington, DC. Architect of the Capitol.

Interior design/composition: Brad Walrod/Kenoza Type, Inc.

Ashbrook Center at Ashland University
401 College Avenue
Ashland, Ohio 44805
www.ashbrook.org

**ABOUT THE ASHBROOK CENTER**

The Ashbrook Center restores and strengthens the capacities of the American people for constitutional self-government. Ashbrook teaches students and teachers across our country what America is and what she represents in the long history of the world. Offering a variety of resources and programs, Ashbrook is the largest university-based educator in the enduring principles and practice of free government. Dedicated in 1983 by President Ronald Reagan, the Ashbrook Center is governed by its own board and responsible for raising all of the funds necessary for its many programs.

**BRING THE DOCUMENTS AND DEBATES OF THE NATION'S PAST INTO THE PRESENT**

Readers of this volume may be particularly interested in Ashbrook's Teaching American History programs which provide an opportunity for secondary educators to explore themes in American history and self-government through the study of original historical documents. Designed especially for teachers, our seminar-style programs are offered online and on location, both on our campus and at sites around the country. We use discussions, not lectures and texts, not textbooks, so that each seminar is a conversation among peers in which each attendee is an active participant in learning.

For more information, please visit us online at Ashbrook.org, TeachingAmericanHistory.org, and ReligionInAmerica.org.

# Contents

General Editor's Introduction ................................................................... xi
Introduction ................................................................................................. xiii

1 James Otis, Speech against Writs of Assistance, February 24, 1761 ..... 3
2 James Otis, "Rights of the British Colonies Asserted and Proved,"
   July 1764 ..................................................................................................... 8
3 Resolutions of the Stamp Act Congress, October 19, 1765 ................. 15
4 "A Farmer" (John Dickinson), "Letters from a Farmer in
   Pennsylvania, No. 2," December 10, 1767 ............................................. 18
5 Charleston Nonimportation Agreement, July 22, 1769 ....................... 22
6 Deacon John Tudor, An Account of the Boston Massacre,
   March 1770 ................................................................................................ 25
7 Samuel Adams, "The Rights of the Colonists," November 20, 1772 .... 29
8 "An Impartial Observer," Account of the Boston Tea Party,
   December 1773 .......................................................................................... 35
9 Gouverneur Morris, "We Shall be under the Domination of a
   Riotous Mob," May 20, 1774 .................................................................... 39
10 Thomas Jefferson, *A Summary View of the Rights of British
    America*, July 1774 .................................................................................... 42
11 Philadelphia Welcomes the First Continental Congress,
    September 16, 1774 ................................................................................... 53
12 Joseph Galloway, Plan of Union, September 28, 1774 ......................... 57
13 The Association Enacted by the First Continental Congress,
    October 20, 1774 ....................................................................................... 61
14 "A. W. Farmer" (Reverend Samuel Seabury), *A View of the
    Controversy Between Great-Britain and her Colonies*... (December
    24, 1774) ..................................................................................................... 66
15 "Friend to America" (Alexander Hamilton), *The Farmer Refuted*...,
    February 23, 1775 ...................................................................................... 70
16 Patrick Henry, "Give me liberty or give me death!," March 23, 1775 ... 75
17 John Andrews, Account of the Battles of Lexington and Concord,
    April 20, 1775 ............................................................................................ 79
18 John Dickinson and Thomas Jefferson, Declaration of the Causes
    and Necessity of Taking Up Arms, July 6, 1775 .................................... 82

vii

19 Lancaster County Committee of Correspondence and Observation, Resolution Regarding Quaker Pacifists, July 11, 1775 ... 87
20 Thomas Paine, *Common Sense*, January 1776 .............................. 90
21 Stratford, Connecticut's Thomas Gage—and Monmouth County, New Jersey's Dunmore, May 30, 1776 .......................................... 97
22 Abigail and John Adams, "Remember the Ladies," March 31–May 26, 1776 .................................................................................... 99
23 John Adams, *Thoughts on Government*, April 1776 ....................... 106
24 George Mason, Virginia Declaration of Rights, June 12, 1776 .......... 114
25 Thomas Jefferson, Draft of the Declaration of Independence, July 2–4, 1776 ................................................................................ 117
26 Celebrations of American Independence in Boston and Watertown, Massachusetts, July 18, 1776 .................................... 125
27 "Common Sense" (Thomas Paine), *The American Crisis*, December 23, 1776 .............................................................. 128
28 Prince Hall, et. al., Massachusetts Antislavery Petition, January 13, 1777 .................................................................................... 133
29 Private Hugh McDonald, The Continentals Encounter Civilians, December 1776–April 1777 ................................................. 135
30 Generals Gates and Burgoyne on the Murder of Jane McCrea, September 2–6, 1777 ............................................................. 138
31 Articles of Confederation, proposed November 15, 1777; ratified March 1, 1781 ........................................................................ 143
32 Private Joseph Plumb Martin, Foraging for Valley Forge, December 1777–April 1778 ................................................. 147
33 Lieutenant Colonel John Laurens, Envisioning an African American Regiment, February 2, 1778 ......................................... 154
34 Benjamin Franklin and the Marquis de Lafayette, List of Prints to Illustrate British Cruelties, ca. May 1779 ............................... 158
35 Eliza Wilkinson, Redcoats in South Carolina, June 1779 ............... 163
36 "Plain Truth," "To the Traitor General Arnold," September 25, 1781 .............................................................. 167
37 Dr. James Thacher, Account of the British Surrender at Yorktown, October 19, 1781 ................................................................... 170
38 Thomas Jefferson, *Notes on the State of Virginia*, 1781–1784 ............ 175
39 George Washington, The Newburgh Address, March 15, 1783 ......... 179
40 Captain Samuel Shaw, An Officer's Account of Washington's Remarks, April 1783 ............................................................ 184

**41** George Washington, Circular Letter to the States, June 8–21, 1783 ... 187
**42** Treaty of Paris, September 3, 1783 ............................................. 195
**43** Haym Salomon, et al., Petition of the Philadelphia Synagogue to the Council of Censors of Pennsylvania, December 23, 1783 .......... 202
**44** George Washington, Cincinnatus Reborn, December 23, 1783 ....... 206

APPENDIX A  Thematic Table of Contents ............................... 209
APPENDIX B  Discussion Questions ......................................... 217
APPENDIX C  Declaration of Independence ............................ 231
APPENDIX D  Constitution of the United States of America ......... 237
APPENDIX E  Suggestions for Further Reading ........................ 253

Illustrations follow page 142

# General Editor's Introduction

This volume is another in the Ashbrook Center's collection of primary document volumes covering major periods, themes, and institutions in American history and government. The documents in this volume explain the political, moral, social, and economic causes of the American Revolution, as well as its effects in those same realms.

When completed, the Ashbrook document collections will be a comprehensive and authoritative account of America's story, told in the words of those who wrote it—America's presidents, labor leaders, farmers, philosophers, industrialists, politicians, workers, explorers, religious leaders, judges, soldiers; its slaveholders and abolitionists; its expansionists and isolationists; its reformers and stand-patters; its strict and broad constructionists; its hard-eyed realists and visionary utopians—all united in their commitment to equality and liberty, yet all also divided often by their different understandings of these most fundamental American ideas. The documents are about all this—the still unfinished American experiment with self-government.

As this volume does, each of the volumes in the series will contain key documents on its period, theme, or institution, selected by an expert and reviewed by an editorial board. Each volume will have an introduction highlighting key documents and themes. In an appendix to each volume, there will also be a thematic table of contents, showing the connections between various documents. Another appendix will provide study questions for each document, as well as questions that refer to other documents in the collection, tying them together as the thematic table of contents does. Each document will be checked against an authoritative original source and have an introduction outlining its significance. We will provide notes to each document to identify people, events, movements, or ideas that may be unfamiliar to non-specialist readers and to improve understanding of the document's historical context. For the same reason, we have modernized spelling, punctuation, and most capitalization.

In sum, our intent is that the documents and their supporting material provide reliable and unique access to the richness of the American story.

Robert M. S. McDonald, Professor of History at the United States Military Academy, selected the documents and wrote the introductions. Holly Southern was the copyeditor. Ali Brosky and Ellen Tucker provided assistance with various aspects of the process. This publication was made possible through the support of a grant by the John Templeton Foundation. The opinions expressed in this publication are those of the editors and do not necessarily reflect the views of the John Templeton Foundation.

Sarah A. Morgan Smith<br>
General Editor and Fellow<br>
The Ashbrook Center

# Introduction

Captain John Parker, commander of the Lexington militia, had received Paul Revere's warning. Great Britain's Boston-based troops were due to pass through his Massachusetts town on their march to seize gunpowder, ammunition, and artillery pieces in nearby Concord. What Parker could not have known was how those Redcoats would react when, at dawn on April 19, 1775, his men stood in their way. "Don't fire unless fired upon," one of his compatriots heard him yell, "but if they mean to have a war, let it begin here!"

No one knows who first pulled a trigger, but no one disputes that eight of the nearly eighty Lexington militiamen—vastly outnumbered by several hundred British regulars—lost their lives that morning. Conflict at Concord a few hours later yielded a different outcome. The king's soldiers found few of the military supplies that had been their objective. Forced into retreat at the Old North Bridge, they began a perilous seventeen-mile journey back to Boston. As thousands of Massachusetts militiamen descended on their route, British casualties mounted. At Menotomy, Massachusetts, 80-year-old Samuel Whittemore stood ready to avenge British aggression with a musket, a pair of pistols, and a sword. As Redcoats marched along the road near his home, he took aim. He downed one British soldier and then another. Dropping his musket, he drew his pistols. He had shot a third Redcoat by the time a detachment of the regulars descended upon him, stabbing him thirteen times with their bayonets and shooting him in the face. As he flailed about with his sword they left him for dead. But Whittemore didn't die. He lived—for another 18 years. In 1793, he took his last breath as a 98-year-old citizen of the free and independent United States.

Parker's famous words—"if they mean to have a war, let it begin here"—helped mark the start of what eventually came to be known as the War for Independence. But people have long taken pains to distinguish this war, which concluded with the signing of the 1783 Treaty of Paris, from the less well-defined and potentially farther-reaching American Revolution. As John Adams wrote to Thomas Jefferson in 1815, "What do we mean by the Revolution? The war? That was no part of the Revolution. It was only an effect and consequence of it. The Revolution was in the minds of the people, and this," Adams insisted, took place "from 1760 to 1775, in the course of fifteen years before a drop of blood was drawn at Lexington." Although Adams believed that the real revolution had taken place before the war, Philadelphia physician Benjamin Rush, a fellow member of the Continental Congress, insisted that it would continue for years after the fighting had ended. "There is nothing more common," Rush wrote in 1787, "than to confound the terms of American Revolution with those of the late American war." But the war and the Revolution were not the same thing. "It remains yet to establish and perfect our new forms of government," Rush observed, "and to prepare the principles, morals, and manners of our citizens, for those forms of government after they are established and brought to perfection." This, the real revolution, had only just begun.

This volume features a selection of primary sources spanning 1760 to 1783. Some of these documents give voice to the sometimes competing philosophies of the Revolutionary generation. Others exemplify them. All originate from either the years of the war or the crucial period preceding the conflict, when "the minds of the people," as Adams wrote, took a decisive turn. Whittemore, a veteran of King George's War (1744–48) and the French and Indian War (1754–63), before taking aim at Redcoats had risked his life fighting alongside them. Similarly, the vast majority of Americans prior to 1760 felt proud of their British heritage. In the minds of American colonists, what made Britain the richest and most powerful of the world's nations was the fact that it was also the most free. This, for them, endured as the source of their British patriotism. As philosopher John Locke had explained when justifying the Glorious Revolution of 1688–89, only a government that protected the people's rights to life, liberty, and property could consider itself legitimate. Soon after the French and Indian War, however, Parliament approved a series of measures that jeopardized colonists' rights. Americans who resisted Britain's "long train of abuses and usurpations," as Jefferson's Declaration of Independence described it, had struggled to hold their government true to its own avowed principles. Only gradually and reluctantly did the belief that Britain had no intention of keeping its promises push Americans to secure these commitments independent of the British government's interference. In this sense the American revolutionaries were better Englishmen than their cousins across the Atlantic.

The conflict that commenced when Parker and his men stood their ground at Lexington tested the principles valued most by these once-loyal Britons. How to deal with those who remained loyal to the king? How best to bear the monetary costs? How to recruit and retain for the army men willing not only to defend, at a minute's notice, their homes and hometowns but also, for multiple years, distant parts of the new United States? Given their love of liberty and the revulsion they felt toward acts of coercion, the War for Independence posed a significant problem. Wars, which necessitate the concentration of force, require the centralization of power. How to defeat (or at least outlast) the world's most formidable military without creating an army posing a threat to the freedom it aimed to defend?

George Washington probably never wrote that government, "like fire, is a dangerous servant, and a fearsome master," but the fact that so many have never questioned this quotation's frequent attribution to him helps to explain his selection as commander of the Continental Army. The members of the Continental Congress recognized in him a multitude of qualifications. He had gained experience as a colonel in the French and Indian War. He possessed relative youth as well as social and physical stature. As a Virginian, he seemed well positioned to transform an army of New Englanders into a truly continental force. Maybe most important, since 1758 he had served in the House of Burgesses. Like them, he was a civilian legislator who understood the importance of civilian control of military power, which, if not properly directed, possessed the greatest potential to consume the people's liberty. He demonstrated respect for civilian leaders and urged his army's restraint when dealing with common citizens. Throughout the war, Washington addressed Congress in the most deferential terms. Near the end, he extinguished his officers' threatened insubordination against this legislative body and the states on whose authority it acted. After the conclusion of peace, Washington's decision to relinquish power, resign as commander-in-chief, and return to Mount Vernon as a private citizen reportedly prompted even George III to describe him as "the most distinguished of any man living" and "the greatest character of the age."

It was not just Washington's willingness to give up power that made the American Revolution a successful struggle for liberty. In addition to exhausting the will of Great Britain to wage war against them, the American revolutionaries transitioned from monarchy and aristocracy to republican government and an emerging spirit of democracy. Embracing representative government within and among the states, they coalesced around the principles that the people are sovereign and that popular consent is a precondition of political legitimacy. They had also internalized the rich lexicon of individual rights that had formed the basis of both their opposition to British imperial policy and their claim on independence. Yet if the "self-evident" "truths" that "all men are created equal, with certain unalienable rights" bolstered their confidence, at the same time, they troubled their collective conscience. What about women, African Americans, members of religious minorities, and other individuals denied their natural rights to life, liberty, and property? What about people denied civil rights bestowing equality under the law?

It is no coincidence that during the years of the War for Independence, people began to question why rights that were said to belong to all mankind were not recognized as the inheritance of all Americans. But it is also no surprise that the Founders' generation—the first to notice the conflict between their newly-expanded principles and their practices reflecting deeply-entrenched prejudices—was not the last to struggle to keep the promises of the Declaration of Independence. Even before the war's conclusion, northern states began either to abolish slavery or to enact plans for gradual emancipation. Soon after, Congress halted the expansion of slavery to parts of the West, and Jefferson, as president in 1807, championed and signed a bill outlawing America's participation in the international slave trade.

In the decades to follow, the issue of slavery became even more central. So did the rights of women, and the voting rights of men who did not own land. Even today, in the United States and around the world, oppressed groups and individuals invoke the philosophies of the American Revolution. As Benjamin Rush predicted in 1787, "the American war is over, but this is far from being the case with the American Revolution. On the contrary, nothing but the first act of the great drama is closed."

In some ways the Revolution would extend far beyond the conclusion of the War for Independence. A few days prior to the fiftieth anniversary of the adoption of his Declaration, Thomas Jefferson observed that "all eyes are opened, or opening, to the rights of man." He expressed his faith that the decision of the Continental Congress to separate from Great Britain would continue to inspire people "to burst the chains under which monkish ignorance and superstition had persuaded them to bind themselves, and to assume the blessings and security of self-government." Awakening the world to the proposition that "the mass of mankind has not been born with saddles on their backs, nor a favored few booted and spurred, ready to ride them, legitimately, by the grace of God," the ideas of the American Revolution could eventually bring liberty to everyone, everywhere, not only in the United States but also around the globe. The freedom for which Americans had stood their ground would come "to some parts sooner" and "to others later." But eventually, Jefferson predicted, real liberty would one day be enjoyed by all.

*Acknowledgments:* A number of friends either suggested documents included in this collection or tracked down information helping me to contextualize them. I am grateful for the assistance of Jeremy Bailey, Veronica Burchard, Benjamin Carp, Mickey Craig, Joe Dooley, Todd Estes, Mary-Jo Kline, Stuart Leibiger, Melanie Miller, Rob Parkinson, Richard Samuelson, and Brian Steele. Sean Sculley performed both these tasks and also reviewed all of the documents' introductions. Sarah Morgan Smith, who served as series editor, lent her considerable expertise to the selection of documents and execution of the finished product. Caleb Cage helped to deepen my appreciation for people who, in the midst of war, share their stories for the benefit of others, present and future. Jefferson McDonald and Grace McDonald helped select illustrations. Christine Coalwell McDonald, a historian in her own right, offered unfailing encouragement and assisted in every way possible.

Robert M. S. McDonald

# The American Revolution

CORE DOCUMENTS

DOCUMENT 1

# Speech Against Writs of Assistance

James Otis

February 24, 1761

By 1760 the British seemed poised for victory in the French and Indian War. But as the expense of the war weighed on the British treasury, Parliament eyed the North American colonies as a source of revenue. To increase the payment of taxes on imports and curtail rampant smuggling, customs officials sought renewal of their writs of assistance, which authorized them to enter and search individuals' homes, ships, shops, and warehouses unannounced and without warrants.

Massachusetts lawyer James Otis (1725–1783) so firmly embraced the principle that "a man's house is his castle" that he resigned as his colony's Admiralty Court advocate general when pressed to defend the writs of assistance. Considering them a violation of "one of the most essential branches of English liberty," he served as attorney for a group of merchants challenging the writs. In a case heard by the Massachusetts Superior Court, Otis spoke for nearly five hours. John Adams, who was in the audience, took notes on Otis's remarks.

Although Otis lost the case, his passionate opposition to the writs launched his career as a leading critic of British imperial policy. In May 1761, Bostonians elected him to represent them in the legislature. He helped orchestrate resistance to the 1765 Stamp Act and 1767 Townshend Acts. In 1769, however, a tax collector clubbed him in the head during a barroom brawl, prompting (or exacerbating) a mental illness that continued until 1783, when he was struck by lightning and died. Adams considered Otis a great patriot, perhaps "the greatest orator" of his era, and "a man whom none who ever knew him, can ever forget."

SOURCE: John Adams's Reconstruction of Otis's Speech in the Writs of Assistance Case, in *The Collected Political Writings of James Otis*, ed. Richard A. Samuelson (Indianapolis: Liberty Fund, 2015), 11–14. http://oll.libertyfund.org/titles/2703

---

MAY IT PLEASE YOUR HONORS,

I was desired by one of the Court to look into the books, and consider the question now before them concerning writs of assistance. I have accordingly

3

considered it, and now appear, not only in obedience to your order, but likewise in behalf of the inhabitants of this town, who have presented another petition, and out of regard to the liberties of the subject. And I take this opportunity to declare, that whether under a fee or not (for in such a cause as this I despise a fee) I will to my dying day oppose with all the powers and faculties God has given me, all such instruments of slavery on the one hand, and villainy on the other, as this writ of assistance is.

It appears to me the worst instrument of arbitrary power, the most destructive of English liberty and the fundamental principles of law, that ever was found in an English law book. I must, therefore, beg your honors' patience and attention to the whole range of an argument, that may perhaps appear uncommon in many things, as well as to points of learning that are more remote and unusual; that the whole tendency of my design may the more easily be perceived, the conclusions better discerned, and the force of them be better felt. I shall not think much of my pains in this cause, as I engaged in it from principle. I was solicited to argue this cause as advocate general; and because I would not, I have been charged with desertion from my office. To this charge I can give a very sufficient answer. I renounced that office, and I argue this cause, from the same principle; and I argue it with the greater pleasure, as it is in favor of British liberty, at a time when we hear the greatest monarch upon earth declaring from his throne that he glories in the name of Briton, and that the privileges of his people are dearer to him than the most valuable prerogatives of his crown; and as it is in opposition to a kind of power, the exercise of which, in former periods of English history, cost one king of England his head,[1] and another his throne.[2] I have taken more pains in this cause, than I ever will take again, although my engaging in this and another popular cause has raised much resentment. But I think I can sincerely declare, that I cheerfully submit myself to every odious name for conscience's sake; and from my soul I despise all those, whose guilt, malice, or folly has made them my foes. Let the consequences be what they will, I am determined to proceed. The only principles of public conduct, that are worthy of a gentleman or a man, are to sacrifice estate, ease, health, and applause, and even life to the sacred calls of his country. These manly sentiments, in private life, make the good citizen; in public life, the patriot and the hero. I do not say, that when brought to the test, I shall be invincible. I pray God I

---

[1] Charles I (1600–1649) served as king from 1625 until his execution in 1649.
[2] James II (1633–1701) served as king from 1685 until his ouster during the Glorious Revolution of 1688.

SPEECH AGAINST WRITS OF ASSISTANCE

may never be brought to the melancholy trial; but if ever I should, it will be then known how far I can reduce to practice principles, which I know to be founded in truth. In the mean time I will proceed to the subject of this writ.

In the first place, may it please your honors, I will admit that writs of one kind may be legal; that is, special writs, directed to special officers, and to search certain houses, etc., specially set forth in the writ, may be granted by the Court of Exchequer at home, upon oath made before the lord treasurer by the person who asks it, that he suspects such goods to be concealed in those very places he desires to search. The act of 14 Charles II, which Mr. Gridley[3] mentions, proves this. And in this light the writ appears like a warrant from a Justice of the Peace to search for stolen goods. Your honors will find in the old books concerning the office of a justice of the peace, precedents of general warrants to search suspected houses. But in more modern books you will find only special warrants to search such and such houses specially named, in which the complainant has before sworn that he suspects his goods are concealed; and you will find it adjudged that special warrants only are legal. In the same manner I rely on it, that the writ prayed for in this petition, being general, is illegal. It is a power that places the liberty of every man in the hands of every petty officer. I say I admit that special writs of assistance, to search special places, may be granted to certain person on oath; but I deny that the writ now prayed for can be granted, for I beg leave to make some observations on the writ itself, before I proceed to other acts of Parliament. In the first place, the writ is universal, being directed "to all and singular Justices, Sheriffs, Constables, and all other officers and subjects"; so, that, in short, it is directed to every subject in the king's dominions. Everyone with this writ may be a tyrant; if this commission be legal, a tyrant in a legal manner also may control, imprison, or murder anyone within the realm. In the next place, it is perpetual; there is no return. A man is accountable to no person for his doings. Every man may reign secure in his petty tyranny, and spread terror and desolation around him. In the third place, a person with this writ, in the daytime, may enter all houses, shops, etc., at will, and command all to assist him. Fourthly, by this writ not only deputies, etc., but even their menial servants, are allowed to lord it over us. Now one of the most essential branches of English liberty is the freedom of one's house. A man's house is his castle; and while he is quiet, he is as well guarded as a prince in his castle. This writ, if it should be declared legal, would totally annihilate

---

[3] Massachusetts lawyer Jeremiah Gridley (1702–1767) represented the government in this case.

this privilege. Custom-house officers may enter our houses, when they please; we are commanded to permit their entry. Their menial servants may enter, may break locks, bars, and everything in their way; and whether they break through malice or revenge, no man, no court, can inquire. Bare suspicion without oath is sufficient. This wanton exercise of this power is not a chimerical suggestion of a heated brain. I will mention some facts. Mr. Pue[4] had one of these writs, and when Mr. Ware[5] succeeded him, he endorsed this writ over to Mr. Ware; so that these writs are negotiable from one officer to another; and so your Honors have no opportunity of judging the person to whom this vast power is delegated. Another instance is this: Mr. Justice Walley[6] had called this same Mr. Ware before him, by a constable, to answer for a breach of Sabbath-day acts, or that of profane swearing. As soon as he had finished, Mr. Ware asked him if he had done. He replied, Yes. Well then, said Mr. Ware, I will show you a little of my power. I command you to permit me to search your house for uncustomed goods.[7] And [Ware] went on to search his house from the garret to the cellar; and then served the constable in the same manner. But to show another absurdity in this writ; if it should be established, I insist upon it, every person by the [act of the] 14[th year of the reign of] Charles II has this power as well as custom-house officers. The words are, "It shall be lawful for any person or persons authorized," etc. What a scene does this open! Every man, prompted by revenge, ill humor, or wantonness, to inspect the inside of his neighbor's house, may get a writ of assistance. Others will ask it from self-defence; one arbitrary exertion will provoke another, until society be involved in tumult and in blood.

Again, these writs are not returned. Writs in their nature are temporary things. When the purposes for which they are issued are answered, they exist no more; but these live forever; no one can be called to account. Thus reason and the constitution are both against this writ. Let us see what authority there is for it. Not more than one instance can be found of it in all our law books; and that was in the zenith of arbitrary power namely in the reign of Charles II, when star-chamber powers were pushed to extremity by some ignorant clerk of the exchequer. But had this writ been in any book whatever,

---

[4] Jonathan Pue (died 1760) served as surveyor of customs for the Port of Salem.
[5] Nathaniel Ware (died 1767) served as comptroller of customs from 1750 to 1764 for the Port of Boston.
[6] Abiel Walley (1710–1759) in 1740 became justice of the quorum of Suffolk County, Massachusetts.
[7] Uncustomed: not having passed through customs; smuggled.

it would have been illegal. All precedents are under the control of the principles of law. Lord Talbot says it is better to observe these than any precedents, though in the House of Lords, the last resort of the subject. No acts of Parliament can establish such a writ; though it should be made in the very words of the petition, it would be void. An act against the constitution is void.... But these prove no more than what I before observed, that special writs may be granted *on oath and probable suspicion.* The act of 7 and 8 William III that the officers of the plantations shall have the same powers, etc., is confined to this sense; that an officer should show probable ground; should take his oath of it; should do this before a magistrate; and that such magistrate, if he think proper, should issue a special warrant to a constable to search the places.

DOCUMENT 2

# Rights of the British Colonies Asserted and Proved

James Otis

*July 1764*

Boston lawyer James Otis (1725–1783) made a name for himself as a leading critic of British imperial policy. In 1761, he had opposed as unjust and unconstitutional British officials' searches and seizures of colonists' property by declaring that "a man's house is his castle." In his 1764 pamphlet, Rights of the British Colonies Asserted and Proved, *he explained why taxation without representation amounted to tyranny. Making use of principles spelled out in the* Two Treatises of Government, *written in 1689 by John Locke (1632–1704), which helped to legitimize the Glorious Revolution of 1688–89 and a line of British monarchs stretching from William and Mary to George III, Otis reminded readers that individual rights were a gift from God and not governments, whose duty it was to acknowledge and protect them. He argued that the property of British Americans could only be taxed by Parliament if colonists enjoyed representation in London. His pamphlet helped to clarify Americans' beliefs, positioning them to oppose the 1765 Stamp Act and 1767 Townshend Acts.*

SOURCE: *Rights of the British Colonies Asserted and Proved*, in *The Collected Political Writings of James Otis*, ed. Richard A. Samuelson (Indianapolis: Liberty Fund, 2015), 124–28, 141, 145–8, 152, 155–6, 158, 169–70. https://oll.libertyfund.org/titles/2703#Otis_1644-573

---

... I affirm that government is founded on the necessity of our natures; and that an original supreme sovereign, absolute, and uncontrollable *earthly* power *must* exist in and preside over every society; from whose final decisions there can be no appeal but directly to Heaven. It is therefore *originally* and *ultimately* in the people. I say supreme absolute power is *originally* and *ultimately* in the people; and they never did in fact *freely*, nor can they *rightfully* make an absolute, unlimited renunciation of this divine right. It is ever in the nature of the thing given in *trust*, and on a condition, the performance of which no mortal can dispense with; namely, that the person or persons on whom the sovereignty is conferred by the people, shall *incessantly* consult *their* good. Tyranny of all kinds is to be abhorred, whether it be in the hands of one, or of the few, or of the many. And though "in the last age a generation of men sprung up that would flatter Princes with an opinion that *they* have a *divine right* to absolute power"; yet "slavery is so vile and miserable an estate of man, and so directly opposite to the generous temper and courage of our nation, that it is hard to be conceived that an *Englishman*, much less a *gentleman*, should plead for it": especially at a time when the finest writers of the most polite nations on the continent of *Europe*, are enraptured with the beauties of the civil constitution of *Great Britain;* and envy her, no less for the *freedom* of her sons, than for her immense *wealth* and *military* glory.

But let the *origin* of government be placed where it may, the *end* of it is manifestly the good of *the whole. Salus populi supreme lex esto,*[1] is of the law of nature, and part of that grand charter given the human race (although too many of them are afraid to assert it), by the only monarch in the universe, who has a clear and indisputable right to *absolute* power; because he is the *only* One who is *omniscient* as well as *omnipotent.*

It is evidently contrary to the first principles of reason that supreme *unlimited* power should be in the hands of *one* man. It is the greatest "*idolatry,* begotten by *flattery,* on the body of *pride,*" that could induce one to think that *single mortal* should be able to hold so great a power, if ever so well inclined. Hence the origin of *deifying* princes: It was from the trick of gulling the vulgar into a belief that their tyrants were *omniscient,* and that it was therefore right, that they should be considered as *omnipotent*....

The *end* of government being the *good* of mankind, points out its great duties: It is above all things to provide for the security, the quiet, and happy enjoyment of life, liberty, and property. There is no one act which a government can have a *right* to make, that does not tend to the advancement of the security, tranquility, and prosperity of the people....

The first principle and great end of government being to provide for the best good of all the people, this can be done only by a supreme legislative and executive ultimately in the people, or whole community, where God has placed it; but the inconveniencies, not to say impossibility, attending the consultations and operations of a large body of people have made it necessary to transfer the power of the whole to a *few*: This necessity gave rise to deputation, proxy, or a right of representation.

... There is nothing more evident, says Mr. Locke, than "that creatures

---

[1] *Latin*: Let the highest law be the people's well being.

of the same species and rank promiscuously born to all the same advantages of nature, and the use of the same faculties, should also be equal one among another, without subordination and subjection, unless the master of them all should by any manifest declaration of his will set one above another, and confer on him by an evident and clear appointment, and undoubted right to dominion and sovereignty." "The natural liberty of man is to be free from any superior power on earth, and not to be under the will or legislative authority of man, but only to have the law of nature for his rule."[2] This is the liberty of independent states; this is the liberty of every man out of society, and who has a mind to live so; which liberty is only abridged in certain instances, not lost to those who are born in or voluntarily enter into society; this gift of God cannot be annihilated.

... Every British subject born on the continent of America, or in any other of the British dominions, is by the law of God and nature, by the common law, and by act of Parliament (exclusive of all charters from the crown), entitled to all the natural, essential, inherent, and inseparable rights of our fellow subjects in Great Britain. Among those rights are the following, which it is humbly conceived no man or body of men, not excepting the Parliament—justly, equitably, and consistently with their own rights and the constitution—can take away.

1st. *That the supreme and subordinate powers of the legislation should be free and sacred in the hands where the community ... rightfully placed them.*

2dly. *The supreme national legislative cannot be altered justly until the commonwealth is dissolved, nor a subordinate legislative taken away without forfeiture or other good cause.* Nor then can the subjects in the subordinate government be reduced to a state of slavery, and subject to the despotic rule of others. A state has no right to make slaves of the conquered. Even when the subordinate right of legislature is forfeited, and so declared, this cannot affect the natural persons either of those who were invested with it, or the inhabitants, so far as to deprive them of the rights of subjects and of men. The colonists will have an equitable right notwithstanding any such forfeiture of charter, to be represented in Parliament, or to have some new subordinate legislature among themselves. It would be best if they had both. Deprived, however, of their common rights as subjects, they cannot lawfully be, while they remain such. A representation in Parliament from the several colonies, since they are become so large and numerous, as to be called on not to maintain provincial

---

[2] *The Works of John Locke, Esq.*, 3 vols. (London: D. Browne and others, 1759), 2:168, 173.

government, civil and military, among themselves, for this they have cheerfully done, but to contribute towards the support of a national standing army, by reason of the heavy national debt, when they themselves owe a large one, contracted in the common cause, can't be thought an unreasonable thing, nor if asked, could it be called an immodest request. *Qui sentis commodum sentire debet et onus*,[3] has been thought a maxim of equity. But that a man should bear a burden for other people, as well as himself, without a return, never long found a place in any law book or decrees, but those of the most despotic princes. Besides the equity of an American representation in Parliament, a thousand advantages would result from it. It would be the most effectual means of giving those of both countries a thorough knowledge of each other's interests; as well as that of the whole, which are inseparable.

... No representation of the colonies in Parliament alone, would, however, be equivalent to a subordinate legislature among themselves; nor so well answer the ends of increasing their prosperity and the commerce of Great Britain. It would be impossible for the Parliament to judge so well, of their abilities to bear taxes, impositions on trade, and other duties and burdens, or of the local laws that might be really needful, as a legislature here.

3dly. *No legislature, supreme or subordinate, has a right to make itself arbitrary.*

It would be a most manifest contradiction, for a free legislature, like that of Great Britain, to make itself arbitrary.

4thly. *The supreme legislature cannot justly assume a power of ruling by extempore arbitrary decrees, but is bound to dispense justice by known settled rules,* and by duly *authorized independent judges.*

5thly. *The supreme power cannot take from any man any part of his property, without his consent in person, or by representation.*

6thly. *The legislature cannot transfer the power of making laws to any other hands.*

These are their bounds, which by God and nature are fixed, hitherto have they a right to come, and no further.

1. *To govern by stated laws.*
2. *Those laws should have no other end ultimately, but the good of the people.*
3. *Taxes are not to be laid on the people, but by their consent in person, or by deputation.*
4. *Their whole power is not transferable.*

---

[3] *Latin*: He who agrees to enjoy the benefit of something ought also to bear the cost of it.

These are the first principles of law and justice, and the great barriers of a free state, and of the British constitution in particular. I ask, I want no more. Now let it be shown how it is reconcilable with these principles, or to many other fundamental maxims of the British constitution, as well as the natural and civil rights, which by the laws of their country, all British subjects are entitled to, as their best inheritance and birthright, that all the northern colonies, who are without one representative in the House of Commons, should be taxed by the British Parliament.

That the colonists, black and white, born here, are freeborn British subjects, and entitled to all the essential civil rights of such, is a truth not only manifest from the provincial charters, from the principles of the common law, and acts of Parliament; but from the British constitution, which was reestablished at the revolution,[4] with a professed design to lecture the liberties of all the subjects to all generations.

... Now can there be any liberty, where property is taken away without consent? Can it with any color of truth, justice, or equity, be affirmed, that the northern colonies are represented in Parliament? Has this whole continent of near three thousand miles in length, and in which and his other American dominions, his majesty has, or very soon will have, some millions of as good, loyal, and useful subjects, white and black, as any in the three kingdoms, the election of one member of the House of Commons?

Is there the least difference, as to the consent of the colonists, whether taxes and impositions are laid on their trade, and other property, by the crown alone, or by the Parliament? As it is agreed on all hands, the crown alone cannot impost them. We should be justifiable in refusing to pay them, but must and ought to yield obedience to an act of Parliament, although erroneous, until repealed.

I can see no reason to doubt, but that the imposition of taxes, whether on trade, or on land, or houses, or ships, on real or personal, fixed or floating property, in the colonies, is absolutely irreconcilable with the rights of the colonists, as British subjects, and as men. I say men, for in a state of nature, no man can take my property from me, without my consent: If he does, he deprives me of my liberty, and makes me a slave. If such a proceeding is a breach of the law of nature, no law of society can make it just. The very act of taxing, exercised over those who are not represented, appears to me to be depriving them of one of their most essential rights, as freemen; and if

---

[4] The Glorious Revolution (1688–89), in which James II was deposed and William III and Mary II became king and queen.

continued, seems to be in effect an entire disfranchisement of every civil right. For what one civil right is worth a rush, after a man's property is subject to be taken from him at pleasure, without his consent. If a man is not his *own assessor* in person, or by deputy, his liberty is gone, or lays entirely at the mercy of others.

... I am aware it will be objected, that the Parliament of *England,* and of Great Britain, since the union, have from early days to this time, made acts to bind if not to tax Ireland: I answer, Ireland is a *conquered* country. I do not, however, lay so much stress on this; for it is my opinion, that a *conquered* country has, upon submission and good behavior, the same right to be free, under a conqueror, as the rest of his subjects....

To say the Parliament is absolute and arbitrary, is a contradiction. The Parliament cannot make 2 and 2, 5; omnipotency cannot do it. The supreme power in a state, is *jus dicere*[5] only; *jus dare,*[6] strictly speaking, belongs alone to God.... There must be in every instance, a higher authority—that is, GOD. Should an act of Parliament be against any of *his* natural laws, which are *immutably* true, their declaration would be contrary to eternal truth, equity, and justice, and consequently void: and so it would be adjudged by the Parliament itself, when convinced of their mistake. Upon this great principle, parliaments repeal such acts, as soon as they find they have been mistaken, in having declared them to be for the public good, when in fact they were not so .... See here the grandeur of the British constitution! See the wisdom of our ancestors! The supreme *legislative,* and the supreme *executive,* are a perpetual check and balance to each other. If the supreme executive errs, it is informed by the supreme legislative in Parliament: If the supreme legislative errs, it is informed by the supreme executive in the king's courts of law. Here, the king appears, as represented by his judges, in the highest luster and majesty, as supreme executor of the commonwealth; and he never shines brighter, but on his throne, at the head of the supreme legislative. This is government! This, is a constitution! To preserve which, either from foreign or domestic foes, has cost oceans of blood and treasure in every age; and the blood and the treasure have upon the whole been well spent. British America, has been bleeding in this cause from its settlement: We have spent all we could raise, and more; for notwithstanding the parliamentary reimbursement of part, we still remain much in debt....

We all think ourselves happy under Great Britain. We love, esteem, and

---

[5] *Latin*: to acknowledge a right.
[6] *Latin*: to grant a right.

reverence our mother country, and adore our king. And could the choice of independency be offered the colonies, or subjection to Great Britain upon any terms above absolute slavery, I am convinced they would accept the latter. The ministry, in all future generations may rely on it, that British America will never prove undutiful, until driven to it, as the last fatal resort against ministerial oppression, which will make the wisest mad, and the weakest strong....

The sum of my argument is that civil government is of God—that the administrators of it were originally the whole people—that they might have devolved it on whom they pleased—that this devolution is fiduciary, for the good of the whole—that by the British constitution, this devolution is on the king, lords and commons, the supreme, sacred and uncontrollable legislative power, not only in the realm, but thro' the dominions—that by the abdication, the original compact was broken to pieces—that by the revolution, it was renewed and more firmly established, and the rights and liberties of the subject in all parts of the dominions, more fully explained and confirmed—that in consequence of this establishment, and the acts of succession and union his majesty GEORGE III is rightful king and sovereign, and with his Parliament, the supreme legislative of Great Britain, France, and Ireland, and the dominions thereto belonging—that this constitution is the most free one, and by far the best, now existing on earth—that by this constitution, every man in the dominion is a free man—that no parts of his majesty's dominions can be taxed without their consent—that every part has a right to be represented in the supreme or some subordinate legislature—that the refusal of this, would seem to be a contradiction in practice to the theory of the constitution—that the colonies are subordinate dominions, and are now in such a state, as to make it best for the good of the whole, that they should not only be continued in the enjoyment of subordinate legislation, but be also represented in some proportion to their number and estates, in the grand legislature of the nation—that this would firmly unite all parts of the British empire, in the greatest peace and prosperity; and render it invulnerable and perpetual.

DOCUMENT 3

# Resolutions of the Stamp Act Congress
*October 19, 1765*

The stunning irony of the French and Indian War (1754–1763), which resulted in Great Britain gaining from France a vast North American empire, is that it set in motion events causing Britain to lose that hard-won empire—as well as the thirteen Atlantic seaboard colonies that had contributed mightily to its victory. During the course of the Seven Years' War, as this conflict was known globally, Britain's debt doubled. In 1765, hoping to boost revenue, Parliament imposed on its colonies the Stamp Act, which taxed everything from contracts to newspapers, stationery, playing cards, and dice. Americans rose up in indignation. It was bad enough that this measure increased taxes and required payment in hard-to-find British currency. Even worse, the Stamp Act amounted to taxation without representation since Parliament included not a single member elected by Americans. If the protection of private property stood as one of the first goals of government—a premise the colonists thought England's Glorious Revolution of 1688–89 had sanctified—then the British government was not merely failing to do its job. By reaching into Americans' pockets without their permission, it had committed an act of theft.

Colonists did not take kindly to what they perceived as this violation of their rights. They boycotted goods subject to the stamp tax; ostracized and intimidated stamp tax collectors; and protested, petitioned, and organized resistance not only on the local level but also through an intercolonial network of activists known as Sons of Liberty. In October of 1765, in an unprecedented display of colonial unity, thirty-seven delegates from nine colonies gathered in New York City for the Stamp Act Congress, which issued these resolutions and sent petitions to the king and both houses of Parliament. Although British officials dismissed the Congress as an extralegal body, they could not ignore the economic damage done by the boycott. In February 1766, Parliament voted to repeal the Stamp Act.

SOURCE: Hezekiah Niles, ed., *Principles and Acts of the Revolution in America*... (Baltimore: William Ogden Niles, 1822), 456–57.

*Saturday, Oct. 19th, 1765, A. M.*—The congress met... and upon mature deliberation, agreed to the following declarations of the rights and grievances of the colonists in America....

The members of this congress, sincerely devoted, with the warmest sentiments of affection and duty, to his majesty's person and government; inviolably attached to the present happy establishment of the Protestant succession [*to the throne*], and with minds deeply impressed by a sense of the present and impending misfortunes of the British colonies on this continent; having considered as maturely as time would permit, the circumstances of the said colonies, esteem it our indispensable duty to make the following declarations, of our humble opinion, respecting the most essential rights and liberties of the colonists, and of the grievances under which they labor, by reason of several late acts of Parliament.

1st. That his majesty's subjects in these colonies, owe the same allegiance to the crown of Great Britain, that is owing from his subjects born within the realm, and all due subordination to that august body, the parliament of Great Britain.

2d. That his majesty's liege[1] subjects in these colonies are entitled to all the inherent rights and privileges of his natural born subjects within the kingdom of Great Britain.

3d. That it is inseparably essential to the freedom of a people, and the undoubted rights of Englishmen, that no taxes should be imposed on them, but with their own consent, given personally, or by their representatives.

4th. That the people of these colonies are not, and from their local circumstances cannot be, represented in the House of Commons in Great Britain.

5th. That the only representatives of the people of these colonies, are persons chosen therein, by themselves; and that no taxes ever have been, or can be constitutionally imposed on them, but by their respective legislatures.

6th. That all supplies to the crown, being free gifts of the people, it is unreasonable and inconsistent with the principles and spirit of the British constitution, for the people of Great Britain to grant to his majesty the property of the colonists.

7th. That trial by jury is the inherent and invaluable right of every British subject in these colonies.[2]

8th. That the late act of Parliament, entitled, An act for granting and

---

[1] Loyal.
[2] People accused of violating the Stamp Act were to face trial in vice admiralty courts, which lacked juries.

applying certain stamp duties, and other duties in the British colonies and plantations in America, etc.,[3] by imposing taxes on the inhabitants of these colonies, and the said act, and several other acts, by extending the jurisdiction of the courts of admiralty beyond its ancient limits, have a manifest tendency to subvert the rights and liberties of the colonists.

9th. That the duties imposed by several late acts of Parliament, from the peculiar circumstances of these colonies, will be extremely burdensome and grievous, and from the scarcity of specie,[4] the payment of them absolutely impracticable.

10th. That as the profits of the trade of these colonies ultimately center in Great Britain, to pay for the manufactures which they are obliged to take from thence,[5] they eventually contribute very largely to all supplies granted there to the crown.

11th. That the restrictions imposed by several late acts of parliament, on the trade of these colonies, will render them unable to purchase the manufactures of Great Britain.

12th. That the increase, prosperity, and happiness of these colonies, depend on the full and free enjoyment of their rights and liberties, and an intercourse, with Great Britain, mutually affectionate and advantageous.

13th. That it is the right of the British subjects in these colonies to petition the king or either house of Parliament.

Lastly, That it is the indispensable duty of these colonies to the best of sovereigns, to the mother country, and to themselves, to endeavor, by a loyal and dutiful address to his majesty, and humble application to both houses of Parliament, to procure the repeal of the act for granting and applying certain stamp duties, of all clauses of any other acts of Parliament, whereby the jurisdiction of the admiralty is extended as aforesaid, and of the other late acts for the restriction of the American commerce.

---

[3] George III gave his assent to the Stamp Act on March 22, 1765.
[4] Coined money; the legal tender—in short supply in the colonies—required for payment of the stamp tax.
[5] From that place.

DOCUMENT 4

# "Letters from a Farmer in Pennsylvania, No. 2"

"A Farmer" (John Dickinson)
December 10, 1767

Colonists who celebrated the 1766 repeal of the Stamp Act turned a blind eye to the Declaratory Act, which accompanied the Stamp Act's termination and asserted Parliament's "full power and authority" to impose its will on the American colonies "in all cases whatsoever." The 1767 Townshend Acts, promoted by Chancellor of the Exchequer Charles Townshend (1725–1767), alerted them to Parliament's commitment to increasing revenue from America, which still contributed only about a tenth of what it cost to station British troops on its frontiers.

Philadelphia lawyer John Dickinson (1732–1808) picked up his pen in opposition to Townshend's laws, which imposed taxes on lead, glass, paint, paper, and tea. Posing as an ordinary farmer, this former (and future) Pennsylvania legislator, who had drafted the resolutions of the Stamp Act Congress, made the case that colonists who acquiesced to these taxes would be allowing Parliament to "take money out of our pockets, without our consent." Newspapers up and down the Atlantic coast published his "Farmer's Letters," which also appeared bound together as a pamphlet. Thomas Jefferson (1743–1826), who would serve with Dickinson in the Continental Congress, later described him as "among the first of the advocates for the rights of his country." When Dickinson died in 1808, Jefferson wrote that a "truer patriot... could not have left us."

SOURCE: Paul Leicester Ford, ed., *The Writings of John Dickinson* (Philadelphia: Historical Society of Pennsylvania, 1895), 1:312–22. https://archive.org/details/writingsofjohndioodickrich/page/312

---

My dear countrymen,

There is another late act of Parliament, which appears to me to be unconstitutional, and as destructive to the liberty of these colonies, as that mentioned in my last letter;[1] that is, the act for granting the duties on paper, glass, etc.

The Parliament unquestionably possesses a legal authority to *regulate* the trade of *Great Britain*, and all her colonies. Such an authority is essential to the relation between a mother country and her colonies; and necessary for the common good of all. He, who considers these provinces as states distinct from the *British Empire*, has very slender notions of *justice*, or of their *interests*. We are but parts of a *whole*; and therefore there must exist a power somewhere to preside and preserve the connection in due order. This power is lodged in the Parliament; and we are as much dependent on *Great Britain*, as a perfectly free people can be on another.

I have looked over *every statute* relating to these colonies, from their first settlement to this time; and I find every one of them founded on this principle, till the *Stamp Act* administration. *All before*, are calculated to regulate trade, and preserve or promote a mutually beneficial intercourse between the several constituent parts of the empire; and though many of them imposed duties on trade, yet those duties were always imposed *with design* to restrain the commerce of one part, that was injurious to another, and thus to promote the general welfare. The raising a revenue thereby was never intended .... Never did the *British* Parliament, till the period above mentioned, think of imposing duties in *America*, FOR THE PURPOSE OF RAISING A REVENUE....

This I call an innovation; and a most dangerous innovation. It may perhaps be objected, that *Great Britain* has a right to lay what duties she pleases upon her exports, and it makes no difference to us, whether they are paid here or there.

To this I answer. These colonies require many things for their use, which the laws of *Great Britain* prohibit them from getting anywhere but from her. Such are paper and glass.

That we may legally be bound to pay any *general* duties on these commodities, relative to the regulation of trade, is granted; but we being *obliged by the laws* to take from *Great Britain*, any *special* duties imposed on their

---

[1] The 1767 New York Restraining Act prohibited the governor and legislature of New York from passing any legislation until they agreed to comply with the 1765 Quartering Act, which required colonial governments to pay for the food, housing, and supplies of British troops stationed within their borders.

exportations *to us only, with intention to raise a revenue from us only,* are as much *taxes,* upon us, as those imposed by the *Stamp Act*....

Some persons perhaps may say, that this act lays us under no necessity to pay the duties imposed, because we may ourselves manufacture the articles on which they are laid; whereas by the *Stamp Act* no instrument of writing could be good, unless made on *British* paper, and that too stamped.

Such an objection amounts to no more than this, that the injury resulting to these colonies, from the total disuse of *British* paper and glass, will not be *so afflicting* as that which would have resulted from the total disuse of writing among them; for by that means even the *Stamp Act* might have been eluded. Why then was it universally detested by them as slavery itself? Because it presented to these devoted provinces nothing but a choice of calamities, embittered by indignities, each of which it was unworthy of freemen to bear. But is no injury a violation of right but the *greatest* injury? If... eluding the payment of the taxes imposed by the *Stamp Act,* would have subjected us to a more dreadful inconvenience, than... eluding the payment of those imposed by the late act; does it therefore follow, that the last is *no violation* of our rights, though it is calculated for the same purpose the other was, that is, *to raise money upon us,* WITHOUT OUR CONSENT?...

But the objectors may further say, that we shall suffer no injury at all by the disuse of *British* paper and glass. We might not, if we could make as much as we want. But can any man, acquainted with *America,* believe this possible? I am told there are but two or three *glasshouses* on this continent, and but very few *paper mills;* and suppose more should be erected, a long course of years must elapse, before they can be brought to perfection. This continent is a country of planters, farmers, and fishermen; not of manufacturers. The difficulty of establishing particular manufactures in such a country is almost insuperable. For one manufacture is connected with others in such a manner that it may be said to be impossible to establish one or two without establishing several others. The experience of many nations may convince us of this truth....

*Great Britain* has prohibited the manufacturing *iron* and *steel* in these colonies, without any objection being made to her *right* of doing it. The *like* right she must have to prohibit any other manufacture among us. Thus she is possessed of an undisputed *precedent* on that point. This authority, she will say, is founded on the *original intention* of settling these colonies; that is, that we should manufacture for them, and that they should supply her with materials. The *equity* of this policy, she will also say, has been universally acknowledged by the colonies, who never have made the least objection to statutes for that purpose; and will further appear by the *mutual benefits* flowing from this usage ever since the settlement of these colonies....

Here then, my dear countrymen, ROUSE yourselves, and behold the ruin hanging over your heads....

Upon the whole, the single question is, whether the Parliament can legally impose duties to be paid *by the people of these colonies only,* FOR THE SOLE PURPOSE OF RAISING A REVENUE, *on commodities which she obliges us to take from her alone,* or, in other words, whether the Parliament can legally take money out of our pockets, without our consent....

A FARMER

DOCUMENT 5

# Charleston Nonimportation Agreement
July 22, 1769

While John Dickinson's *Letters from a Farmer in Pennsylvania* helped establish the principles around which colonists united against the 1767 Townshend Acts, the widespread use of economic sanctions to punish the British united Americans in action. To protest Parliament's imposition of taxes on lead, glass, paint, paper, and tea, by 1769 nearly every colony had agreed to boycott British goods. The general success of the movement for nonimportation, which reduced British exports to the colonies by one-third, resulted partly because its implementation occurred on the local level. Agreements could be tailored to the specific circumstances of the individuals pledging to abstain from commerce with Great Britain—and to treat with "the utmost contempt" (as subscribers to this South Carolina nonimportation agreement promised) any neighbors who failed to comply.

SOURCE: Charles McLean Andrews, "Boston Merchants and the Non-Importation Agreement," *Publications of the Colonial Society of Massachusetts* 19 (1916–17): 217–19. https://archive.org/details/cu31924030152437/page/n65

---

We, his majesty's dutiful and loving subjects, the inhabitants of South Carolina, being sensibly affected with the great prejudice done to Great Britain, and the abject and wretched condition to which the British colonies are reduced by several acts of Parliament[1] lately passed; by *some of which* the monies that the colonists usually and cheerfully spent in the purchase of all sorts of goods imported from Great Britain, are now, to their great grievance, wrung from them, without their consent, or even their being represented, and applied by the ministry, in prejudice of, and without regard to, the real interest of Great Britain, or the manufactures thereof, almost totally, to the support of new[ly] created commissioners of customs, placemen, parasitical and novel ministerial officers; and *by others of which acts,* we are not only

---

[1] The 1767 Townshend Acts.

deprived of those invaluable rights, trial by our peers and the common law, but are also made subject to the arbitrary and oppressive proceedings of the civil law, justly abhorred and rejected by our ancestors, the free men of England; and finding, that the most dutiful and loyal petitions from the colonies alone, for redress of those grievances, have been rejected with contempt, so that no relief can be expected from that method of proceedings; and, being fully convinced of the absolute necessity, of stimulating our fellow subjects and sufferers in Great Britain to aid us, in this, our distress, and of joining the rest of the colonies, in some other loyal and vigorous methods, that may most probably procure such relief, which we believe may be most effectually promoted by strict economy, and by encouraging the manufactures of America in general, and of this province in particular. We, therefore, whose names are underwritten, do solemnly promise, and agree to and with each other, that, until the colonies be restored to their former freedom, by the repeal of the said acts, we will most strictly abide by the following

## RESOLUTIONS

I. That we will encourage and promote the use of North American manufactures in general, and those of this province in particular. And any of us, who are vendors thereof, do engage to sell and dispose of them, at the same rates as heretofore.

II. That we will, upon no pretense whatsoever, either upon our own account or on commission, import into this province any of the manufactures of Great Britain, or any other European or East India goods, either from Great Britain, Holland, or any other place, other than such as may have been shipped in consequence of former orders; excepting only Negro cloth, commonly called white and colored plains, not exceeding one shilling and six pence sterling per yard, canvas, bolting cloths, drugs and family medicines, plantation and workmen's tools, nails, firearms, bar steel, gunpowder, shot, lead, flints, wire cards and card wire,[2] mill and grindstones, fish hooks, printed books and pamphlets, salt, coals, and saltpeter.[3] And exclusive of these articles, we do solemnly promise and declare, that we will immediately countermand all orders to our correspondents in

---

[2] Material used to establish patterns in the weaving of fabrics.

[3] Potassium nitrate; a chemical compound used for fertilizer, in medicine, and in the making of gunpowder.

Great Britain, for shipping any such goods, wares, and merchandise. And we will sell and dispose of the goods we have on hand, or that may arrive in consequence of former orders at the same rates as heretofore.

III. That we will use the utmost economy, in our persons, houses, and furniture; particularly, that we will give no mourning, or gloves, or scarves at funerals.[4]

IV. That, from and after the 1st. day of January, 1770, we will not import, buy, or sell any Negroes that shall be brought into this province from Africa; nor, after the 1st. day of October next, any Negroes that shall be imported from the West Indies, or any other place excepting from Africa as aforesaid. And that, if any goods or Negroes shall be sent to us, contrary to our agreement in this subscription, such goods shall be reshipped or stored, and such Negroes reshipped from this province, and not by any means offered for sale therein.

V. That we will not purchase from or sell for, any masters of vessels, transient persons, or non-subscribers, any kind of European or East India goods whatever, excepting coals and salt, after the 1st. day of November next:

VI. That as wines are subject to a heavy duty, we agree, not to import any on our account or commission, or purchase from any master of vessel, transient person, or non-subscriber, after the 1st. day of January next.

VII. Lastly, That we will not purchase any Negroes imported, or any goods or merchandise whatever, from any resident in this province, that refuses or neglects to sign this agreement, within one month from the date hereof; excepting it shall appear he has been unavoidably prevented from doing the same. And every subscriber who shall not, strictly and literally, adhere to this agreement, according to the true intent and meaning hereof, ought to be treated with the utmost contempt.

---

[4] Eighteenth-century Americans who attended funerals sometimes received gloves, scarves, or other items as mementos of the deceased.

DOCUMENT 6

# Account of the Boston Massacre

Deacon John Tudor

*March 1770*

The Townshend Acts resulted in colonists' nonimportation agreements. The enforcement of these pacts sometimes resulted in violence. On February 22, 1770, when a group of Boston teenagers placed a sign in front of the shop of merchant Theophilus Lillie noting his status as an "IMPORTER," an angry crowd gathered. Ebenezer Richardson (1718–?), a customs employee who tried but failed to remove the sign, succeeded in attracting the scorn of the mob, which followed him home. As his house shook and his windows shattered, Richardson panicked and fired his shotgun into the crowd, killing 10-year-old Christopher Seider (1759–1770).

Seider's death sparked outrage in Boston. The presence of British troops, who had arrived in 1768, did nothing to defuse tensions. By 1770, there was one Redcoat for every four of the city's 16,000 inhabitants. Off-duty soldiers and civilians sometimes brawled in the streets, as on the nights of Friday, March 2, and Saturday, March 3. On Monday, March 5, Lord North (1732–1792), the new prime minister (1770–1782), introduced in Parliament a bill repealing most of the taxes imposed by the Townshend Acts. Yet this act, meant to improve relations between Britain and its colonies, would be overshadowed by the Boston Massacre, which occurred that same evening.

Taken together, accounts of the night's events make clear the basic details of the "massacre." Angry Bostonians surrounded a Redcoat sentry who stood at the door of the customhouse. They hurled snowballs, ice, and insults. He returned the crowd's strong words. The crowd grew—and grew angrier. Church bells rang, summoning additional people, many of whom carried buckets because they thought the bells signaled a nearby fire. Captain Thomas Preston (c. 1722–c. 1798), who had been watching from a distance, marched with seven soldiers, bayonets fixed to their muskets, to rescue the sentry. Soon all nine of these Redcoats had their backs to the wall of the customhouse. In this chaos, Preston later testified, he ordered his men not to fire their half-cocked muskets. Meanwhile, people in the noisy crowd yelled "Fire!" One soldier, hit by a chunk of ice, discharged his musket. The other soldiers then fired as well. The soldiers wounded 11 members of the mob. Three died within minutes. Another died hours later. A fifth died after several days.

In October and November, in two separate trials, John Adams (1735–1826) served as defense attorney for Preston and his men. Presented with the testimony of multiple witnesses, a jury found Preston not guilty. Another jury found all but two of his men not guilty; the others were convicted of manslaughter, branded with an "M" between the thumb and index finger, and released. The British fared more poorly in the court of public opinion. A depiction popularized by the engraving of Paul Revere (1734–1818) showed Preston ordering his men to fire and the victims with their backs against the wall (see illustration). Meanwhile, merchant John Tudor (1709–1795), a deacon at the Second Church of Boston, recorded in his diary what he had seen and heard about the incident and its aftermath. As news of the massacre spread, more and more Americans wondered if the British government, entrusted to protect their lives, liberty, and property, in fact posed a grievous threat to those essential rights.

SOURCE: William Tudor, ed., *Deacon Tudor's Diary*.... (Boston: Wallace Spooner, 1896), 30–34. https://archive.org/details/deacontudorsdiarootudo/page/n79

---

On Monday evening, the 5th current, a few minutes after 9 o'clock, a most horrid murder was committed in King Street before the customhouse door by 8 or 9 soldiers under the command of Captain Thomas Preston, drawn off from the main guard on the south side of the townhouse.

## March 5 [*Monday*]

This unhappy affair began by some boys and young fellows throwing snowballs at the sentry placed at the customhouse door. On which 8 or 9 soldiers came to his assistance. Soon after a number of people collected, when the captain commanded the soldiers to fire, which they did and 3 men were killed on the spot and several mortally wounded, one of which died [*the*] next morning. The captain soon drew off his soldiers up to the main guard, or the consequences might have been terrible, for on the guns firing the people were alarmed and set the bells ringing as if for fire, which drew multitudes to the place of action. Lieutenant Governor [*Thomas*] Hutchinson, who was commander in chief, was sent for and came to the council chamber, where some of the magistrates attended. The [*lieutenant*] governor desired the multitude about 10 o'clock to separate and go home peaceable and he would do all in his power that justice should be done, etc.... The people insisted that the soldiers should be ordered to their barracks 1st before they would separate, which being done the people separated about 1 o'clock....

Captain Preston was taken up by a warrant... and we sent him to jail soon after 3, having evidence sufficient to commit him, on his ordering the soldiers to fire....

## [March 6, Tuesday]

The next forenoon the 8 soldiers that fired on the inhabitants were also sent to jail. Tuesday A.M. the inhabitants met at Faneuil Hall and after some pertinent speeches, chose a committee of 15 gentlemen to wait on the lieutenant governor in council to request the immediate removal of the troops. The message was in these words. That it is the unanimous opinion of this meeting that the inhabitants and soldiery can no longer live together in safety; that nothing can rationally be expected to restore the peace of the town and prevent blood and carnage but the removal of the troops; and that we most fervently pray his honor that his power and influence may be exerted for their instant removal. His honor's reply was, gentlemen I am extremely sorry for the unhappy difference and especially of the last evening, and signifying that it was not in his power to remove the troops, etc., etc.

The above reply was not satisfactory to the inhabitants, as but one regiment should be removed to the Castle Barracks.[1] In the afternoon the town adjourned to Dr. Sewill's Meetinghouse,[2] for Faneuil Hall was not large enough to hold the people, there being at least 3,000, some supposed near 4,000, when they chose a committee to wait on the lieutenant governor to let him and the council know that nothing less will satisfy the people than a total and immediate removal of the troops out of the town.

His honor laid before the council the vote of the town. The council thereon expressed themselves to be unanimously of [the] opinion that it was absolutely necessary for his majesty's service, the good order of the town, etc., that the troops should be immediately removed out of the town.

His honor communicated this advice of the council to Colonel Dalrymple[3]

---

[1] The barracks were located at Castle William (renamed Fort Independence in 1797) on Castle Island in Boston Harbor.
[2] The Old South Church.
[3] Colonel William Dalrymple (1736–1807), commander of the British troops in Boston.

and desired he would order the troops down to Castle William. After the colonel had seen the vote of the council he gave his word and honor to the town's committee that both the regiments should be removed without delay. The committee returned to the town meeting and Mr. Hancock,[4] chairman of the committee, read their report as above, which was received with a shout and clap of hands, which made the meetinghouse ring....

## March 8 (Thursday)

Agreeable to a general request of the inhabitants, were followed to the grave (for they were all buried in one) in succession the 4 bodies of Messrs. Samuel Gray, Samuel Maverick, James Caldwell, and Crispus Attucks, the unhappy victims who fell in the bloody massacre.[5] On this sorrowful occasion most of the shops and stores in town were shut, all the bells were ordered to toll a solemn peal in Boston, Charleston, Cambridge, and Roxbury. The several hearses forming a junction in King Street, the theater of that inhuman tragedy, proceeded from thence through the main street, lengthened by an immense concourse of people so numerous as to be obliged to follow in ranks of 4 and 6 abreast and brought up by a long train of carriages. The sorrow visible in the countenances, together with the peculiar solemnity, surpass description; it was supposed that the spectators and those that followed the corps amounted to 15,000, some supposed 20,000. Note [that] Captain Preston was tried for his life on the affair of the above [on] October 24, 1770. The trial lasted 5 days, but the jury brought him in not guilty.

---

[4] John Hancock (1737–1793).
[5] The fifth fatality, Patrick Carr, died on March 14 and was buried alongside the other victims on March 17.

DOCUMENT 7

# "The Rights of the Colonists"

Samuel Adams
November 20, 1772

In the 1760s, Samuel Adams (1722–1803) emerged as a key leader of Boston's radicals. Although his second cousin, John Adams (1735–1826), described him as "zealous, ardent, and keen" in his defense of Americans' liberties, Royal Governor Thomas Hutchinson (1711–1780) doubted "whether there is a greater incendiary in the king's dominion or a man of greater malignity of heart."

It is no surprise that Hutchinson possessed a negative opinion of Samuel Adams. Beginning with the Stamp Act crisis and continuing with colonists' resistance to the Townshend Acts and efforts to propagandize the Boston Massacre, Adams had been a thorn in Hutchinson's side. By 1772, the issue was who should pay royal officials' salaries. Adams perceived that whoever held the purse strings would be able to use these officials as puppets; so did Hutchinson and his English allies, who in 1768 arranged for part of Hutchinson's salary to be paid from the proceeds of customs revenues. In 1770 Great Britain added the tea tax as a source of Hutchinson's income. Two years later, it directed that superior court judges be paid from these sources as well. Adams insisted that the Massachusetts assembly, which answered to voters, should compensate these judges in order to maintain its leverage over them.

The controversy allowed Adams to prompt the Town of Boston to appoint a committee of correspondence that would produce a broad statement of colonists' rights. The resulting document, drafted primarily by Adams, helps to underscore the importance to American revolutionaries of the ideas of John Locke (1632–1704), who justified England's Glorious Revolution (1688–1689) by arguing that ousted King James II had failed to uphold government's obligation to protect individuals' fundamental rights to life, liberty, and property.

SOURCE: Samuel Adams, "The Rights of the Colonists," in Harry Alonzo Cushing, ed., *The Writings of Samuel Adams*, 4 vols. (New York: G. P. Putnam's Sons, 1904–08), 2:350–59. https://archive.org/details/writitngssamadam02adamrich/page/350

## 1st. Natural Rights of the Colonists as Men

Among the natural rights of the colonists are these: First, a right to *life;* secondly to *liberty;* thirdly to *property;* together with the right to support and defend them in the best manner they can. These are evident branches of, rather than deductions from, the duty of self-preservation, commonly called the first law of nature.

All men have a right to remain in a state of nature as long as they please. And in case of intolerable oppression, civil or religious, to leave the society they belong to, and enter into another.

When men enter into society, it is by voluntary consent; and they have a right to demand and insist upon the performance of such conditions, and previous limitations as form an equitable *original compact.*

Every natural right not expressly given up or from the nature of a social compact necessarily ceded remains.

All positive and civil laws, should conform as far as possible, to the law of natural reason and equity.

As neither reason requires, nor religion permits the contrary, every man living in or out of a state of civil society, has a right peaceably and quietly to worship God according to the dictates of his conscience.

"Just and true liberty, equal and impartial liberty" in matters spiritual and temporal, is a thing that all men are clearly entitled to, by the eternal and immutable laws of God and nature, as well as by the law of nations, and all well-grounded municipal laws, which must have their foundation in the former.

In regard to religion, mutual toleration in the different professions thereof, is what all good and candid minds in all ages have ever practiced; and both by precept and example inculcated on mankind. And it is now generally agreed among Christians that this spirit of toleration in the fullest extent consistent with the being of civil society "is the chief characteristic mark of the true church" and, insomuch that Mr. Locke[1] has asserted and proved beyond the possibility of contradiction on any solid ground, that such toleration ought to be extended to all whose doctrines are not subversive of society. The only sects which he thinks ought to be, and which by all wise laws are excluded from such toleration, are those who teach doctrines subversive of the civil government under which they live. The Roman Catholics or Papists

---

[1] English philosopher John Locke (1632–1704).

are excluded by reason of such doctrines as these, that princes excommunicated may be deposed, and those they call *heretics* may be destroyed without mercy; besides their recognizing the pope in so absolute a manner, in subversion of government, by introducing as far as possible into the states, under whose protection they enjoy life, liberty, and property, that solecism in politics, *imperium in imperio*,[2] leading directly to the worst anarchy and confusion, civil discord, war, and bloodshed.

The natural liberty of men by entering into society is abridged or restrained so far only as is necessary for the great end of society, the best good of the whole.

In the state of nature, every man is, under God, judge and sole judge of his own rights and the injuries done him. By entering into society, he agrees to an arbiter or indifferent judge between him and his neighbors; but he no more renounces his original right, than by taking a cause out of the ordinary course of law, and leaving the decision to referees or indifferent arbitrations. In the last case he must pay the referees for time and trouble; he should be also willing to pay his just quota for the support of government, the law, and constitution; the end of which is to furnish indifferent and impartial judges in all cases that may happen, whether civil, ecclesiastical, marine, or military.

"The natural liberty of man is to be free from any superior power on earth, and not to be under the will or legislative authority of man; but only to have the law of nature for his rule."[3]

... In short it is the greatest absurdity to suppose it in the power of one or any number of men, at the entering into society, to renounce their essential natural rights, or the means of preserving those rights, when the great end of civil government from the very nature of its institution is for the support, protection, and defense of those very rights: the principal of which ... are life, liberty, and property. If men, through fear, fraud, or mistake, should *in terms* renounce and give up any essential natural right, the eternal law of reason and the great end of society, would absolutely vacate such renunciation; the right to freedom being *the gift* of God almighty, it is not in the power of man to alienate this gift, and voluntarily become a slave.

---

[2] *Latin*: a government within a government.
[3] John Locke, *Two Treatises of Government*, ed. Thomas Hollis (London: A. Millar et al., 1764), 212.

### 2d. The Rights of the Colonists as Christians

These may be best understood by reading—and carefully studying the institutes of the great Lawgiver and head of the Christian church—which are to be found clearly written and promulgated in the *New Testament.*

By the act of the British Parliament commonly called the Toleration Act,[4] every subject in England except Papists, etc., was restored to, and reestablished in, his natural right to worship God according to the dictates of his own conscience. And by the charter of this province it is granted ordained and established ( . . . as an original right) that there shall be liberty of conscience allowed in the worship of God, to all Christians except Papists.... Magna Charta[5] itself is in substance but a constrained declaration, or proclamation, and promulgation in the name of king, Lords, and Commons of the sense the latter had of their original inherent, indefeasible[6] natural rights, as also those of free citizens equally perdurable[7] with the other. That great author, that great jurist, and even that court writer, Mr. Justice Blackstone,[8] holds that this recognition was justly obtained of King John,[9] sword in hand. And peradventure it must be one day, sword in hand, again rescued and preserved from total destruction and oblivion.

### 3d. The Rights of the Colonists as Subjects

A commonwealth or state is a body politic or civil society of men, united together to promote their mutual safety and prosperity, by means of their union.

The absolute rights of Englishmen, and all freemen in or out of civil society, are principally personal security, personal liberty, and private property.

All persons born in the British American colonies are by the laws of God and nature, and by the common law of England, exclusive of all charters

---

[4] William and Mary gave royal assent to the Toleration Act on May 24, 1689.
[5] The 1215 *Magna Carta* (*Latin*: Great Charter) limited the English king's power and established protections for the church and noblemen.
[6] Inalienable; inseparable.
[7] Enduring forever; imperishable.
[8] Sir William Blackstone (1723–1780) was an English lawyer, judge, and Tory politician best known as author of the four-volume *Commentaries on the Laws of England* (1765–1769).
[9] John of England (1166–1216) served as king between 1199 and 1216. In 1215 he reluctantly agreed to approve the *Magna Carta*.

from the crown, well entitled, and by the acts of the British Parliament are declared to be entitled, to all the natural, essential, inherent, and inseparable rights, liberties, and privileges of subjects born in Great Britain, or within the realm. Among those rights are the following, which no man, or body of men, consistently with their own rights as men and citizens or members of society, can for themselves give up or take away from others.

First, "The first fundamental, positive law of all commonwealths or states, is the establishing [*of*] the legislative power. [*And*] the first fundamental natural law also, which is to govern even the legislative power itself, is the preservation of the Society."[10]

Secondly, The legislative has no right to absolute arbitrary power over the lives and fortunes of the people. Nor can mortals assume a prerogative, not only too high for men, but for angels, and therefore reserved for the exercise of the Deity alone.

"The legislative cannot justly assume to itself a power to rule by extempore arbitrary decrees; but it is bound to see that justice is dispensed, and that the rights of the subjects be decided, by promulgated, standing, and known laws, and authorized independent judges;" that is, independent, as far as possible, of prince or people. "There shall be one rule of justice for rich and poor, for the favorite in court, and the countryman at the plough."[11]

Thirdly, the supreme power cannot justly take from any man any part of his property without his consent, in person or by his representative.

These are some of the first principles of natural law and justice, and the great barriers of all free states and of the British Constitution in particular. It is utterly irreconcilable to these principles, and to many other fundamental maxims of the common law, common sense, and reason, that a British House of Commons should have a right, at pleasure, to give and grant the property of the colonists. That these colonists are well entitled to all the essential rights, liberties, and privileges of men and freemen, born in Britain, is manifest, not only from the colony charter... but acts of the British Parliament...." Now what liberty can there be, where property is taken away without consent? Can it be said with any color of truth and justice, that this continent of three thousand miles in length, and of a breadth as yet unexplored, in which ... there are five millions of people, has the least voice, vote, or influence in the decisions of the British Parliament? Have they, all together, any more right or power to return a single number to that House of Commons, who

---

[10] Locke, *Two Treatises of Government*, 312–13.
[11] Ibid., 323.

have not inadvertently, but deliberately, assumed a power to dispose of their lives, liberties, and properties, then to choose an emperor of China? Had the colonists a right to return members to the British Parliament, it would only be hurtful; as from their local situation and circumstances it is impossible they should be ever truly and properly represented there. The inhabitants of this country in all probability in a few years will be more numerous, than those of Great Britain and Ireland together; yet it is absurdly expected by the promoters of the present measures, that these, with their posterity to all generations, should be easy, while their property, shall be disposed of by a House of Commons at three thousand miles' distant from them; and who cannot be supposed to have the least care or concern for their real interest; who have not only no natural care for their interest, but must be in effect bribed against it, as every burden they lay on the colonists is so much saved or gained to themselves. Hitherto many of the colonists have been free from quitrents;[12] but if the breath of a British House of Commons can originate an act for taking away all our money, our lands will go next or be subject to rack rents[13] from haughty and relentless landlords who will ride at ease, while we are trodden in the dirt. The colonists have been branded with the odious names of traitors and rebels, only for complaining of their grievances....

---

[12] Annual fees, based on acreage, paid by a landowner to the person (a colony's proprietor or the king or queen) or the heir of the person who originally granted title to the land.
[13] Excessively high quitrents.

DOCUMENT 8

## Account of the Boston Tea Party

"An Impartial Observer"
*December 1773*

Although Parliament in 1770 repealed most of the taxes associated with the Townshend Acts, the duty on tea remained. Colonists continued their boycott of the product, and by 1773 nearly 10,000 tons of tea sat in the East India Company's London warehouses. Parliament's passage of the Tea Act aimed to rescue the near-bankrupt company, which had many well-connected shareholders and owed money to both the Bank of England and the British government. The act awarded the company a monopoly on the legal sale of tea in America and eliminated the duty the company paid to land tea in England. The tax to be paid by colonists who imported tea from England remained, but the law would tempt them to violate their boycott by making East India Company tea less expensive than Dutch tea smuggled into the colonies.

As in Philadelphia, New York, and other American ports, Bostonians viewed the Tea Act as a challenge to their virtue and a trick to cause them to accept taxation without representation. As a result, the November 28 arrival of the Dartmouth and its shipment of tea triggered a crisis. The Sons of Liberty stationed guards at Griffin's Wharf to prevent the unloading of the Dartmouth's cargo. Yet Governor Thomas Hutchinson, who had at his disposal British troops as well as British warships, refused to allow the Dartmouth to leave. By law the vessel had twenty days—until December 17—to pay the duty, after which the tea could be seized and then dispersed to sellers who might not know or care about its origins. The subsequent arrival of two additional ships carrying tea—the Eleanor and the Beaver—compounded the situation.

The account of "An Impartial Observer" described for newspaper readers how Bostonians, through a series of massive public meetings and then the concerted efforts of about fifty local men disguised as "Aboriginal Natives" (Mohawks, as others specified), confronted the crisis. Orchestrated by Sam Adams and the Sons of Liberty, the December 16 Tea Party destroyed 90,000 pounds of tea worth nearly £10,000. The following day, John Adams praised it in his diary as an act "so bold, so daring, so firm" that "it must have ... important consequences." It did. Parliament, which had repealed the Stamp Act and Townshend Acts in response to colonial protests, this time doubled down. Rather than attempting to prosecute individuals for the destruction of the tea, in early 1774 the British government punished all of Massachusetts with the Coercive Acts (Americans called them the "Intolerable Acts"), which closed Boston Harbor, hobbled the legislature, banned most town meetings, curtailed jury trials, expanded the quartering of British troops, and put America and Great Britain on a path toward war.

SOURCE: "An Impartial Observer," *Boston Gazette*, December 20, 1773.

---

Having accidentally arrived at Boston upon a visit to a friend the evening before the meeting of the body of the people on the 29th of November, curiosity, and the pressing invitations of my most kind host, induced me to attend the meeting.

I must confess that I was most agreeably, and I hope that I shall be forgiven by the people if I say so, unexpectedly, entertained and instructed by the regular, reasonable, and sensible conduct and expression of the people there collected, that I should rather have entertained an idea of being transported to the British senate[1] than to an adventurous and promiscuous assembly of people of a remote colony, were I not convinced by the genuine and uncorrupted integrity and manly hardihood of the rhetoricians of that assembly that they were not yet corrupted by venality or debauched by luxury....

The body of the people determined the tea should not be landed. The determination was deliberate, was judicious; the sacrifice of their rights, of the union of all the colonies, would have been the effect had they conducted [*themselves*] with less resolution. On the committee of correspondence they devolved the care of seeing their resolutions reasonably executed. That body, as I had been informed by one of their members, had taken every step which prudence and patriotism could suggest, to effect the desirable purpose, but were defeated.

The body once more assembled [*on December 14*], I was again present. Such a collection of the people was to me a novelty; near seven thousand persons[2] from several towns, gentlemen, merchants, yeomen, and others, respectable for their rank and abilities, and venerable for their age and

---

[1] The House of Lords.
[2] The Old South Meeting House was the largest building in Boston. Given its size, attendance was probably not more than 5,000—still an impressive number given that Boston had about 16,000 residents and nearby towns had only a few thousand more.

character, constituted the assembly. They decently, unanimously, and firmly adhered to their former resolution, that the baleful commodity which was to rivet and establish the duty should never be landed.

To prevent the mischief, they repeated the desires of the committee of the towns, that the owner of the ship should apply for a clearance; it appeared that Mr. Rotch[3] had been managed and was still under the influence of the opposite party; he resisted the request of the people to apply for a clearance for his ship with an obstinacy which, in my opinion, bordered on stubbornness. Subdued at length by the peremptory demand of the body, he consented to apply, a committee of ten respectable gentlemen were appointed to attend him to the collector.

The succeeding morning the application was made and the clearance refused with all the insolence of office; the body meeting the same morning by adjournment, Mr. Rotch was directed to protest in form, and then apply to the governor for a pass.... Mr. Rotch executed his commission with fidelity, but a pass could not be obtained, his excellency excusing himself in his refusal that he should not make the precedent of granting a pass till the clearance was obtained, which was indeed a fallacy as it had been usual with him in ordinary cases.

Mr. Rotch, returning in the evening [*of December 16*], reported as above; the body then voted his conduct to be satisfactory, and recommending order and regularity to the people, dissolved.

Previous to the dissolution, a number of persons, supposed to be the Aboriginal Natives from their complexion, approaching near the door of the assembly, gave the war whoop, which was answered by a few in the galleries of the house where the assembly was convened; silence was commanded, and a prudent and peaceable deportment again enjoined.

The savages repaired to the ships which entertained the pestilential teas, and had began their ravage previous to the dissolution of the meeting—they applied themselves to the destruction of this commodity in earnest, and in the space of about two hours broke up 342 chests, and discharged their contents into the sea.

A watch, as I am informed, was stationed to prevent embezzlement and not a single ounce of teas was suffered to be purloined or carried off. It is worthy [*of*] remark that, although a considerable quantity of goods of different kinds were still remaining on board the vessels, no injury was sustained; such attention to private property was observed, that a small padlock belonging

---

[3] Francis Rotch (1750–1822), whose family owned the *Dartmouth*.

to the capt[*ain*] of one of the ships being broke, another was procured and sent to him.

I cannot but express my admiration of the conduct of this people! Uninfluenced by party or any other attachment, I presume I shall not be suspected of misrepresentation.

The East India Company must console themselves with this reflection, that if they have suffered, the prejudice they sustain does not arise from enmity to them; a fatal necessity has rendered this catastrophe inevitable.

The landing the tea would have been fatal, as it would have saddled the colonies with a duty imposed without their consent, and which no power on earth can affect. Their strength, numbers, spirit, and illumination render the experiment dangerous, the defeat certain.

The consignees must attribute to themselves the loss of the property of the East India Company. Had they reasonably quieted the minds of the people by a resignation, all [*would have*]... been well. The customhouse, and the man who disgraces [*his*] majesty by *representing* him, acting in confederacy with the inveterate enemies of America, stupidly opposed every measure concerted to return the tea.

That American virtue may defeat every attempt to enslave them, is the warmest wish of my heart....

AN IMPARTIAL OBSERVER.

DOCUMENT 9

# "We Shall be under the Domination of a Riotous Mob"

Gouverneur Morris to John Penn
May 20, 1774

When news of the first measures that came to be known as the Coercive Acts reached New York City, the Sons of Liberty sprang to action, calling a large public meeting in Fraunces Tavern. Moderates within the city, fearing that this radical group would take things too far by imposing an embargo that would cripple the finances of local merchants, schemed to coopt the proceedings. Radicals learned of the moderates' plan, however, forcing a compromise that resulted in the appointment of the "Committee of Fifty-one." This body, which included members of both factions, would direct New York's resistance efforts and call for a Continental Congress.

Since working people constituted the majority of the radicals and most of the moderates were men of some wealth, it was easy for Gouverneur Morris (1752–1816), a well-heeled New York attorney whose family owned a large portion of the Bronx, to view this episode as more than a minor dustup over the tactics of resistance. As Morris revealed in this letter to friend John Penn (ca. 1728–1795), he saw the controversy as evidence of rising tensions between the talented and educated "aristocracy" and the "shepherds" and "sheep" of the mob.

The fact that Morris and many other propertied men demonstrated a willingness to work with common people probably helps to explain why the American Revolution did not devolve into the sort of class conflict witnessed in the subsequent French Revolution. Morris would end up supporting independence, serving in the Continental Congress, signing the Articles of Confederation, and helping to draft the 1787 Constitution.

SOURCE: Peter Force, ed., *American Archives: A Documentary History of the English Colonies*, 4th ser., 6 vols. (Washington, D.C., 1837–53), 1:342–43.

Gouverneur Morris to John Penn New York, May 20, 1774

You have heard, and you will hear, a great deal about politics, and in the heap of chaff you may find some grains of good sense. Believe me, sir, freedom and religion are only watchwords. We have appointed a committee, or rather we have nominated one. Let me give you the history of it. It is needless to premise, that the lower orders of mankind are more easily led by specious appearances than those of a more exalted station. This, and many similar propositions, you know better than your humble servant.

The troubles in America, during Grenville's administration[1] ... stimulated some daring coxcombs to rouse the mob into an attack upon the bounds of order and decency. These fellows became ... the leaders in all the riots, the bellwethers[2] of the flock..... On the whole, the shepherds were not much to blame in a politic point of view. The bellwethers jingled merrily, and roared out liberty, and property, and religion, and a multitude of cant terms, which everyone thought he understood, and was egregiously mistaken.... That we have been in hot water with the British Parliament ever since everybody knows.... The port of Boston has been shut up. These sheep, simple as they are, cannot be gulled as heretofore. In short, there is no ruling them; and now ... the heads of the mobility[3] grow dangerous to the gentry, and how to keep them down is the question. While they correspond with the other colonies, call and dismiss popular assemblies, make resolves to bind the consciences of the rest of mankind, bully poor printers, and exert with full force all their other tribunitial[4] powers, it is impossible to curb them.

But art sometimes goes farther than force, and, therefore, to trick them handsomely a committee of patricians was to be nominated, and into their hands was to be committed the majesty of the people, and the highest trust was to be reposed in them.... The tribunes, through the want of good legerdemain[5] in the senatorial order, perceived the finesse; and yesterday I was present at a grand division of the city, and there I beheld my fellow citizens very accurately counting all their chickens, not only before any of them were hatched, but before above one half of the eggs were laid. In short, they fairly

---

[1] George Grenville (1712–1770) served as prime minister from 1763 to 1765.
[2] A flock's leading sheep; the bellwether wears a bell on its neck.
[3] The mob, with perhaps a play on the word "nobility."
[4] Tribune-like. Tribunes in the Roman republic were officials who represented and protected the interests of the common people.
[5] Magic.

contended about the future forms of our government, whether it should be founded upon aristocratic or democratic principles.

I stood in the balcony, and on my right hand were ranged all the people of property, with some few poor dependents, and on the other all the tradesmen, etc., who thought it worth their while to leave daily labor for the good of the country. The spirit of the English Constitution has yet a little influence left, and but a little. The remains of it, however, will give the wealthy people a superiority this time, but would they secure it they must banish all schoolmasters and confine all knowledge to themselves. This cannot be. The mob begins to think and to reason. Poor reptiles! It is with them a vernal morning; they are struggling to cast off their winter's slough, they bask in the sunshine, and before noon they will bite, depend upon it. The gentry begin to fear this. Their committee will be appointed, they will deceive the people, and again forfeit a share of their confidence. And if these instances of what with one side is policy, with the other perfidy, shall continue to increase, and become more frequent, farewell aristocracy. I see, and I see it with fear and trembling, that if the disputes with Great Britain continue, we shall be under the worst of all possible dominions; we shall be under the domination of a riotous mob.

DOCUMENT 10

# A Summary View of the Rights of British America

Thomas Jefferson

July 1774

The Coercive Acts not only sparked outrage among the common people whom Gouverneur Morris (1752–1816) derided as members of the mob; they also inflamed the indignation of Americans who occupied positions of power and influence. One such person was Thomas Jefferson (1743–1826), a member of Virginia's House of Burgesses who helped write a May 1774 resolution designating a day of fasting and prayer to show solidarity with the people of Massachusetts. Soon after, Lord Dunmore (1730–1809), the royal governor, showed his solidarity with Parliament by dissolving the House of Burgesses. As the elected members of that body prepared to regroup as the extralegal Virginia Convention, Jefferson drafted for its consideration his Summary View of the Rights of British America.

The 31-year-old's argument represented the next step in the progression of radical thought. While earlier critiques of British measures had denied the authority of Parliament to tax the colonies, Jefferson's Summary View held that "the British Parliament has no right to exercise authority over us" in any circumstance. While earlier opponents of Britain's policies had laid blame on Parliament, Jefferson's argument elevated responsibility to the level of the king. "Let not the name of George the third be a blot in the page of history," Jefferson wrote, reminding the monarch that "kings are the servants, not the proprietors of the people."

While stirring, Jefferson's words struck many as too much, too soon. The Virginia Convention declined to adopt his statement as its own. Several of its members, however, arranged to have it published in Williamsburg as a pamphlet. Soon presses in Philadelphia and London printed their own editions of the Summary View, which, like most political pamphlets of the era, appeared without its author's name on the title page. Even so, word spread of Jefferson's role. In the summer of 1775 his reputation preceded his arrival as a delegate to the Second Continental Congress, where Rhode Island representative Samuel Ward (1725–1776) recorded his first impression of "the famous Mr. Jefferson," whom he sized up as "a very sensible, spirited, fine fellow—and by the pamphlet he wrote last summer, he certainly is one."

SOURCE: [Thomas Jefferson,] *A Summary View of the Rights of British America: Set Forth in Some Resolutions Intended for the Inspection of the Present Delegates of the People of Virginia, Now in Convention* (Williamsburg, Va.: Clementina Rind, 1774). https://www.wdl.org/en/item/117/

---

RESOLVED, that it be an instruction to the said deputies, when assembled in general congress with the deputies from the other states of British America, to propose to the said congress that a humble and dutiful address be presented to his majesty, begging leave to lay before him, as chief magistrate of the British empire, the united complaints of his majesty's subjects in America; complaints which are excited by many unwarrantable encroachments and usurpations, attempted to be made by the legislature of one part of the empire, upon those rights which God and the laws have given equally and independently to all. To represent to his majesty that these his states have often individually made humble application to his imperial throne to obtain, through its intervention, some redress of their injured rights, to none of which was ever even an answer condescended; humbly to hope that this their joint address, penned in the language of truth, and divested of those expressions of servility which would persuade his majesty that we are asking favors, and not rights, shall obtain from his majesty a more respectful acceptance. And this his majesty will think we have reason to expect when he reflects that he is no more than the chief officer of the people, appointed by the laws, and circumscribed with definite powers, to assist in working the great machine of government, erected for their use, and consequently subject to their superintendence. And in order that these our rights, as well as the invasions of them, may be laid more fully before his majesty, to take a view of them from the origin and first settlement of these countries.

To remind him that our ancestors, before their emigration to America, were the free inhabitants of the British dominions in Europe, and possessed a right which nature has given to all men, of departing from the country in which chance, not choice, has placed them, of going in quest of new habitations, and of there establishing new societies, under such laws and regulations as to them shall seem most likely to promote public happiness.... Nor was ever any claim of superiority or dependence asserted over them by that mother country from which they had migrated; and were such a claim made, it is believed that his majesty's subjects in Great Britain have too firm a feeling of the rights derived to them from their ancestors, to bow down the sovereignty of their state before such visionary pretensions..... America was conquered, and her settlements made, and firmly established, at the expense of individuals, and not of the British public. Their own blood was spilt in acquiring lands for their settlement, their own fortunes expended in making that settlement effectual; for themselves they fought, for themselves they conquered, and for themselves alone they have right to hold. Not a shilling was ever issued from the public treasures of his majesty, or his ancestors, for their assistance, until of very late times, after the colonies had become established on a firm and permanent footing.... Settlements having been thus effected in the wilds of America, the emigrants thought proper to adopt that system of laws under which they had hitherto lived in the mother country, and to continue their union with her by submitting themselves to the same common sovereign, who was thereby made the central link connecting the several parts of the empire thus newly multiplied.

But that not long were they permitted, however far they thought themselves removed from the hand of oppression, to hold undisturbed the rights thus acquired, at the hazard of their lives, and loss of their fortunes. A family of princes was then on the British throne, whose treasonable crimes against their people brought on them afterwards the exertion of those sacred and sovereign rights of punishment reserved in the hands of the people for cases of extreme necessity, and judged by the constitution unsafe to be delegated to any other judicature.[1] While every day brought forth some new and unjustifiable exertion of power over their subjects on that side the water, it was not to be expected that those here, much less able at that time to oppose the designs of despotism, should be exempted from injury.

Accordingly that country, which had been acquired by the lives, the labors, and the fortunes, of individual adventurers, was by these princes, at several times, parceled out and distributed among the favorites and... by an assumed right of the crown alone, was erected into distinct and independent governments; a measure which it is believed his majesty's prudence and understanding would prevent him from imitating at this day, as no exercise of such a power, of dividing and dismembering a country, has ever occurred in his majesty's realm of England, though now of very ancient standing; nor

---

[1] Charles I (1600–1649), of the House of Stuart, reigned as king of England, Scotland, and Ireland (1625–1649) prior to his execution during the English Civil War (1642–1651). His marriage to a French Roman Catholic, belief in the divine right of kings, and hostile relationship with Parliament had helped to provoke that war.

could it be justified or acquiesced under there, or in any other part of his majesty's empire.

That the exercise of a free trade with all parts of the world, possessed by the American colonists, as of natural right, and which no law of their own had taken away or abridged, was next the object of unjust encroachment. ... The Parliament for the commonwealth ... assumed upon themselves the power of prohibiting their trade with all other parts of the world, except the island of Great Britain. This arbitrary act, however, they soon recalled, and by solemn treaty, entered into on the 12th day of March, 1651, between the said commonwealth by their commissioners, and the colony of Virginia by their House of Burgesses, it was expressly stipulated, by the 8th article of the said treaty, that they should have "free trade as the people of England do enjoy to all places and with all nations, according to the laws of that commonwealth." But that, upon the restoration of his majesty King Charles the second, their rights of free commerce fell once more a victim to arbitrary power; and by several acts ... of his reign, as well as of some of his successors, the trade of the colonies was laid under such restrictions, as show what hopes they might form from the justice of a British Parliament, were its uncontrolled power admitted over these states. History has informed us that bodies of men, as well as individuals, are susceptible of the spirit of tyranny. A view of these acts of Parliament for regulation, as it has been affectedly called, of the American trade, if all other evidence were removed out of the case, would undeniably evince the truth of this observation.... That to heighten still the idea of parliamentary justice, and to show with what moderation they are like to exercise power, where themselves are to feel no part of its weight, we take leave to mention to his majesty certain other acts of British Parliament, by which they would prohibit us from manufacturing for our own use the articles we raise on our own lands with our own labor. By an act ... passed in the 5th year of the reign of his late majesty King George the second, an American subject is forbidden to make a hat for himself of the fur which he has taken perhaps on his own soil; an instance of despotism to which no parallel can be produced in the most arbitrary ages of British history. By one other act ... passed in the 23d year of the same reign, the iron which we make we are forbidden to manufacture, and heavy as that article is, and necessary in every branch of husbandry, besides commission and insurance, we are to pay freight for it to Great Britain, and freight for it back again, for the purpose of supporting not men, but machines, in the island of Great Britain.... But that we do not point out to his majesty the injustice of these acts, with intent to rest on that principle the cause of their nullity; but to show that experience confirms the propriety of those political principles which exempt us from the jurisdiction of the British Parliament. The true ground on which we declare these acts void is, that the British Parliament has no right to exercise authority over us....

That thus have we hastened through the reigns which preceded his majesty's, during which the violations of our right were less alarming, because repeated at more distant intervals than that rapid and bold succession of injuries which is likely to distinguish the present from all other periods of American story. Scarcely have our minds been able to emerge from the astonishment into which one stroke of parliamentary thunder has involved us, before another more heavy, and more alarming, is fallen on us. Single acts of tyranny may be ascribed to the accidental opinion of a day; but a series of oppressions, begun at a distinguished period, and pursued unalterably through every change of ministers, too plainly prove a deliberate and systematical plan of reducing us to slavery....

[One such] act... passed in the same 7th year of his reign, having been a peculiar attempt, must ever require peculiar mention; it is entitled "An act for suspending the legislature of New York." One free and independent legislature hereby takes upon itself to suspend the powers of another, free and independent as itself; thus exhibiting a phenomenon unknown in nature, the creator and creature of its own power. Not only the principles of common sense, but the common feelings of human nature, must be surrendered up before his majesty's subjects here can be persuaded to believe that they hold their political existence at the will of a British Parliament. Shall these governments be dissolved, their property annihilated, and their people reduced to a state of nature, at the imperious breath of a body of men, whom they never saw, in whom they never confided, and over whom they have no powers of punishment or removal, let their crimes against the American public be ever so great? Can any one reason be assigned why 160,000 electors in the island of Great Britain should give law to four millions in the states of America, every individual of whom is equal to every individual of them, in virtue, in understanding, and in bodily strength? Were this to be admitted, instead of being a free people, as we have hitherto supposed, and mean to continue ourselves, we should suddenly be found the slaves, not of one, but of 160,000 tyrants, distinguished too from all others by this singular circumstance, that they are removed from the reach of fear, the only restraining motive which may hold the hand of a tyrant.

That by "an act... to discontinue in such manner and for such time as are therein mentioned the landing and discharging, lading[2] or shipping, of goods, wares, and merchandize, at the town and within the harbor of Boston, in the province of Massachusetts Bay, in North America," which was passed at the last session of British Parliament; a large and populous town, whose trade was their sole subsistence, was deprived of that trade, and involved in utter ruin. Let us for a while suppose the question of right suspended, in order to examine this act on principles of justice: An act of Parliament had been passed imposing duties on teas, to be paid in America, against which act the Americans had protested as inauthoritative. The East India Company, who until that time had never sent a pound of tea to America on their own account, step forth on that occasion the asserters of parliamentary right, and send hither many shiploads of that obnoxious commodity. The masters of their several vessels, however, on their arrival in America, wisely attended to admonition, and returned with their cargoes. In the province of Massachusetts alone the remonstrances of the people were disregarded, and a compliance, after being many days waited for, was flatly refused. Whether in this the master of the vessel was governed by his obstinacy, or his instructions, let those who know, say. There are extraordinary situations which require extraordinary interposition. An exasperated people, who feel that they possess power, are not easily restrained within limits strictly regular. A number of them assembled in the town of Boston, threw the tea into the ocean, and dispersed without doing any other act of violence. If in this they did wrong, they were known and were amenable to the laws of the land, against which it could not be objected that they had ever, in any instance, been obstructed or diverted from their regular course in favor of popular offenders. They should therefore not have been distrusted on this occasion. But that ill fated colony had formerly been bold in their enmities against the house of Stuart, and were now devoted to ruin by that unseen hand which governs the momentous affairs of this great empire. On the partial representations of a few worthless ministerial dependents, whose constant office it has been to keep that government embroiled, and who, by their treacheries, hope to obtain the dignity of the British knighthood,[3] without calling for a party accused, without asking a proof, without attempting a distinction between

---

[2] The loading of cargo onto a ship.
[3] Jefferson notated his personal copy of this pamphlet: "alluding to the knighting of Francis Bernard" (1712–1779), who had served as royal governor of Massachusetts (1760–1769).

the guilty and the innocent, the whole of that ancient and wealthy town is in a moment reduced from opulence to beggary. Men who had spent their lives in extending the British commerce, who had invested in that place the wealth their honest endeavors had merited, found themselves and their families thrown at once on the world for subsistence by its charities. Not the hundredth part of the inhabitants of that town had been concerned in the act complained of; many of them were in Great Britain and in other parts beyond sea; yet all were involved in one indiscriminate ruin, by a new executive power, unheard of until then, that of a British Parliament. A property, of the value of many millions of money, was sacrificed to revenge, not repay, the loss of a few thousands. This is administering justice with a heavy hand indeed!...

By the act... for the suppression of riots and tumults in the town of Boston, passed also in the last session of Parliament, a murder committed there is, if the governor pleases, to be tried in the court of King's Bench, in the island of Great Britain, by a jury of Middlesex. The witnesses, too, on receipt of such a sum as the governor shall think it reasonable for them to expend, are to enter into recognizance to appear at the trial. This is, in other words, taxing them to the amount of their recognizance, and that amount may be whatever a governor pleases; for who does his majesty think can be prevailed on to cross the Atlantic for the sole purpose of bearing evidence to a fact? His expenses are to be borne, indeed, as they shall be estimated by a governor; but who are to feed the wife and children whom he leaves behind, and who have had no other subsistence but his daily labor?... And the wretched criminal, if he happen to have offended on the American side, stripped of his privilege of trial by peers of his vicinage, removed from the place where alone full evidence could be obtained, without money, without counsel, without friends, without exculpatory proof, is tried before judges predetermined to condemn. The cowards who would suffer a countryman to be torn from the bowels of their society, in order to be thus offered a sacrifice to parliamentary tyranny, would merit that everlasting infamy now fixed on the authors of the act!... That these are the acts of power, assumed by a body of men, foreign to our constitutions, and unacknowledged by our laws, against which we do, on behalf of the inhabitants of British America, enter this our solemn and determined protest; and we do earnestly entreat his majesty, as yet the only mediatory power between the several states of the British empire, to recommend to his Parliament of Great Britain the total revocation of these acts, which, however nugatory they be, may yet prove the cause of further discontents and jealousies among us.

That we next proceed to consider the conduct of his majesty, as holding the executive powers of the laws of these states, and mark out his deviations from the line of duty: By the constitution of Great Britain, as well as of the several American states, his majesty possesses the power of refusing to pass into a law any bill which has already passed the other two branches of legislature. His majesty, however, and his ancestors, conscious of the impropriety of opposing their single opinion to the united wisdom of two houses of Parliament, while their proceedings were unbiased by interested principles, for several ages past have modestly declined the exercise of this power in that part of his empire called Great Britain. But by change of circumstances, other principles than those of justice simply have obtained an influence on their determinations; the addition of new states to the British empire has produced an addition of new, and sometimes opposite interests. It is now, therefore, the great office of his majesty, to resume the exercise of his negative power, and to prevent the passage of laws by any one legislature of the empire, which might bear injuriously on the rights and interests of another. Yet this will not excuse the wanton exercise of this power, which we have seen his majesty practice on the laws of the American legislatures. For the most trifling reasons, and sometimes for no conceivable reason at all, his majesty has rejected laws of the most salutary tendency. The abolition of domestic slavery is the great object of desire in those colonies, where it was unhappily introduced in their infant state. But previous to the enfranchisement of the slaves we have, it is necessary to exclude all further importations from Africa; yet our repeated attempts to effect this by prohibitions, and by imposing duties which might amount to a prohibition, have been hitherto defeated by his majesty's negative: Thus preferring the immediate advantages of a few British corsairs[4] to the lasting interests of the American states, and to the rights of human nature, deeply wounded by this infamous practice. Nay, the single interposition of an interested individual against a law was scarcely ever known to fail of success, although in the opposite scale were placed the interests of a whole country. That this is so shameful an abuse of a power trusted with his majesty for other purposes, as if not reformed, would call for some legal restrictions....

Since the establishment... of the British constitution, at the glorious revolution, on its free and ancient principles, neither his majesty, nor his ancestors, have exercised such a power of dissolution [*of Parliament*] in the island of Great Britain; and when his majesty was petitioned, by the united voice of his people there, to dissolve the present Parliament, who had become

---

[4] Pirates.

obnoxious to them, his ministers were heard to declare, in open Parliament, that his majesty possessed no such power by the constitution. But how different their language and his practice here! To declare, as their duty required, the known rights of their country, to oppose the usurpations of every foreign judicature, to disregard the imperious mandates of a minister or governor, have been the avowed causes of dissolving houses of representatives in America. But if such powers be really vested in his majesty, can he suppose they are there placed to awe the members from such purposes as these? When the representative body have lost the confidence of their constituents, when they have notoriously made sale of their most valuable rights, when they have assumed to themselves powers which the people never put into their hands, then indeed their continuing in office becomes dangerous to the state, and calls for an exercise of the power of dissolution. Such being the causes for which the representative body should, and should not, be dissolved, will it not appear strange to an unbiased observer, that that of Great Britain was not dissolved, while those of the colonies have repeatedly incurred that sentence?...

That in order to enforce the arbitrary measures before complained of, his majesty has from time to time sent among us large bodies of armed forces, not made up of the people here, nor raised by the authority of our laws: Did his majesty possess such a right as this, it might swallow up all our other rights whenever he should think proper. But his majesty has no right to land a single armed man on our shores, and those whom he sends here are liable to our laws made for the suppression and punishment of riots, routs, and unlawful assemblies; or are hostile bodies, invading us in defiance of law. When in the course of the late war it became expedient that a body of Hanoverian troops should be brought over for the defense of Great Britain, his majesty's grandfather, our late sovereign, did not pretend to introduce them under any authority he possessed. Such a measure would have given just alarm to his subjects in Great Britain, whose liberties would not be safe if armed men of another country, and of another spirit, might be brought into the realm at any time without the consent of their legislature. He therefore applied to Parliament, who passed an act for that purpose, limiting the number to be brought in and the time they were to continue. In like manner is his majesty restrained in every part of the empire. He possesses, indeed, the executive power of the laws in every state; but they are the laws of the particular state which he is to administer within that state, and not those of any one within the limits of another. Every state must judge for itself the number of armed men which they may safely trust among them, of whom they are to consist, and under what restrictions they shall be laid.

To render these proceedings still more criminal against our laws, instead of subjecting the military to the civil powers, his majesty has expressly made the civil subordinate to the military. But can his majesty thus put down all law under his feet? Can he erect a power superior to that which erected himself? He has done it indeed by force; but let him remember that force cannot give right.

That these are our grievances which we have thus laid before his majesty, with that freedom of language and sentiment which becomes a free people claiming their rights, as derived from the laws of nature, and not as the gift of their chief magistrate: Let those flatter who fear; it is not an American art. To give praise which is not due might be well from the venal, but would ill beseem those who are asserting the rights of human nature. They know, and will therefore say, that kings are the servants, not the proprietors of the people. Open your breast, sire, to liberal and expanded thought. Let not the name of George the third be a blot in the page of history. You are surrounded by British counselors, but remember that they are parties. You have no ministers for American affairs, because you have none taken from among us, nor amenable to the laws on which they are to give you advice. It behooves you, therefore, to think and to act for yourself and your people. The great principles of right and wrong are legible to every reader; to pursue them requires not the aid of many counselors. The whole art of government consists in the art of being honest. Only aim to do your duty, and mankind will give you credit where you fail. No longer persevere in sacrificing the rights of one part of the empire to the inordinate desires of another; but deal out to all equal and impartial right. Let no act be passed by any one legislature which may infringe on the rights and liberties of another. This is the important post in which fortune has placed you, holding the balance of a great, if a well-poised empire. This, sire, is the advice of your great American council, on the observance of which may perhaps depend your felicity and future fame, and the preservation of that harmony which alone can continue both to Great Britain and America the reciprocal advantages of their connection. It is neither our wish, nor our interest, to separate from her. We are willing, on our part, to sacrifice every thing which reason can ask to the restoration of that tranquility for which all must wish. On their part, let them be ready to establish union on a generous plan. Let them name their terms, but let them be just.... The God who gave us life gave us liberty at the same time; the hand of force may destroy, but cannot disjoin them. This, sire, is our last, our determined resolution; and that you will be pleased to interpose with that efficacy which your earnest endeavors may ensure to procure redress of these our great grievances, to quiet the minds of your subjects in British America, against any apprehensions of future encroachment, to establish fraternal love and harmony through the whole empire, and that these may continue to the latest ages of time, is the fervent prayer of all British America!

DOCUMENT 11

# Philadelphia Welcomes the First Continental Congress

*Dunlap's Pennsylvania Packet*
*September 16, 1774*

One manifestation of Americans' outrage over the Coercive Acts was the convening in Philadelphia of the First Continental Congress, which met from September 5 to October 26, 1774. Although the Coercive Acts were aimed primarily at Massachusetts (which the hardline administration [1770–1782] of Lord North [1732–1792] sought to punish for the Boston Tea Party), colonists throughout America understood that if these laws could deny basic English liberties there, then these rights could be denied anywhere. As a result, the delegates to Congress came from everywhere except Georgia, which needed the help of the British army to fight Creek Indians on its frontier. Virginia's delegation included Patrick Henry (1736–1799) and George Washington (1732–1799). New York's included John Jay (1745–1829). Samuel Adams (1722–1803) and his second cousin John Adams (1735–1826) sat among the representatives of Massachusetts. In total, fifty-six men from twelve colonies gathered to debate and decide what to do next.

Philadelphians extended an enthusiastic welcome with a celebration on September 16. This account of the festivities, which took place in the City Tavern and the Pennsylvania State House (later known as Independence Hall), makes clear that, although united against the Coercive Acts, it might not be easy for Congress to help bring about the "happy reconciliation between Great Britain and her colonies" to which they raised their wine glasses. Just about every sympathetic British politician was a Whig—and Lord North, a Tory, enjoyed widespread support within Parliament.

SOURCE: *Dunlap's Pennsylvania Packet or, the General Advertiser* (Philadelphia), September 19, 1774.

On Friday last[1] the honorable delegates, now met in General Congress, were elegantly entertained by the gentlemen of this city. Having met at the City Tavern about 3 o'clock, they were conducted from thence to the State House by the managers of the entertainment, where they were received by a very large company composed of the clergy, such genteel strangers as happened to be in town, and a number of respectable citizens, making in the whole near 500. After dinner the following toasts were drank, accompanied by music and a discharge of cannon.

1. The KING.
2. The QUEEN.
3. The Duke of Gloucester.[2]
4. The Prince of Wales[3] and Royal Family.
5. Perpetual union to the colonies.
6. May the colonies faithfully execute what the Congress shall wisely resolve.
7. The much injured town of Boston, and province of Massachusetts Bay.
8. May Great Britain be just, and America free.
9. No unconstitutional standing armies.
10. May the cloud which hangs over Great Britain and the colonies, burst only on the heads of the present ministry.
11. May every American hand down to posterity pure and untainted liberty he has derived from his ancestors.
12. May no man enjoy freedom, who has not spirit to defend it.
13. May the persecuted genius of liberty find a lasting asylum in America.
14. May British swords never be drawn in defense of tyranny.
15. The arts and manufactures of America.
16. Confusion to the authors of the Canada bill.[4]
17. The liberty of the press.

---

[1] September 16, 1774.
[2] Prince William Henry (1743-1805), younger brother of King George III (1738-1820).
[3] Prince George Augustus Frederick (1762-1830), son of George III, who in 1820 became King George IV.
[4] The Quebec Act of June 22, 1774, which included several objectionable provisions, expanded Quebec's territory into lands claimed by New York, Pennsylvania, and Virginia.

18. A happy reconciliation between Great Britain and her colonies, on a constitutional ground.
19. The virtuous few in both houses of Parliament.
20. The city of London.
21. Lord Chatham.[5]
22. Lord Camden.[6]
23. Bishop of St. Asaph.[7]
24. Duke of Richmond.[8]
25. Sir George Savile.[9]
26. Mr. Burke.[10]
27. General Conway.[11]
28. Mr. Dunning.[12]
29. Mr. Sawbridge.[13]
30. Dr. Franklin.
31. Mr. Dulany.[14]
32. Mr. Hancock.

---

[5] William Pitt (1708–1778), Earl of Chatham, was a Whig who led Parliament during the French and Indian War and from 1766 to 1768.

[6] Charles Pratt (1714–1794), Earl of Camden, was a Whig politician and civil libertarian who served as advisor to Pitt.

[7] Jonathan Shipley (1714–1788), who served as Bishop of St. Asaph (1769–1788), was a Whig who published a 1774 pamphlet criticizing Britain's treatment of America.

[8] Charles Lennox (1735–1806), 3rd Duke of Richmond, was a Whig politician known as "the radical duke" because of his support for American colonists in Parliament.

[9] George Savile (1726–1784), 8th Baronet of Thornhill, was a Whig member of the House of Commons (1759–1783) who frequently voiced his sympathy for American colonists.

[10] Edmund Burke (1730–1797) was a Whig member of the House of Commons (1766–1794) who defended Americans' rights.

[11] Henry Seymour Conway (1721–1795) was a British army officer and Whig politician who opposed the Stamp Act and Townshend Acts as well as attempts to crush American resistance to British policies.

[12] John Dunning (1731–1783) was a Whig member of the House of Commons (1768–1782) who opposed the 1774 Massachusetts Government Act, a key component of the Coercive Acts.

[13] John Sawbridge (1732–1795) was a Whig member of the House of Commons (1768–1780) known for his support of the radical John Wilkes (1725–1797) and the plight of American colonists.

[14] Daniel Dulaney (1722–1797), a member of the Maryland Governor's Council (1757–1776), had authored an influential 1765 pamphlet opposing taxation without

The acclamations with which several of them were received, not only testified the sense of the honor conferred by such worthy guests, but the fullest confidence in their wisdom and integrity, and a firm resolution to adopt and support such measures as they shall direct for the public good at this alarming crisis.

---

representation. While he had criticized British imperial policies, he would also oppose American independence.

DOCUMENT 12

# Plan of Union

Joseph Galloway
September 28, 1774

Of all the tragic figures of the American Revolution, few major officeholders experienced such a reversal of fortunes as Joseph Galloway (1731–1803). A lawyer who married into wealth, in 1756 Galloway became a member of the Pennsylvania General Assembly, which he led as speaker beginning in 1766. As a delegate to the First Continental Congress, Galloway proposed a constitutional solution to the imperial crisis through his Plan of Union, which would create "an inferior and distinct branch" of Parliament in the form of a "Grand Council" with representatives from each of the colonies. This legislature would elect its own speaker but serve under a "president general" appointed by the king. This intermediary layer of government between Parliament and the colonies would have the power to block measures of Parliament affecting the American colonies, which would retain their charters and control of their internal affairs.

Whether Britain would have accepted Galloway's Plan of Union is a matter for speculation. What is certain is that the First Continental Congress did not. Although his proposal appealed to many moderate delegates, after a day's debate a motion was made to table the plan for consideration at some future date. The delegates seemed to recognize this as a polite way of killing Galloway's idea. With the Rhode Island delegation divided, the states voted six to five in favor of the motion. This defeated not only Galloway's plan but also his hopes for compromise. When the Second Continental Congress met the following year, he was not among its members. When it declared independence in 1776, Galloway, once a leader in the resistance movement, became a Loyalist. After aiding and abetting the British Army in its 1777–1778 capture and occupation of Philadelphia, he moved to Great Britain and never returned to his native land.

SOURCE: Worthington C. Ford, et al., eds., *Journals of the Continental Congress, 1774–1789*, 34 vols. (Washington, D.C.: Government Printing Office, 1904–37), 1:49–51. https://archive.org/details/journalsofcontino1unit/page/48

*Resolved,* That the Congress will apply to his majesty for a redress of grievances under which his faithful subjects in America labor; and assure him, that the colonies hold in abhorrence the idea of being considered independent communities on the British government, and most ardently desire the establishment of a political union, not only among themselves, but with the mother state, upon those principles of safety and freedom which are essential in the constitution of all free governments, and particularly that of the British legislature; and as the colonies from their local circumstances, cannot be represented in the Parliament of Great Britain,[1] they will humbly propose to his majesty and his two houses of Parliament, the following plan, under which the strength of the whole empire may be drawn together on any emergency, the interest of both countries advanced, and the rights and liberties of America secured.

## A plan of a proposed union between Great Britain and the colonies

That a British and American legislature, for regulating the administration of the general affairs of America, be proposed and established in America, including all the said colonies; within, and under which government, each colony shall retain its present constitution, and powers of regulating and governing its own internal police, in all cases whatsoever.

That the said government be administered by a president general, to be appointed by the king, and a Grand Council, to be chosen by the representatives of the people of the several colonies, in their respective assemblies, once in every three years.

That the several assemblies shall choose members for the Grand Council in the following proportions:[2]

New Hampshire.
Massachusetts Bay.

---

[1] Among the several objections to the idea that colonists could enjoy effective representation in Parliament was the fact that it took at least six to eight weeks to sail between London and major American seaports. As a result, it might have taken more than four months for American colonists to learn of measures being considered by Parliament and communicate their views in response.

[2] Galloway did not specify how many members of the Grand Council each colony would be assigned.

Rhode Island.
Connecticut.
New York.
New Jersey.
Pennsylvania.
Delaware Counties.
Maryland.
Virginia.
North Carolina.
South Carolina.
Georgia.

Who shall meet at the city of _____[3] for the first time, being called by the president general, as soon as conveniently may be after his appointment.

That there shall be a new election of members for the Grand Council every three years; and on the death, removal, or resignation of any member, his place shall be supplied by a new choice, at the next sitting of assembly of the colony he represented.

That the Grand Council shall meet once in every year, if they shall think it necessary, and oftener, if occasions shall require, at such time and place as they shall adjourn to, at the last preceding meeting, or as they shall be called to meet at, by the president general, on any emergency.

That the Grand Council shall have power to choose their speaker, and shall hold and exercise all the like rights, liberties and privileges, as are held and exercised by and in the House of Commons of Great Britain.

That the president general shall hold his office during the pleasure of the king, and his assent shall be requisite to all acts of the Grand Council, and it shall be his office and duty to cause them to be carried into execution.

That the president general, by and with the advice and consent of the Grand Council, hold and exercise all the legislative rights, powers, and authorities, necessary for regulating and administering all the general police and affairs of the colonies, in which Great Britain and the colonies, or any of them, the colonies in general, or more than one colony, are in any manner concerned, as well civil and criminal as commercial.

That the said president general and the Grand Council, be an inferior and

---

[3] Galloway also did not specify in which city the Grand Council would meet, supplying this blank instead.

distinct branch of the British legislature, united and incorporated with it, for the aforesaid general purposes; and that any of the said general regulations may originate and be formed and digested, either in the Parliament of Great Britain, or in the said Grand Council, and being prepared, transmitted to the other for their approbation or dissent; and that the assent of both shall be requisite to the validity of all such general acts or statutes.

That in time of war, all bills for granting aid to the crown, prepared by the Grand Council, and approved by the president general, shall be valid and passed into a law, without the assent of the British Parliament.

DOCUMENT 13

# The Association Enacted by the First Continental Congress
*October 20, 1774*

*The rejection of Joseph Galloway's Plan of Union (Document 12) gave more radical members of the Continental Congress the opportunity to propose an alternative action. Rather than attempting to compromise with Great Britain, they sought to punish it with economic sanctions. Knowing that colonial boycotts and nonimportation agreements had helped pressure Parliament to repeal the Stamp Act and most of the taxes imposed through the Townshend Acts, members of the Congress voted in favor of this intercolonial Association, which would first end the importation of British goods, then their consumption, and finally all exports from the colonies to other parts of the British empire.*

*Throughout the colonies, local committees, which eventually included about 7,000 total members, would enforce the Association. Since many imported goods were expensive and considered luxuries, the Association helped to bridge the gap between rich and poor in America. For well-off Americans, clothing made of homespun fabrics, which replaced finer British textiles, remained fashionable symbols of resistance; colonists of more modest fortunes, for whom homespun had long been an economic necessity, now not only dressed like leaders of the colonial resistance but also joined with them in celebrating the virtue of austerity.*

SOURCE: Worthington Chauncey Ford, et al., eds., *Journals of the Continental Congress, 1774–1789*, 34 vols. (Washington, D.C.: Government Printing Office, 1904–37), 1:75–80. https://archive.org/details/journalsofcontino1unit/page/n97

---

We, his majesty's most loyal subjects ... find that the present unhappy situation of our affairs is occasioned by a ruinous system of colony administration, adopted by the British ministry about the year 1763, evidently calculated for enslaving these colonies, and, with them, the British empire. In prosecution of which system, various acts of Parliament have been passed, for raising a revenue in America, for depriving the American subjects, in many instances, of the constitutional trial by jury, exposing their lives to danger, by directing a new and illegal trial beyond the seas, for crimes alleged to have been committed in America; and in prosecution of the same system, several late, cruel, and oppressive acts have been passed, respecting the town of Boston and the Massachusetts Bay [colony], and also an act for extending the province of Quebec, so as to border on the western frontiers of these colonies, establishing an arbitrary government therein, and discouraging the settlement of British subjects in that wide extended country; thus, by the influence of civil principles and ancient prejudices, to dispose the inhabitants to act with hostility against the free Protestant colonies, whenever a wicked ministry shall choose so to direct them.

To obtain redress of these grievances, which threaten destruction to the lives, liberty, and property of his majesty's subjects, in North America, we are of opinion, that a non-importation, non-consumption, and non-exportation agreement, faithfully adhered to, will prove the most speedy, effectual, and peaceable measure; and, therefore, we do, for ourselves, and the inhabitants of the several colonies, whom we represent, firmly agree and associate, under the sacred ties of virtue, honor, and love of our country, as follows:

1. That from and after the first day of December next, we will not import, into British America, from Great Britain or Ireland, any goods, wares, or merchandise whatsoever, or from any other place, any such goods, wares, or merchandise, as shall have been exported from Great Britain or Ireland; nor will we, after that day, import any East India tea from any part of the world; nor any molasses, syrups, paneles,[1] coffee, or pimento, from the British plantations or from Dominica; nor wines from Madeira, or the Western Islands; nor foreign indigo.

2. We will neither import nor purchase, any slave imported after the first day of December next; after which time, we will wholly discontinue the slave trade, and will neither be concerned in it ourselves, nor will we hire our vessels, nor sell our commodities or manufactures to those who are concerned in it.

3. As a non-consumption agreement, strictly adhered to, will be an effectual security for the observation of the non-importation, we, as above, solemnly agree and associate, that, from this day, we will not purchase or use any tea, imported on account of the East India company, or any on which a duty hath been or shall be paid; and from and after the first day of March next, we will not purchase or use any East India tea whatever; nor will we, nor shall

---

[1] Brown unpurified sugar.

any person for or under us, purchase or use any of those goods, wares, or merchandise, we have agreed not to import, which we shall know, or have cause to suspect, were imported after the first day of December, except such as come under the rules and directions of the tenth article hereafter mentioned.

4. The earnest desire we have, not to injure our fellow subjects in Great Britain, Ireland, or the West Indies, induces us to suspend a non-exportation, until the tenth day of September, 1775; at which time, if the said acts and parts of acts of the British parliament herein after mentioned are not repealed, we will not, directly or indirectly, export any merchandise or commodity whatsoever to Great Britain, Ireland, or the West Indies, except rice to Europe.

5. Such as are merchants, and use the British and Irish trade, will give orders, as soon as possible, to their factors, agents, and correspondents in Great Britain and Ireland, not to ship any goods to them, on any pretense whatsoever, as they cannot be received in America; and if any merchant, residing in Great Britain or Ireland, shall directly or indirectly ship any goods, wares, or merchandise, for America, in order to break the said non-importation agreement, or in any manner contravene the same, on such unworthy conduct being well attested, it ought to be made public; and, on the same being so done, we will not, from thenceforth, have any commercial connection with such merchant.

6. That such as are owners of vessels will give positive orders to their captains, or masters, not to receive on board their vessels any goods prohibited by the said non-importation agreement, on pain of immediate dismissal from their service.

7. We will use our utmost endeavors to improve the breed of sheep, and increase their number to the greatest extent; and to that end, we will kill them as seldom as may be, especially those of the most profitable kind; nor will we export any to the West Indies or elsewhere; and those of us, who are or may become overstocked with or can conveniently spare any sheep, will dispose of them to our nèighbors, especially to the poorer sort, on moderate terms.

8. We will, in our several stations, encourage frugality, economy, and industry, and promote agriculture, arts, and the manufactures of this country, especially that of wool; and will discountenance and discourage every species of extravagance and dissipation, especially all horseracing, and all kinds of gaming, cockfighting, exhibition of shows, plays, and other expensive diversions and entertainments; and on the death of any relation or friend, none of us, or any of our families, will go into any further mourning dress, than a black crape or ribbon on the arm or hat, for gentlemen, and a black

ribbon and necklace for ladies, and we will discontinue the giving of gloves and scarves at funerals.

9. Such as are venders of goods or merchandise will not take advantage of the scarcity of goods that may be occasioned by this association, but will sell the same at the rates we have been respectively accustomed to do, for twelve months last past. And if any vender of goods or merchandise shall sell any such goods on higher terms, or shall, in any manner, or by any device whatsoever violate or depart from this agreement, no person ought, nor will any of us deal with any such person, or his or her factor or agent, at any time thereafter, for any commodity whatever.

10. In case any merchant, trader, or other person, shall import any goods or merchandise, after the first day of December, and before the first day of February next, the same ought forthwith, at the election of the owner, to be either reshipped or delivered up to the committee of the county or town, wherein they shall be imported, to be stored at the risk of the importer, until the non-importation agreement shall cease, or be sold under the direction of the committee aforesaid; and in the last mentioned case, the owner or owners of such goods shall be reimbursed out of the sales, the first cost and charges, the profit, if any, to be applied towards relieving and employing such poor inhabitants of the town of Boston, as are immediate sufferers by the Boston port bill....

11. That a committee be chosen in every county, city, and town, by those who are qualified to vote for representatives in the legislature, whose business it shall be attentively to observe the conduct of all persons touching this association; and when it shall be made to appear, to the satisfaction of a majority of any such committee, that any person within the limits of their appointment has violated this association, that such majority do forthwith cause the truth of the case to be published in the gazette; to the end, that all such foes to the rights of British America may be publicly known, and universally contemned[2] as the enemies of American liberty; and thenceforth we respectively will break off all dealings with him or her.

12. That the committee of correspondence, in the respective colonies, do frequently inspect the entries of their customhouses, and inform each other, from time to time, of the true state thereof, and of every other material circumstance that may occur relative to this association.

13. That all manufactures of this country be sold at reasonable prices, so that no undue advantage be taken of a future scarcity of goods.

---

[2] Scorned; treated with contempt.

14. And we do further agree and resolve, that we will have no trade, commerce, dealings, or intercourse whatsoever, with any colony or province, in North America, which shall not accede to, or which shall hereafter violate this association, but will hold them as unworthy of the rights of freemen, and as inimical to the liberties of their country.

And we do solemnly bind ourselves and our constituents, under the ties aforesaid, to adhere to this association, until such parts of the several acts of Parliament passed since the close of the last war ... are repealed.... And we recommend it to the provincial conventions, and to the committees in the respective colonies, to establish such farther regulations as they may think proper, for carrying into execution this association.

**DOCUMENT 14**

# A View of the Controversy between Great Britain and her Colonies

"A. W. Farmer" (Reverend Samuel Seabury)

December 24, 1774

The Continental Congress's October 1774 passage of the Association (Document 13), which promised to end trade with Great Britain, sparked outrage among moderate colonists wishing for reconciliation with the mother country. Among them was the Reverend Samuel Seabury (1729–1796), an Anglican priest who in the 1760s and early 1770s had supported a controversial proposal to bring a British bishop to America to preside over its churches. Now, writing under the pseudonym "A. W. Farmer" ("A Westchester Farmer"), this New York clergyman lashed out against the Association in a November pamphlet, Free Thoughts on the Proceedings of the Continental Congress. This prompted young Alexander Hamilton (1755/57–1804), a student at King's College (now Columbia University), to pick up his pen in response. Hamilton's efforts resulted in the 35-page Full Vindication of the Measures of Congress, signed "A Friend to America" and published on December 15. Less than ten days later, Seabury published this rejoinder.

In 1776, Seabury cast his lot with the Loyalists. He took refuge in British-occupied New York City and in 1778 became chaplain to the King's American Regiment. After the war Seabury returned to his native Connecticut; in 1784 he became the state's first Anglican bishop.

SOURCE: A. W. Farmer, *A View of the Controversy between Great-Britain and her Colonies* (New York: James Rivington, 1774), 17–21, 32–33. https://books.google.com/books/about/A_View_of_the_Controversy_Between_Great.html?id=bqVbAAAAQAAJ

---

... You, sir, affect to consider the gentlemen that went from this province to the Congress as the *representatives* of the province. You know in your conscience that they were not chosen by a hundredth part of the people. You know also, that their appointment was in a way unsupported by any *law*, *usage*, or *custom* of the province. You know also, that the people of this province had already delegated their power to the members of their Assembly, and therefore had no right to choose delegates, to contravene the authority of the Assembly, by introducing a foreign power of legislation. Yet you consider those delegates, in a point of light equal to our *legal* representatives; for you say, that "our *representatives* in General Assembly cannot take any wiser or better course to settle our differences, than our *representatives* in the Continental Congress have taken." Then I affirm, that our representatives ought to go to school for seven years, before they are returned to serve again. No wiser or better course? Then they must take just the course that the Congress have taken; for a *worse*, or more *foolish* [*course*], they cannot take, should they try. If they act any way different from the Congress, they must act *better* and *wiser*....

... You, sir, argue through your whole pamphlet, upon an assumed point .... That the British government—the *King, Lords,* and *Commons,* have laid a regular plan to enslave America; and that they are now deliberately putting it in execution. This point has never been proved, though it has been asserted over, and over, and over again. If you say, that they have declared their right of making laws, to *bind us in all cases whatsoever,* I answer; that the declarative act[1] here referred to, means no more than to assert the supreme authority of Great Britain over all her dominions. If you say, that they have exercised this power in a wanton, oppressive manner, it is a point, that I am not enough acquainted with the *minutiae* of government to determine. It may be true. The colonies are undoubtedly alarmed on account of their liberties. Artful men have availed themselves of the opportunity, and have excited such scenes of contention between the parent state and the colonies, as afford none but dreadful prospects. Republicans[2] smile at the confusion that they themselves have, in a great measure made, and are exerting all their influence, by sedition and rebellion, to shake the British empire to its very basis, that they may have an opportunity of erecting their beloved commonwealth on its ruins. If greater security to our rights and liberties be necessary than the present form and administration of the government can give us, let us endeavor to obtain it; but let our endeavors be regulated by prudence and probability of success. In this attempt all good men will join, both in England and America. All, who love their country, and wish the prosperity of the British empire, will be glad to see it accomplished.

... Every man who wishes well, either to America or Great Britain, must

---

[1] The Declaratory Act, assented to by George III on March 18, 1766.
[2] Those opposed to monarchy; people who do not support a government led by the king.

wish to see a hearty and firm union subsisting between them, and between every part of the British empire. The first object of his desire will be to heal the unnatural breach that now subsists, and to accomplish a speedy reconciliation. All parties declare the utmost willingness to live in union with Great Britain. They profess the utmost loyalty to the king; the warmest affection to their fellow subjects in England, Ireland, and the West Indies; and their readiness to do everything to promote their welfare that can reasonably be expected from them. Even those republicans, who wish the destruction of every species and appearance of monarchy in the world, find it necessary to put on a fair face, and make the same declaration.

What steps, sir, I beseech you, has the Congress taken to accomplish these good purposes? Have they fixed any determined point for us to aim at? They have, and the point marked out by them, is *absolute* independence [*from*] Great Britain—a perfect discharge from all subordination to the supreme authority of the British empire. Have they proposed any method of cementing our union with the mother country? Yes, but a queer one, ... to break off all dealings and intercourse with her. Have they done anything to show their love and affection to their fellow subjects in England, Ireland, and the West Indies? Undoubtedly they have—they have endeavored to starve them all to death. Is this *"Equity"*? Is this *"Wisdom"*? Then murder is equity, and folly, wisdom.

... Do you think, sir, that Great Britain is like an old, wrinkled, withered, worn-out hag, whom every jackanapes[3] that truants along the streets may insult with impunity? You will find her a vigorous matron, just approaching a green old age; and with spirit and strength sufficient to chastise her undutiful and rebellious children. Your measures have as yet produced none of the effects you looked for. Great Britain is not as yet intimidated. She has already a considerable fleet and army in America. More ships and troops are expected in the spring. Every appearance indicates a design in her to support her claim with vigor. You may call it *infatuation, madness, frantic extravagance*, to hazard so small a number of troops as she can spare, against the thousands of New England. Should the dreadful contest once begin—But God forbid! Save, heavenly Father! O save my country from perdition![4]

Consider, sir, is it right to risk the valuable blessings of property, liberty, and life, to the single chance of war? Of the worst kind of war—a civil war? A civil war founded on rebellion? Without ever attempting the peaceable

---

[3] A rude, mischievous person.
[4] Eternal damnation.

mode of accommodation? Without ever asking a redress of our complaints, from the only power on earth who can redress them? When disputes happen between nations independent of each other, they first attempt to settle them by their ambassadors; they seldom run hastily to war, until they have tried what can be done by treaty and mediation. I would make many more concessions to a parent, than were justly due to him, rather than engage with him in a duel. But we are rushing into a war with our parent state, without offering the least concession; without even deigning to propose an accommodation. You, sir, have employed your pen, and exerted your abilities, invindicating,[5] and recommending measures which you know must, if persisted in, have a direct tendency to produce and accelerate this dreadful event. The Congress also foresaw the horrid tragedy that must be acted in America, should their measures be generally adopted. Why else did they advise us "to extend our views to *mournful* events," and be in *all* "respects prepared for *every* contingency?"

May God forgive *them*, but may he confound *their* devices: and may he give *you* repentance and a better mind!...

A. W. Farmer

---

[5] Maligning, vilifying, smearing.

DOCUMENT 15

## *The Farmer Refuted...*

"Friend to America" (Alexander Hamilton)
*February 23, 1775*

Born to unmarried parents on the Caribbean island of Nevis, the early life of Alexander Hamilton (1755/57–1804) is so obscure that not even the year of his birth is known with certainty. At some point his father abandoned his family— possibly to shield his mother, still legally married to another man, from charges of bigamy. Even before his mother succumbed to yellow fever in 1768, Hamilton had become a clerk for merchants on the island of St. Croix.

Full of ambition, in 1769 Hamilton confessed that he "would willingly risk my life though not my character to exalt my station.... I wish there was a war." With funds for his education contributed by patrons on St. Croix, in 1773 Hamilton arrived in New York City, where he enrolled at King's College (now Columbia University) and quickly embraced the cause of resistance to British imperial policies.

In December 1774, in response to an attack on the Continental Association titled *Free Thoughts on the Proceedings of the Continental Congress* by "A. W. Farmer" (Reverend Samuel Seabury), Hamilton, writing as a "Friend to America," published *A Full Vindication of the Measures of Congress.* Shortly thereafter, Seabury authored his rejoinder to Hamilton's pamphlet, *A View of the Controversy Between Great-Britain and her Colonies* (Document 14). Eager to have the last word, Hamilton responded again with *The Farmer Refuted.* Here, Hamilton's discussion of "natural rights" and the "state of nature," together with his recounting of the "vengeance" heaped on Boston by the 1774 Coercive Acts, makes clear that mounting tensions between Britain and the American colonies had raised the stakes. Was Hamilton's 1769 wish for a war on the verge of being fulfilled?

SOURCE: Alexander Hamilton, *The Farmer Refuted, &c.,* [February 23,] 1775, Founders Online, National Archives. https://founders.archives.gov/documents/Hamilton/01-01-02-0057

---

... I shall, for the present, pass over to that part of your pamphlet, in which you endeavor to establish the supremacy of the British Parliament over America.

After a proper eclaircissement[1] of this point, I shall draw such inferences, as will sap the foundation of everything you have offered.

The first thing that presents itself is a wish, that "I had, explicitly, declared to the public my ideas of the *natural rights* of mankind. Man, in a state of nature (you say) may be considered, as perfectly free from all restraints of *law* and *government*, and, then, the weak must submit to the strong."

I shall, henceforth, begin to make some allowance for that enmity, you have discovered to the *natural rights* of mankind. For, though ignorance of them in this enlightened age cannot be admitted, as a sufficient excuse for you; yet, it ought, in some measure, to extenuate your guilt. If you will follow my advice, there still may be hopes of your reformation. Apply yourself, without delay, to the study of the law of nature. I would recommend to your perusal Grotius, Pufendorf, Locke, Montesquieu, and Burlamaqui.[2] I might mention other excellent writers on this subject; but if you attend, diligently, to these, you will not require any others.

There is so strong a similitude between your political principles and those maintained by Mr. Hobbes,[3] that, in judging from them, a person might very easily *mistake* you for a disciple of his. His opinion was, exactly, coincident with yours, relative to man in a state of nature. He held, as you do, that he was, then, perfectly free from all restraint of *law* and *government*. Moral obligation, according to him, is derived from the introduction of civil society; and there is no virtue, but what is purely artificial, the mere contrivance of politicians, for the maintenance of social intercourse. But the reason he run into this absurd and impious doctrine, was, that he disbelieved the existence of an intelligent superintending principle, who is the governor, and will be the final judge of the universe.

As you, sometimes, swear *by him that made you*, I conclude, your sentiment does not correspond with his, in that which is the basis of the doctrine, you both agree in; and this makes it impossible to imagine whence this congruity between you arises. To grant, that there is a supreme intelligence, who rules the world, and has established laws to regulate the actions of his creatures, and, still, to assert, that man, in a state of nature, may be considered as

---

[1] An explanation of something previously difficult to understand.
[2] Political philosophers Hugo Grotius (1583–1645); Samuel von Pufendorf (1632–1694); John Locke (1632–1704); Charles-Louis de Secondat, Baron de La Brède et de Montesquieu (1689–1755); and Jean-Jacques Burlamaqui (1694–1748).
[3] Political philosopher Thomas Hobbes (1588–1679).

perfectly free from all restraints of *laws* and *government*, appear to a common understanding, altogether irreconcilable.

Good and wise men, in all ages, have embraced a very dissimilar theory. They have supposed, that the deity, from the relations, we stand in, to himself and to each other, has constituted an eternal and immutable law, which is, indispensably, obligatory upon all mankind, prior to any human institution whatever.

This is what is called the law of nature, "which, being coeval[4] with mankind, and dictated by God himself, is, of course, superior in obligation to any other. It is binding over all the globe, in all countries, and at all times. No human laws are of any validity, if contrary to this; and such of them as are valid, derive all their authority, mediately[5] or immediately, from this original." BLACKSTONE.[6]

Upon this law, depend the natural rights of mankind, the supreme being gave existence to man, together with the means of preserving and beatifying that existence. He endowed him with rational faculties, by the help of which, to discern and pursue such things, as were consistent with his duty and interest, and invested him with an inviolable right to personal liberty, and personal safety.

Hence, in a state of nature, no man had any *moral* power to deprive another of his life, limbs, property or liberty; nor the least authority to command, or exact obedience from him; except that which arose from the ties of consanguinity.

Hence also, the origin of all civil government, justly established, must be a voluntary compact, between the rulers and the ruled; and must be liable to such limitations, as are necessary for the security of the *absolute rights* of the latter; for what original title can any man or set of men have, to govern others, except their own consent? To usurp dominion over a people, in their own despite, or to grasp at a more extensive power than they are willing to entrust, is to violate that law of nature, which gives every man a right to his personal liberty; and can, therefore, confer no obligation to obedience.

"The principal aim of society is to protect individuals, in the enjoyment of those absolute rights, which were vested in them by the immutable laws of nature; but which could not be preserved, in peace, without that mutual

---

[4] Emerging from the same point of origin.
[5] Through a sometimes slow process of negotiation.
[6] William Blackstone, *Commentaries on the Laws of England*, 4 vols. (1765–70; Philadelphia: Robert Bell, 1771–72), 1:41.

assistance, and intercourse, which is gained by the institution of friendly and social communities. Hence it follows, that the first and primary end of human laws, is to maintain and regulate these *absolute rights* of individuals." BLACKSTONE.[7]

If we examine the pretensions of Parliament, by this criterion, which is evidently a good one, we shall presently detect their injustice. First, they are subversive of our natural liberty, because an authority is assumed over us, which we by no means assent to. And secondly, they divest us of that moral security, for our lives and properties, which we are entitled to, and which it is the primary end of society to bestow. For such security can never exist, while we have no part in making the laws that are to bind us and while it may be the interest of our uncontrolled legislators to oppress us as much as possible.

To deny these principles will be not less absurd, than to deny the plainest axioms: I shall not, therefore, attempt any further illustration of them....

...I have taken a pretty general survey of the American charters,[8] and proved to the satisfaction of every unbiased person, that they are entirely discordant with that sovereignty of Parliament, for which you are an advocate. The disingenuity[9] of your extracts (to give it no harsher name) merits the severest censure, and will no doubt serve to discredit all your former, as well as future, labors in your favorite cause of despotism....

...Boston was the first victim to the meditated vengeance. An act was passed to block up her ports and destroy her commerce with every aggravating circumstance that can be imagined. It was not left at her option to elude the stroke by paying for the tea, but she was also to make such satisfaction to the officers of his majesty's revenue and others who might have suffered as should be judged *reasonable by the governor.* Nor is this all, before her commerce could be restored, she must have submitted to the authority claimed and exercised by the Parliament.

Had the rest of America passively looked on, while a sister colony was subjugated, the same fate would gradually have overtaken all. The safety of the whole depends upon the mutual protection of every part. If the sword of oppression be permitted to lop off one limb without opposition, reiterated strokes will soon dismember the whole body. Hence it was the duty and interest of all the colonies to succor and support the one which was suffering. It is sometimes sagaciously urged, that we ought to commiserate the distresses

---

[7] Ibid., 124.
[8] The colonies' constitutions.
[9] Disingenuousness, dishonesty, untruthfulness.

of the people of Massachusetts, but not intermeddle in their affairs, so far as perhaps to bring ourselves into like circumstances with them. This might be good reasoning, if our neutrality would not be more dangerous, than our participation. But I am unable to conceive how the colonies in general would have any security against oppression if they were once to content themselves with barely *pitying* each other, while Parliament was prosecuting and enforcing its demands. Unless they continually protect and assist each other, they must all inevitably fall a prey to their enemies.

Extraordinary emergencies require extraordinary expedients. The best mode of opposition was that in which there might be an union of councils. This was necessary to ascertain the boundaries of our rights; and to give weight and dignity to our measures, both in Britain and America. A Congress was accordingly proposed, and universally agreed to.

You, sir, triumph in the supposed *illegality* of this body; but, granting your supposition were true, it would be a matter of no real importance. When the first principles of civil society are violated, and the rights of a whole people are invaded, the common forms of municipal law are not to be regarded. Men may then betake themselves to the law of nature; and, if they but conform to their actions, to that standard, all cavils[10] against them, betray either ignorance or dishonesty. There are some events in society, to which human laws cannot extend; but when applied to them lose all their force and efficacy. In short, when human laws contradict or discountenance the means ... necessary to preserve the essential rights of any society, they defeat the proper end of all laws, and so become null and void....

A sincere Friend to America

---

[10] Frivolous objections.

DOCUMENT 16

# "Give me liberty or give me death!"

Patrick Henry

March 23, 1775

*In March of 1775, a month before fighting began at Lexington and Concord, colonists braced for war. Scottish traveler William Mylne (1734–1790) observed that "as to politics I think most of the people are mad [i.e., insane]; in South and North Carolina, Virginia, Maryland, they muster... as if they were going to be attacked." Cooler heads seemed poised to prevail at the meeting of the Second Virginia Convention. Held in Richmond's St. John's Church, safely distant from Williamsburg and Lord Dunmore (who had disbanded the House of Burgesses in 1774), the Convention considered the proposal of Patrick Henry (1736–1799) to form in every county a company of cavalry or infantry. After some delegates urged caution, Henry rose to address the assembly.*

*William Wirt (1772–1834), who published a biography of Henry in 1817, reconstructed his speech based on the recollections of Thomas Jefferson (1743–1826) and others who were present. After Henry concluded his remarks and took his seat, Wirt noted, "no murmur of applause was heard. The effect [of Henry's address] was too deep. After the trance of a moment, several members started from their seats. The cry, 'to arms!' seemed to quiver on every lip, and gleam from every eye" as the assembly erupted in cheers, shouts, and tears. "Their souls," he wrote, "were on fire for action."*

SOURCE: Patrick Henry, Speech on a Resolution to Put Virginia into a State of Defense, in Selim H. Peabody, comp., *American Patriotism: Speeches, Letters, and Other Papers which Illustrate the Foundation, the Development, [and] the Preservation of the United States of America* (New York: American Book Exchange, 1880), 108–10. https://babel.hathitrust.org/cgi/pt?id=mdp.39015027038259;view=1up;seq=122

---

Mr. President[1]—No man thinks more highly than I do, of the patriotism, as well as abilities, of the very worthy gentlemen who have just addressed the

---

[1] Peyton Randolph (1721–1775) served as president (1774–1775) of the Virginia Convention.

house. But different men often see the same subject in different lights; and therefore, I hope it will not be thought disrespectful to those gentlemen, if, entertaining, as I do, opinions of a character very opposite to theirs, I shall speak forth my sentiments freely and without reserve. This is no time for ceremony. The question before the house was one of awful moment to this country. For my own part, I consider it as nothing less than a question of freedom or slavery; and in proportion to the magnitude of the subject ought to be the freedom of the debate. It is only in this way that we can hope to arrive at truth, and fulfill the great responsibility which we hold to God and our country. Should I keep back my opinions at such a time, through fear of giving offense, I should consider myself as guilty of treason towards my country, and of an act of disloyalty toward the majesty of heaven, which I revere above all earthly kings.

Mr. President, it is natural to man to indulge in the illusions of hope. We are apt to shut our eyes against a painful truth, and listen to the song of that siren, till she transforms us into beasts. Is this the part of wise men, engaged in a great and arduous struggle for liberty? Are we disposed to be of the number of those, who, having eyes, see not, and having ears, hear not, the things which so nearly concern their temporal salvation? For my part, whatever anguish of spirit it may cost, I am willing to know the whole truth; to know the worst, and to provide for it.

I have but one lamp by which his feet are guided, and that is the lamp of experience. I know of no way of judging of the future, but by the past. And judging by the past, I wish to know what there has been in the conduct of the British ministry for the last ten years, to justify those hopes with which gentlemen had been pleased to solace themselves and the house? Is it that insidious smile with which our petition has been lately received? Trust it not, sir; it will prove a snare to your feet. Suffer not yourselves to be betrayed with a kiss. Ask yourselves how this gracious reception of our petition comports with those warlike preparations which cover our waters and darken our land. Are fleets and armies necessary to a work of love and reconciliation? Have we shown ourselves so unwilling to be reconciled, that force must be called in to win back our love? Let us not deceive ourselves, sir. These are the implements of war and subjugation—the last arguments to which kings resort. I ask gentlemen, sir, what means this martial array, if its purpose be not to force us to submission? Can gentlemen assign any other possible motive for it? Has Great Britain any enemy, in this quarter of the world, to call for all this accumulation of navies and armies? No, sir: she has none. They are meant for us: they can be meant for no other. They are sent over to bind and rivet upon us those chains, which the British ministry have been so long forging. And what have we to oppose to them? Shall we try argument? Sir, we have been trying that for the last ten years. Have we anything new to offer upon the subject? Nothing. We have held the subject up in every light of which it is capable; but it has been all in vain. Shall we resort to entreaty and humble supplication? What terms shall we find, which have not been already exhausted? Let us not, I beseech you, sir, deceive ourselves longer. Sir, we have done everything that could be done, to avert the storm which is now coming on. We have petitioned, we have remonstrated, we have supplicated, we have prostrated ourselves before the throne, and have implored its interposition to arrest the tyrannical hands of the ministry and Parliament. Our petitions have been slighted; our remonstrances have produced additional violence and insult; our supplications have been disregarded; and we have been spurned, with contempt, from the foot of the throne! In vain, after these things, may we indulge the fond hope of peace and reconciliation. There is no longer any room for hope. If we wish to be free—if we mean to preserve inviolate those inestimable privileges for which we have been so long contending—if we mean not basely to abandon the noble struggle in which we have been so long engaged, and which we have pledged ourselves never to abandon, until the glorious object of our contest shall be obtained—we must fight! I repeat it, sir, we must fight! An appeal to arms and to the God of Hosts is all that is left us!

They tell us, sir, that we are weak: unable to cope with so formidable an adversary. But when shall we be stronger? Will it be the next week, or the next year? Will it be when we are totally disarmed, and when a British guard shall be stationed in every house? Shall we gather strength by irresolution and inaction? Shall we acquire the means of effectual resistance, by lying supinely on our backs and hugging the delusive phantom of hope, until our enemies shall have bound us hand and foot? Sir, we are not weak, if we make a proper use of those means which the God of nature hath placed in our power. Three millions of people, armed in the holy cause of liberty, and in such a country as that which we possess, are invincible by any force which our enemy can send against us. Besides, sir, we shall not fight our battles alone. There is a just God who presides over the destinies of nations, and who will raise up friends to fight our battles for us. The battle, sir, is not to the strong alone; it is to the vigilant, the active, the brave. Besides, sir, we have no election. If we were base enough to desire it, it is now too late to retire from the contest. There is no retreat, but in submission and slavery! Our chains are forged. Their clanking may be heard on the plains of Boston! The war is inevitable—and let it come! I repeat it, sir, let it come.

It is in vain, sir, to extenuate the matter. Gentlemen may cry, peace, peace—but there is no peace. The war is actually begun! The next gale, that sweeps from the north, will bring to our ears the clash of resounding arms! Our brethren are already in the field! Why stand we here idle? What is it that gentlemen wish? What would they have? Is life so dear, or peace so sweet, as to be purchased at the price of chains and slavery? Forbid it, Almighty God! I know not what course others may take; but as for me, give me liberty or give me death!

DOCUMENT 17

# Account of the Battles of Lexington and Concord

John Andrews
April 20, 1775

*In the decade prior to the Coercive Acts, many colonists greeted with skepticism radicals' claims that Great Britain's imperial policy aimed to "enslave" them. After all, nearly every time they pushed back against objectionable measures, Parliament had repealed them. The hardline approach taken by the British government after the Boston Tea Party, however, had the effect of making men such as James Otis (1725–1783) and Samuel Adams (1722–1803) seem more like prophets than conspiracy theorists. Even fewer colonists harbored doubts about Britain's intentions after Lieutenant General Thomas Gage (1721–1787), acting on orders passed down from George III (1738–1820), dispatched hundreds of Redcoats to seize gunpowder and artillery pieces that colonists had stored in Concord, about eighteen miles from Boston—and to capture, if possible, John Hancock (1737–1793) and Adams, leaders of the Massachusetts Provincial Congress (which had been the colony's elected legislature prior to October 1774, when Gage decided to dissolve it). The attack was premised on the belief in London that Americans were cowards who would not fight. Gage feared otherwise, but hoped to preserve the secrecy of the mission in order to capitalize on the element of surprise.*

*During the April 19 Battles of Lexington and Concord, Redcoats learned that many Massachusetts men were itching for a fight—and had been informed of their mission hours before their arrival. Hancock, Adams, and most of the military supplies evaded capture, and by the end of the day the British had suffered more than three times as many casualties as the colonists. This April 20 letter from Boston merchant John Andrews (1743–1822) to his brother-in-law, Philadelphia merchant William Barrell (d. 1776), reveals the shock and uncertainty resulting from the initiation of warfare as well as the speed with which a Bostonian not directly involved in the fighting could grasp the essential elements, if not all the exact details, of what had just happened.*

SOURCE: Winthrop Sargent, ed., "Letters of John Andrews, Esq., of Boston," *Proceedings of the Massachusetts Historical Society* 8 (1864–65): 403–5. https://archive.org/details/proceedingsofmaso8mass/page/402

---

Yesterday[1] produced a scene the most shocking New England ever beheld. Last Saturday P.M.[2] orders were sent to the several regiments quartered here not to let their grenadiers or light infantry do any duty until further orders, upon which the inhabitants conjectured that some secret expedition was afoot, and being on the lookout, they observed those bodies upon the move between ten and eleven o'clock the evening before last,[3] observing a perfect silence in their march towards a point opposite Phipps's farm, where [boats?] were in waiting that conveyed them over [*the Charles River to Cambridge*]. The men appointed to alarm the country[4] upon such occasions got over by stealth as early as they [could] and took their different routes. The first advice we had was about eight o'clock in the morning, when it was reported that the troops had fired upon and killed five men in Lexington—previous to which an officer came express to his excellency Governor Gage, when between eight and nine o'clock a brigade marched out under the command of Earl Percy,[5] consisting of the marines, the Welsh fusiliers, the 4th Regiment, the 47th [regiment], and two field pieces. About twelve o'clock it was gave [*sic*] out by the general's aide [de] camps that no person was killed, and that a single gun had not been fired, which report was variously believed—but between one and two, certain accounts came that eight were killed outright and fourteen wounded of the inhabitants of Lexington—who had about forty men drawn out early in the morning near the meetinghouse[6] to exercise. The party of the light infantry and grenadiers, to the number of about eight hundred, came up to them and ordered them to disperse. The commander of them[7] replied that they were only innocently amusing themselves with exercise, that they had

---

[1] This portion of Andrews's letter, dated April 19 in the *Proceedings of the Massachusetts Historical Society*, had to have been written on April 20 since "yesterday" referred to April 19—the date of the Battles of Lexington and Concord.
[2] April 15, 1775.
[3] Tuesday, April 18, 1775.
[4] Paul Revere (1735–1818) and William Dawes (1745–1799).
[5] Brigadier General Hugh Percy (1742–1817), son of the Duke of Northumberland.
[6] The Congregational church at the southeastern corner of Lexington Green.
[7] Captain John Parker (1729–1775).

not any ammunition with them, and therefore should not molest or disturb them. Which answer not satisfying, the troops fired upon and killed three or four, the others took to their heels and the troops continued to fire. A few took refuge in the meeting[*house*], when the soldiers shoved up the windows and pointed their guns in and killed three there. Thus much is best account I can learn of the beginning of this fatal day.

    You must naturally suppose that such a piece would rouse the country (allowed the report to be true). The troops continued their march to Concord, entered the town, and refreshed themselves in the meeting and town house. In the latter place they found some ammunition and stores belonging to the country, which they found they could not bring away by reason that the country people had occupied all the posts around them. They therefore set fire to the house, which the people extinguished. They set fire a second time, which brought on a general engagement at about eleven o'clock. The troops took two pieces [of] cannon from the peasants, but their numbers increasing they soon regained them, and the troops were obliged to retreat towards town. About noon they were joined by the other brigade under Earl Percy, when another very *warm* engagement came on at Lexington, which the troops could not stand; therefore [*they*] were obliged to continue their retreat, which they did with the bravery becoming British soldiers—but the country [*militia*] were in a manner desperate, not regarding their cannon (any more) in the least, and followed them till seven in the evening, by which time they got into Charlestown, when they left off the pursuit, lest they might injure the inhabitants. I stood upon the hills in town and saw the engagement very plain. It was very bloody for seven hours. It's conjectured that one half the soldiers at least are killed. The last brigade was sent over the ferry in the evening to secure their retreat—where they are this morning entrenching themselves upon Bunker's Hill [to] get a safe retreat to this town. It's impossible to learn any particulars, as the communication between town and country is at present broke off. They were till ten o'clock last night bringing over their wounded, several of which are since [dead], two officers in particular. When I reflect and consider that the fight was between those whose parents but a few generations ago were brothers, I shudder at the thought, and there's no knowing where our calamities will end.

DOCUMENT 18

# Declaration of the Causes and Necessity of Taking Up Arms

John Dickinson and Thomas Jefferson

July 6, 1775

When the second Continental Congress convened in Philadelphia on May 10, 1775, less than a month had passed since the Battles of Lexington and Concord. Almost immediately Congress took steps to create the Continental Army. On June 19 it appointed George Washington (1732–1799), a delegate from Virginia who had led his colony's provincial forces during the French and Indian War, to serve as the army's commander-in-chief. The subsequent arrival of news of Britain's June 17 Pyrrhic victory at Bunker Hill made it impossible to deny that the fighting near Boston was quickly escalating into a full-fledged war. Yet many Americans—including most delegates to the Congress—still wished for peace. How best to provide Great Britain an opportunity for reconciliation while also making clear to officials in London (and people throughout America) that colonists would not cower in the face of British aggression?

The Continental Congress decided to offer the British both a carrot and a stick. The Olive Branch Petition, authored chiefly by Pennsylvania moderate John Dickinson (1732–1808), served as the carrot. Issued on July 5, it pledged Americans' loyalty to the king but called on him to repudiate the measures of Parliament that had violated colonists' rights. The stick was Congress's July 6 Declaration of the Causes and Necessity of Taking Up Arms. Written by Dickinson and 32-year-old Virginia delegate Thomas Jefferson (1743–1826), it aimed not only to impress Britain with America's seriousness of purpose but also to reinforce Americans' resolve by convincing them of the justice of their cause. On August 23 George III (1738–1820) dashed the hopes of Dickinson and others who wished for reconciliation by proclaiming the colonies in a state of rebellion. Viewing the Continental Congress as an illegal body, he responded to neither document.

SOURCE: The Declaration as Adopted by Congress, [6 July 1775], *Founders Online*, National Archives). https://founders.archives.gov/documents/Jefferson/01-01-02-0113-0005

IF IT was possible for men, who exercise their reason, to believe that the Divine Author of our existence intended a part of the human race to hold an absolute property in, and an unbounded power over others, marked out by his infinite goodness and wisdom, as the objects of a legal domination never rightfully resistible, however severe and oppressive, the inhabitants of these colonies might at least require from the Parliament of Great Britain some evidence that this dreadful authority over them has been granted to that body. But a reverence for our great Creator, principles of humanity, and the dictates of common sense must convince all those who reflect upon the subject, that government was instituted to promote the welfare of mankind, and ought to be administered for the attainment of that end. The legislature of Great Britain, however, stimulated by an inordinate passion for a power not only unjustifiable, but which they know to be peculiarly reprobated by the very constitution of that kingdom, and desperate of success in any mode of contest, where regard should be had to truth, law, or right, have at length, deserting those, attempted to effect their cruel and impolitic purpose of enslaving these colonies by violence, and have thereby *rendered it necessary for us to close with their last appeal from reason to arms.* Yet, however blinded that assembly may be ... we esteem ourselves bound by obligations of respect to the rest of the world, to make known the justice of our cause.

*Our forefathers, inhabitants of the island of Great Britain, left their native land to seek on these shores a residence for civil and religious freedom. At the expense of their blood, at the hazard of their fortunes,* with the least charge to the country from which they removed, by unceasing labor and an unconquerable spirit, *they effected settlements in the distant and inhospitable wilds of America,* then filled with numerous and warlike nations of barbarians. Societies or governments, vested with perfect legislatures, were formed under charters from the crown, and a harmonious intercourse was established between the colonies and the kingdom from which they derived their origin. The mutual benefits of this union became in a short time so extraordinary, as to excite astonishment. It is universally confessed, that the amazing increase of the wealth, strength, and navigation of the realm, arose from this source; and the minister, who so wisely and successfully directed the measures of Great Britain in the late war, publicly declared, that these colonies enabled her to triumph over her enemies. Towards the conclusion of that war, *it pleased our sovereign to make a change in his counsels.* From that fatal moment, the affairs of the British empire began to fall into confusion....

... *Parliament was influenced to adopt the pernicious project, and assuming a new power over [the colonies], have in the course of eleven years given such decisive specimens of the spirit and consequences attending this power, as to leave no doubt concerning the effects of acquiescence under it. They have undertaken to give and grant our money without our consent, though we have ever exercised an exclusive right to dispose of our own property; statutes have been passed for extending the jurisdiction of courts of admiralty and vice-admiralty beyond their ancient limits; for depriving us of the accustomed and inestimable privilege of trial by jury in cases affecting both life and property;* for suspending the legislature of one of the colonies; *for interdicting all commerce to the capital of another; and for altering fundamentally the form of government established by charter, and secured by acts of its own legislature solemnly confirmed by the crown;* for exempting the "murderers" of colonists from legal trial, and in effect, from punishment; *for erecting in a neighboring province, acquired by the joint arms of Great Britain and America, a despotism dangerous to our very existence;* and for quartering soldiers upon the colonists in time of profound peace. It has also been resolved in Parliament, that *colonists charged with committing certain offences, shall be transported to England to be tried.*

*But why should we enumerate our injuries in detail? By one statute it is declared that Parliament can "of right make laws to bind us in all cases whatsoever." What is to defend us against so enormous, so unlimited a power? Not a single man of those who assume it, is chosen by us....* We saw the misery to which such despotism would reduce us. *We for ten years incessantly and ineffectually besieged the throne as supplicants; we reasoned, we remonstrated with Parliament in the most mild and decent language.*

Administration sensible that we should regard these oppressive measures as freemen ought to do, sent over fleets and armies to enforce them. The indignation of the Americans was roused, it is true; but it was the indignation of a virtuous, loyal, and affectionate people. A congress of delegates from the united colonies was assembled at Philadelphia, on the fifth day of last September. We resolved again to offer a humble and dutiful petition to the king, and also addressed our fellow subjects of Great Britain. *We have pursued every temperate, every respectful measure; we have even proceeded to break off our commercial intercourse with our fellow subjects, as the last peaceable admonition, that our attachment to no nation upon earth should supplant our attachment to liberty. This, we flattered ourselves, was the ultimate step of the controversy: But subsequent events have shown, how vain was this hope of finding moderation in our enemies....*

Fruitless were all the entreaties, arguments, and eloquence of an illustrious band of the most distinguished peers, and commoners, who nobly and strenuously asserted the justice of our cause....

...General Gage, who in the course of the last year had taken possession of the Town of Boston, in the Province of Massachusetts Bay, and still occupied it as a garrison, on the 19th day of April, sent out from that place a large detachment of his army, who made an unprovoked assault on the inhabitants of the said province, at the Town of Lexington...murdered eight of the inhabitants, and wounded many others. From thence the troops proceeded in warlike array to the Town of Concord, where they set upon another party of the inhabitants of the same province, killing several and wounding more, until compelled to retreat by the country people suddenly assembled to repel this cruel aggression. Hostilities, thus commenced by the British troops, have been since prosecuted by them without regard to faith or reputation....

The general, further emulating his ministerial masters, by a proclamation bearing date on the 12th day of June, after venting the grossest falsehoods and calumnies against the good people of these colonies, proceeds to "declare them all, either by name or description, to be rebels and traitors, to supersede the course of the common law, and instead thereof to publish and order the use and exercise of the law martial." His troops have butchered our countrymen, have wantonly burned Charlestown, besides a considerable number of houses in other places; our ships and vessels are seized; the necessary supplies of provisions are intercepted, and he is exerting his utmost power to spread destruction and devastation around him.

...We are reduced to the alternative of choosing an unconditional submission to the tyranny of irritated ministers, or resistance by force. The latter is our choice. We have counted the cost of this contest, and find nothing so dreadful as voluntary slavery. Honor, justice, and humanity, forbid us tamely to surrender that freedom which we received from our gallant ancestors, and which our innocent posterity have a right to receive from us. We cannot endure the infamy and guilt of resigning succeeding generations to that wretchedness which inevitably awaits them, if we basely entail hereditary bondage upon them.

Our cause is just. Our union is perfect. Our internal resources are great, and, if necessary, foreign assistance is undoubtedly attainable. We gratefully acknowledge, as signal instances of the divine favor towards us, that his providence would not permit us to be called into this severe controversy, until we were grown up to our present strength, had been previously exercised in warlike operation, and possessed of the means of defending ourselves. With hearts fortified with these animating reflections, *we most solemnly, before God and the world, declare, that, exerting the utmost energy of those powers, which our beneficent Creator has graciously bestowed upon us, the arms we have been compelled by our enemies to assume, we will, in defiance of every hazard, with unabating firmness and perseverance, employ for the preservation of our liberties;* being with one mind resolved to die freemen rather than to live slaves.

*Lest this declaration should disquiet the minds of our friends and fellow subjects in any part of the empire, we assure them that we mean not to dissolve that union which has so long and so happily subsisted between us, and which we sincerely wish to see restored. Necessity has not yet driven us into that desperate measure, or induced us to excite any other nation to war against them. We have not raised armies with ambitious designs* of separating from Great Britain, and establishing independent states. *We fight not for glory or for conquest. We exhibit to mankind the remarkable spectacle of a people attacked by unprovoked enemies, without any imputation or even suspicion of offense....*

With a humble confidence in the mercies of the supreme and impartial judge and rule of the universe, *we most devoutly implore his Divine Goodness to protect us happily through this great conflict, to dispose our adversaries to reconciliation on reasonable terms, and thereby to relieve the empire from the calamities of civil war.*

DOCUMENT 19

# Resolution Regarding Quaker Pacifists

Lancaster County Committee of Correspondence and Observation

July 11, 1775

William Penn (1644–1718) established Pennsylvania in 1681 as a refuge for religious dissenters, especially fellow members of the Society of Friends. Yet Quakers, as adherents to this faith were sometimes called, constituted a minority of the colony's population by the mid-eighteenth century. Known for their simple attire, commitment to equality, and refusal to swear oaths, it was the Quakers' pacifism that led many to withdraw from Pennsylvania politics during the French and Indian War. By the summer of 1775, as a new war intensified, the Quakers again found themselves in a difficult situation.

Many had sided with the Patriot resistance to Great Britain's imperial policies. They had signed petitions and joined in commercial boycotts protesting Parliament's taxation without representation and other impositions on their rights. They felt great sympathy for the people of Massachusetts, where British aggression had led to bloodshed. But their sincere religious convictions prohibited them from joining their neighbors in taking up arms to resist what many viewed as British oppression.

In July 1775, the Lancaster County Committee of Correspondence and Observation proposed a means by which Quakers might honor their faith while also doing their part in the cause of resistance. Signed by William Barton (1754–1817), the committee's young secretary, the proposal called on Quakers unwilling to fight to volunteer monetary support for those who would. But this measure offered no perfect solution. The 1776 Philadelphia Yearly Meeting of the Society of Friends, for example, expressly prohibited Quakers from paying any compulsory "fine, penalty, or tax, in lieu of their personal services for carrying on war," or even volunteering to "violate our Christian testimony, and by doing so manifest that they are not in religious fellowship with us."

SOURCE: "At a meeting of the Committee of Correspondence and Observation for the County of Lancaster..." (Lancaster, Penn., 1775), Collections of the Lititz Moravian Museum and Archives, Lititz, Pennsylvania.

At a meeting of the Committee of Correspondence and Observation for the County of Lancaster, at the house of Matthias Slough, Esq.; in the borough of Lancaster, on the 11th day of July, 1775.

PRESENT,
WILLIAM HENRY, Esq.; EVERHARD GRUBER, Esq.; EDWARD HAND; JOHN HOPSON; GEORGE MUSSER; SAMUEL BOYD; JOHN WITMER, Jr.; and JAMES JACKS.

EDWARD HAND in the Chair.

A letter from the CONTINENTAL CONGRESS to this committee, bearing date, at Philadelphia, the sixth day of July, 1775, was read, and on motion it was

RESOLVED, THAT the following extract from the same be immediately printed, and distributed in the different townships of this county.

"The Assembly, taking into consideration the situation of many conscientious people of this province, with respect to arms, have, on the thirtieth day of June last, by their recommendation of that date, given to them, as well as others, advice which we hope all persons will most cheerfully follow.[1]

"The Congress, and your Assembly, greatly to their honor, have taken means for the protection of *America* and this *colony*; and we would advise you, gentlemen, to carry into execution the plans recommended by them, that this *colony* may unitedly act upon one and the same principle.

"Those who contribute will put their money into the hands of a person, they shall choose, to be paid over to such treasurer, as the committee shall appoint, for the uses 'recommended by the Assembly.'"

The COMMITTEE have the pleasure to hope, that a measure so very indulgent to all those denominations of people who *are conscientiously scrupulous of bearing arms*—that removes every objection raised against the proceedings of the COMMITTEE of this county in June last, and leaves not a color for complaint—and which comes recommended by the GENERAL ASSEMBLY of this province, as well as by the CONTINENTAL CONGRESS, will have due weight with every good man who wishes well to his country, and to the public cause, in this time of public calamity.

---

[1] In ASSEMBLY, *June* 30th, 1775: *"The House taking into consideration, that many of the good people of the province are conscientiously scrupulous of bearing arms, it is recommended to these conscientious people, that they cheerfully assist, in proportion to their abilities, such persons as cannot spend both time and substance in the service of their country, without great injury to themselves and families."*

The COMMITTEE do therefore join in earnestly recommending it to such denominations of people, in this county, whose religious scruples forbid them to associate or bear arms, that they contribute towards the necessary and unavoidable expenses of the public, in such proportion as may leave no room, with any, to suspect that they would ungenerously avail themselves of the indulgence granted them; or, under a pretense of *conscience* and *religious scruples*, keep their money in their pockets, and thereby throw those burdens upon a *part* of the community, which, in a cause that affects *all*, should be borne by *all*.

*By order of the committee,*
WILLIAM BARTON, *Secretary.*

DOCUMENT 20

# *Common Sense*

Thomas Paine

January 1776

Although a desire for independence did not cause the war with Great Britain, the war with Britain certainly contributed to a desire for independence. In May 1775, after Lexington and Concord, men serving under Benedict Arnold (1741–1801) and Ethan Allen (1738–1789) seized Fort Ticonderoga. In December, Henry Knox (1750–1806) and his troops dragged from the fort 59 artillery pieces 300 miles across the Berkshire Mountains, frozen rivers, and rough terrain to fortify the commanding view of Boston at Dorchester Heights. The fact that the British had not secured Dorchester Heights made their decision to secure Bunker Hill in June 1775 appear even more foolish, as they had suffered more than 1,000 killed or wounded in the process. Americans endured their own embarrassments, such as the ill-fated December 31 Battle of Quebec. Meanwhile, the king and Parliament displayed little interest in compromise. With so much at stake—and so many lives already lost—the Continental Congress's professed goal of repairing relations with Britain seemed increasingly quixotic.

As Thomas Paine (1737–1809) argued in his influential January 1776 pamphlet, *Common Sense*, the reasons for independence were clear and compelling. They included not only the long list of British violations of Americans' rights but also Paine's stunning, unvarnished critiques of monarchy in general, the British monarch in particular, and the fundamental premises of the relationship between the colonies and London. What had until recently been unspeakable and even unthinkable, Paine now put in print. The pamphlet, which gained a massive audience, made a major contribution to the cause of independence. Within three months of its publication, 100,000 copies of *Common Sense* circulated among the thirteen colonies' two million free inhabitants.

SOURCE: Moncure Daniel Conway, ed., *The Writings of Thomas Paine*, 4 vols. (New York: G. P. Putnam's Sons, 1894–96), 1:68, 69, 84–88, 89–90, 101–2, 110–11. http://oll.libertyfund.org/titles/paine-the-writings-of-thomas-paine-4-vols

The cause of America is in a great measure the cause of all mankind. Many circumstances have, and will arise, which are not local, but universal, and through which the principles of all lovers of mankind are affected, and in the event of which their affections are interested. The laying a country desolate with fire and sword, declaring war against the natural rights of all mankind, and extirpating the defenders thereof from the face of the earth, is the concern of every man to whom nature has given the power of feeling; of which class, regardless of party censure, is THE AUTHOR....

SOME writers have so confounded society with government, as to leave little or no distinction between them; whereas they are not only different, but have different origins. Society is produced by our wants, and government by our wickedness; the former promotes our happiness positively by uniting our affections, the latter negatively by restraining our vices. The one encourages intercourse, the other creates distinctions. The first is a patron, the last a punisher.

Society in every state is a blessing, but government, even in its best state, is but a necessary evil; in its worst state an intolerable one; for when we suffer, or are exposed to the same miseries by a government, which we might expect in a country without government, our calamity is heightened by reflecting that we furnish the means by which we suffer. Government, like dress, is a badge of lost innocence; the palaces of kings are built on the ruins of the bowers[1] of paradise. For were the impulses of conscience clear, uniform, and irresistibly obeyed, man would need no other lawgiver; but that not being the case, he finds it necessary to surrender up a part of his property to furnish means for the protection of the rest; and this he is induced to do by the same prudence which in every other case, advises him out of two evils to choose the least. Wherefore security being the true design and end of government ... whatever form thereof appears most likely to ensure it to us, with the least expense and greatest benefit, is preferable to all others....

IN the following pages I offer nothing more than simple facts, plain arguments, and common sense; and have no other preliminaries to settle with the reader, than that he will divest himself of prejudice and prepossession, and suffer his reason and his feelings to determine for themselves; that he will put on, or rather that he will not put off, the true character of a man, and generously enlarge his views beyond the present day.

Volumes have been written on the subject of the struggle between

---

[1] A serene, shady place in a garden or forest; a sanctuary.

England and America. Men of all ranks have embarked in the controversy, from different motives, and with various designs; but all have been ineffectual, and the period of debate is closed. Arms, as the last resource, decide the contest; the appeal was the choice of the king, and the continent has accepted the challenge....

The sun never shined on a cause of greater worth. It is not the affair of a city, a county, a province, or a kingdom; but of a continent—of at least one-eighth part of the habitable globe. It is not the concern of a day, a year, or an age; posterity are virtually involved in the contest, and will be more or less affected even to the end of time, by the proceedings now. Now is the seedtime of continental union, faith, and honor. The least fracture now will be like a name engraved with the point of a pin on the tender rind[2] of a young oak; the wound would enlarge with the tree, and posterity read it in full grown characters.

By referring the matter from argument to arms, a new era for politics is struck—a new method of thinking has arisen. All plans, proposals, etc., prior to the nineteenth of April, *i.e.* to the commencement of hostilities, are like the almanacs of the last year; which, though proper then, are superseded and useless now. Whatever was advanced by the advocates on either side of the question then, terminated in one and the same point,... a union with Great Britain; the only difference between the parties was the method of effecting it; the one proposing force, the other friendship; but it has so far happened that the first has failed, and the second has withdrawn her influence.

As much has been said of the advantages of reconciliation, which, like an agreeable dream, has passed away and left us as we were, it is but right that we should examine the contrary side of the argument, and enquire into some of the many material injuries which these colonies sustain, and always will sustain, by being connected with and dependent on Great Britain. To examine that connection and dependence, on the principles of nature and common sense, [*is*] to see what we have to trust to, if separated, and what we are to expect, if dependent.

I have heard it asserted by some, that as America has flourished under her former connection with Great Britain, the same connection is necessary towards her future happiness, and will always have the same effect. Nothing can be more fallacious than this kind of argument. We may as well assert that because a child has thrived upon milk, that it is never to have meat, or that the first twenty years of our lives is to become a precedent for the next

---

[2] Tree bark; thick outer layer.

twenty. But even this is admitting more than is true; for I answer roundly, that America would have flourished as much, and probably much more, had no European power taken any notice of her. The commerce by which she has enriched herself are the necessaries of life and will always have a market while eating is the custom of Europe.

But she has protected us, say some. That she has engrossed us is true, and defended the continent at our expense as well as her own, is admitted; and she would have defended Turkey... for the sake of trade and dominion.

Alas! We have been long led away by ancient prejudices and made large sacrifices to superstition. We have boasted the protection of Great Britain, without considering that her motive was *interest* not *attachment*; and that she did not protect us from *our enemies* on *our account*, but from *her enemies* on *her own account*; from those who had no quarrel with us on any *other account*; and who will always be our enemies on the *same account*. Let Britain waive her pretensions to the continent, or the continent throw off the dependence, and we should be at peace with France and Spain, were they at war with Britain....

But Britain is the parent country, say some. Then the more shame upon her conduct. Even brutes do not devour their young, nor savages make war upon their families.... This new world has been the asylum for the persecuted lovers of civil and religious liberty from *every part* of Europe.... [*To here*] have they fled, not from the tender embraces of the mother, but from the cruelty of the monster; and it is so far true of England, that the same tyranny, which drove the first emigrants from home, pursues their descendants still....

But, admitting that we were all of English descent, what does it amount to? Nothing. Britain, being now an open enemy, extinguishes every other name and title: and to say that reconciliation is our duty, is truly farcical. The first king of England, of the present line (William the Conqueror)[3] was a Frenchman, and half the peers of England are descendants from the same country; wherefore, by the same method of reasoning, England ought to be governed by France....

Europe is too thickly planted with kingdoms to be long at peace, and whenever a war breaks out between England and any foreign power, the trade of America goes to ruin, *because of her connection with Britain*. The next war may not turn out like the last, and should it not, the advocates for

---

[3] William I (ca. 1028–1087), after the 1066 Norman invasion, became the first Norman king of England (1066–1087).

reconciliation now will be wishing for separation then, because neutrality in that case would be a safer convoy than a man of war. Everything that is right or reasonable pleads for separation. The blood of the slain, the weeping voice of nature cries, 'TIS TIME TO PART. Even the distance at which the Almighty has placed England and America is a strong and natural proof that the authority of the one over the other was never the design of Heaven....

The authority of Great Britain over this continent, is a form of government, which sooner or later must have an end. And a serious mind can draw no true pleasure by looking forward, under the painful and positive conviction, that what he calls "the present constitution" is merely temporary. As parents, we can have no joy, knowing that this government is not sufficiently lasting to ensure anything which we may bequeath to posterity. And by a plain method of argument, as we are running the next generation into debt, we ought to do the work of it, otherwise we use them meanly and pitifully. In order to discover the line of our duty rightly, we should take our children in our hand, and fix our station a few years farther into life; that eminence will present a prospect, which a few present fears and prejudices conceal from our sight.

Though I would carefully avoid giving unnecessary offence, yet I am inclined to believe, that all those who espouse the doctrine of reconciliation, may be included within the following descriptions: Interested men, who are not to be trusted; weak men, who *cannot* see; prejudiced men, who will not see; and a certain set of moderate men, who think better of the European world than it deserves; and this last class, by an ill-judged deliberation, will be the cause of more calamities to this continent than all the other three....

I HAVE never met with a man, either in England or America, who has not confessed his opinion, that a separation between the countries would take place one time or other. And there is no instance in which we have shown less judgment, than in endeavoring to describe, what we call, the ripeness or fitness of the continent for independence.

As all men allow the measure, and vary only in their opinion of the time, let us, in order to remove mistakes, take a general survey of things, and endeavor if possible to find out the *very* time. But I need not go far; the inquiry ceases at once, for the *time has found us*. The general concurrence, the glorious union of all things, proves the fact.

It is not in numbers but in unity that our great strength lies; yet our present numbers are sufficient to repel the force of all the world. The continent has at this time the largest body of armed and disciplined men of any power under Heaven; and is just arrived at that pitch of strength, in which no single colony is able to support itself, and the whole, when united, is able to do anything. Our land force is more than sufficient, and as to naval affairs, we cannot be insensible that Britain would never suffer an American man of war to be built, while the continent remained in her hands. Wherefore, we should be no forwarder a hundred years hence... than we are now; but the truth is, we should be less so, because the timber of the country is every day diminishing, and that which will remain at last, will be far off or difficult to procure....

Debts we have none; and whatever we may contract on this account will serve as a glorious memento of our virtue. Can we but leave posterity with a settled form of government, an independent constitution of its own, the purchase at any price will be cheap. But to expend millions for the sake of getting a few vile acts repealed, and routing the present ministry only, is unworthy the charge, and is using posterity with the utmost cruelty; because it is leaving them the great work to do, and a debt upon their backs from which they derive no advantage. Such a thought is unworthy a man of honor, and is the true characteristic of a narrow heart and a piddling politician.

The debt we may contract does not deserve our regard if the work be but accomplished. No nation ought to be without a debt. A national debt is a national bond; and when it bears no interest, is in no case a grievance. Britain is oppressed with a debt of upwards of one hundred and forty million sterling, for which she pays upwards of four million interest. And as a compensation for her debt, she has a large navy; America is without a debt, and without a navy; yet for the twentieth part of the English national debt, could have a navy as large....

TO CONCLUDE, however strange it may appear to some, or however unwilling they may be to think so, matters not, but many strong and striking reasons may be given to show, that nothing can settle our affairs so expeditiously as an open and determined declaration for independence. Some of which are,

*First*—It is the custom of nations, when any two are at war, for some other powers, not engaged in the quarrel, to step in as mediators, and bring about the preliminaries of a peace. But while America calls herself the subject of Great Britain, no power, however well disposed she may be, can offer her mediation. Wherefore, in our present state we may quarrel on forever.

*Second*—It is unreasonable to suppose, that France or Spain will give us any kind of assistance, if we mean only to make use of that assistance for the purpose of repairing the breach, and strengthening the connection between Britain and America; because, those powers would be sufferers by the consequences.

*Third*—While we profess ourselves the subjects of Britain, we must, in the eyes of foreign nations, be considered as rebels. The precedent is somewhat dangerous to their peace, for men to be in arms under the name of subjects. We, on the spot, can solve the paradox; but to unite resistance and subjection, requires an idea much too refined for common understanding.

*Fourth*—Were a manifesto to be published, and dispatched to foreign courts, setting forth the miseries we have endured, and the peaceful methods which we have ineffectually used for redress; declaring at the same time, that not being able any longer to live happily or safely under the cruel disposition of the British court, we had been driven to the necessity of breaking off all connections with her; at the same time, assuring all such courts of our peaceable disposition towards them, and of our desire of entering into trade with them. Such a memorial would produce more good effects to this continent, than if a ship were freighted with petitions to Britain....

These proceedings may at first seem strange and difficult, but like all other steps which we have already passed over, will in a little time become familiar and agreeable: and until and independence is declared, the continent will feel itself like a man who continues putting off some unpleasant business from day to day, yet knows it must be done, hates to set about it, wishes it over, and is continually haunted with the thoughts of its necessity.

DOCUMENT 21

# Stratford, Connecticut's Thomas Gage—and Monmouth County, New Jersey's Dunmore

New-England Chronicle
May 30, 1776

As war raged and calls for independence mounted, the question of how to galvanize opposition to Britain gained increasing importance. Although historians' estimates of the number of Loyalists vary, most agree that, in 1776, those opposed to independence constituted less than one-quarter of the population. During the course of the war, Loyalists became an even smaller minority. Some left the United States while others, either changing their minds or succumbing to pressure from their neighbors, became Patriots.

One convert appears to have been William Edwards (1730–1814) of Stratford, Connecticut, who in early 1776 reportedly named his newborn son after Lieutenant General Thomas Gage (1721–1787), the former Massachusetts military governor and commander of British forces occupying Boston. Edwards, a member of the Church of England in a predominantly Congregationalist town, was accustomed to being in the minority. But the "petticoat army" of local women who threatened to tar and feather his wife might have caused him to reconsider his Loyalist views, for he later took up arms in behalf of independence. The April 19 issue of New London's Connecticut Gazette, which published a slightly different version of the account below, noted that the women were led by Elizabeth Judson Whiting (1723–1793), wife of Lieutenant Colonel Samuel Whiting (1720–1803), commander of Stratford's militia. Prior to departing the Edwardses' house, according to the Gazette, the women gave "three huzzahs."

Meanwhile, few people cheered the decision of an African American woman in Monmouth County, New Jersey, to name her newborn son in honor of Virginia's royal governor, Lord Dunmore (1730–1809). John Murray, the 4th Earl of Dunmore, attracted the scorn of many white colonists when, in November 1775, he issued a proclamation urging people enslaved on Patriots' plantations to run away and join the British army. Many of the hundreds who answered Dunmore's call were organized into an "Ethiopian Regiment" that suffered defeat in the December 1775 Battle of Great Bridge, which wrested control of Norfolk, Virginia, from

British forces. These African Americans were among the first Loyalists to fight in the American Revolution, but they would not be the last.

SOURCE: *New-England Chronicle* (Boston), May 30, 1776.

---

The following odd affair happened at Stratford on the 10th of March last: A child of Mr. Edwards, of that place, was baptized by the Rev. Mr.——,[1] of Norwalk, and named THOMAS GAGE.[2] This alarmed the neighborhood, and on the 13th, 170 young ladies formed themselves into a battalion, and with solemn ceremony appointed a general and the other officers to lead them on; then the petticoat army marched in the greatest good order to pay their compliments to THOMAS GAGE, and present his mother (the nymphs ought to have deferred this part of the business a few days, says our correspondent) with a suit of tar and feathers; but THOMAS's sire having intelligence of their expedition, *vi et armis*,[3] kept them from entering his house, so that the female soldiers returned to headquarters without effecting what they intended, and disbanded themselves.

As the public were a few days since informed of the honor done General GAGE, by naming a child after him, it may not be amiss to let it be known, that Lord *Dunmore* also comes in for his share in the same way.

On Monday the eighth instant,[4] a lusty, likely NEGRO WENCH was delivered of a male child, who, in memory of a certain notable NEGRO CHIEF, is named DUNMORE.

> Hail! Doughty Ethiopian Chief!
> Thou ignominious Negro-Thief!
> This BLACK *shall prop thy sinking name,*
> *And damn thee to perpetual Fame.*

[*Query*, Is not this, though an act of justice to Dunmore, cruelty to the innocent Negro?]

---

[1] Rev. Jeremiah Leaming (1717–1804), a leading Connecticut Anglican, was rector of St. Paul's Church in Norwalk, Connecticut.
[2] William Edwards's wife, Mary, gave birth to a son, Thomas, on January 3, 1776.
[3] *Latin*: with force and arms.
[4] April 8, 1776. Although "instant" means "this month," the *Chronicle*'s report was reprinted from the May 2, 1776, issue of the *New-York Journal*, where the material on the baby named Dunmore appeared in an unsigned April 20 letter from Monmouth County, New Jersey.

DOCUMENT 22

# "Remember the Ladies"

Abigail Adams and John Adams
March 31—May 26, 1776

*In the spring of 1776, talk of independence had not yet transformed the common understanding that the struggle against Britain was an effort to defend colonists' rights as Englishmen. But what about the rights of America's Englishwomen? What about the rights of people of African descent and Native Americans? These uncomfortable questions could be applied not only to natural rights (such as the freedom from harm to one's life, liberty, and property), but even to civil rights (such as the rights to vote and hold office) related to government decision-making. Maybe nowhere else were these vexing questions more intelligently discussed than in this series of letters written by Abigail Adams (1744–1818) and her husband, Massachusetts Continental Congress delegate John Adams (1735–1826).*

*Abigail Adams's seemingly sincere insistence that Congress "remember the ladies" when making new laws, John Adams's seemingly ham-handed initial response, and his May 1776 message to Massachusetts jurist James Sullivan (1744–1808) highlight the complexity of Americans' thoughts regarding the ends and means of government. While Abigail Adams's letters provided evidence of what Sullivan described, in a May 9 letter, as a "leveling spirit" promoting greater equality, John Adams's letters caution that too much equality could undermine liberty. Given the uncertain experiment in collective self-government on which Americans were about to embark, did it make sense to hand the reins of power to men, women, or even children who lacked the means to fully govern themselves?*

SOURCES: Abigail Adams to John Adams, March 31, 1776, *Founders Online, National Archives,* https://founders.archives.gov/documents/Adams/04-01-02-0241; J. Adams to A. Adams, April 14, 1776, Founders Online, *National Archives,* https://founders.archives.gov/documents/Adams/04-01-02-0248; A. Adams to J. Adams, May 7, 1776, Founders Online, *National Archives,* https://founders.archives.gov/documents/Adams/04-01-02-0259; J. Adams to James Sullivan, May 26, 1776, Founders Online, National Archives, https://founders.archives.gov/documents/Adams/06-04-02-0091.

### Abigail Adams to John Adams | Braintree, Mass., March 31, 1776

I wish you would ever write me a letter half as long as I write you, and tell me, if you may, where your fleet are gone? What sort of defense Virginia can make against our common enemy? Whether it is so situated as to make an able defense? Are not the gentry lords and the common people vassals, are they not like the uncivilized natives Britain represents us to be? I hope their riflemen, who have shown themselves very savage and even bloodthirsty, are not a specimen of the generality of the people.

I am willing to allow the colony great merit for having produced a Washington but they have been shamefully duped by a Dunmore.[1]

I have sometimes been ready to think that the passion for liberty cannot be equally strong in the breasts of those who have been accustomed to deprive their fellow creatures of theirs. Of this I am certain that it is not founded upon that generous and Christian principle of doing to others as we would that others should do unto us....

I long to hear that you have declared an independency—and by the way, in the new code of laws which I suppose it will be necessary for you to make, I desire you would remember the ladies, and be more generous and favorable to them than your ancestors. Do not put such unlimited power into the hands of the husbands. Remember, all men would be tyrants if they could. If particular care and attention is not paid to the ladies, we are determined to foment a rebellion, and will not hold ourselves bound by any laws in which we have no voice, or representation.

That your sex are naturally tyrannical is a truth so thoroughly established as to admit of no dispute, but such of you as wish to be happy willingly give up the harsh title of master for the more tender and endearing one of friend. Why then, not put it out of the power of the vicious and the lawless to use us with cruelty and indignity with impunity. Men of sense in all ages abhor those customs which treat us only as the vassals of your sex. Regard us then as beings placed by providence under your protection and, in imitation of the Supreme Being, make use of that power only for our happiness....

---

[1] Lord John Murray (1730–1809), Earl of Dunmore, last royal governor of Virginia, who reportedly duped the residents of Williamsburg into leaving their powder supplies unguarded (allowing them to be taken for the crown), and who infamously issued a proclamation promising freedom to any enslaved man belonging to a Patriot who would abandon his master and fight for the British.

## John Adams to Abigail Adams | Philadelphia, April 14, 1776

...As to your extraordinary code of laws, I cannot but laugh. We have been told that our struggle has loosened the bands of government everywhere. That children and apprentices were disobedient—that schools and colleges were grown turbulent, that Indians slighted their guardians, and Negroes grew insolent to their masters. But your letter was the first intimation that another tribe, more numerous and powerful than all the rest, were grown discontented. This is rather too coarse a compliment but you are so saucy, I won't blot it out.

Depend upon it, we know better than to repeal our masculine systems. Although they are in full force, you know they are little more than theory. We dare not exert our power in its full latitude. We are obliged to go fair, and softly, and in practice, you know we are the subjects. We have only the name of masters, and rather than give up this, which would completely subject us to the despotism of the petticoat, I hope General Washington, and all our brave heroes would fight. I am sure every good politician would plot, as long as he would against despotism, empire, monarchy, aristocracy, oligarchy, or ochlocracy.[2] A fine story indeed. I begin to think the ministry as deep as they are wicked. After stirring up Tories, land-jobbers, trimmers, bigots, Canadians, Indians, Negroes, Hanoverians, Hessians, Russians, Irish Roman Catholics, Scotch renegades, at last they have stimulated them to demand new privileges and threaten to rebel.

## Abigail Adams to John Adams | Braintree, Mass., May 7, 1776

How many are the solitary hours I spend, ruminating upon the past, and anticipating the future, whilst you, overwhelmed with the cares of state, have but few moments you can devote to any individual. All domestic pleasures and enjoyments are absorbed in the great and important duty you owe your country, "for our country is as it were a secondary God, and the first and greatest parent. It is to be preferred to parents, wives, children, friends, and all things—the Gods only accepted. For if our country perishes it is as impossible to save an individual, as to preserve one of the fingers of a mortified hand."[3]

---

[2] Government by mob rule.
[3] Adams was apparently quoting the second-century Stoic philosopher Hierocles, although in the eighteenth century his fragments were attributed to earlier philosophers.

Thus do I suppress every wish, and silence every murmur, acquiescing in a painful separation from the companion of my youth, and the friend of my heart....

A government of more stability is much wanted in this colony, and they are ready to receive it from the hands of the Congress, and since I have begun with maxims of state I will add another: that a people may let a king fall, yet still remain a people, but if a king let his people slip from him, he is no longer a king. And as this is most certainly our case, why not proclaim to the world in decisive terms your own importance?

Shall we not be despised by foreign powers for hesitating so long at a word?

I cannot say that I think you very generous to the ladies, for whilst you are proclaiming peace and good will to men, emancipating all nations, you insist upon retaining an absolute power over wives. But you must remember that arbitrary power is like most other things which are very hard, very liable to be broken—and notwithstanding all your wise laws and maxims we have it in our power not only to free ourselves but to subdue our masters, and without violence throw both your natural and legal authority at our feet—

Charm by accepting, by submitting sway

Yet have our humor most when we obey....

## John Adams to James Sullivan | Philadelphia, May 26, 1776

Your favors of May 9th. and 17th. are now before me; and I consider them as the commencement of a correspondence, which will not only give me pleasure, but may be of service to the public, as, in my present station I stand in need of the best intelligence, and the advice of every gentleman of abilities and public principles in the colony which has seen fit to place me here.

Our worthy friend, Mr. Gerry,[4] has put into my hand, a letter from you, of the sixth of May, in which you consider the principles of representation and legislation, and give us hints of some alterations, which you seem to think necessary, in the qualification of voters.

I wish, sir, I could possibly find time, to accompany you, in your investigation of the principles upon which a representative assembly stands and ought to stand, and in your examination whether the practice of our colony,

---

[4] Elbridge Gerry (1744–1814), a fellow delegate from Massachusetts to the Continental Congress.

has been conformable to those principles. But alas! Sir, my time is so incessantly engrossed by the business before me that I cannot spare enough, to go through so large a field; and as to books, it is not easy to obtain them here, nor could I find a moment to look into them, if I had them.

It is certain, in theory, that the only moral foundation of government is the consent of the people. But to what an extent shall we carry this principle? Shall we say, that every individual of the community, old and young, male and female, as well as rich and poor, must consent, expressly, to every act of legislation? No, you will say. This is impossible. How then does the right arise in the majority to govern the minority, against their will? Whence arises the right of the men to govern women, without their consent? Whence the right of the old to bind the young, without theirs?

But let us first suppose, that the whole community of every age, rank, sex, and condition, has a right to vote. This community is assembled—a motion is made and carried by a majority of one voice. The minority will not agree to this. Whence arises the right of the majority to govern, and the obligation of the minority to obey? From necessity, you will say, because there can be no other rule. But why exclude women? You will say, because their delicacy renders them unfit for practice and experience, in the great business of life, and the hardy enterprises of war, as well as the arduous cares of state. Besides, their attention is so much engaged with the necessary nurture of their children, that nature has made them fittest for domestic cares. And children have not judgment or will of their own. True. But will not these reasons apply to others? Is it not equally true, that men in general in every society, who are wholly destitute of property, are also too little acquainted with public affairs to form a right judgment, and too dependent upon other men to have a will of their own? If this is a fact, if you give to every man, who has no property, a vote, will you not make a fine encouraging provision for corruption by your fundamental law? Such is the frailty of the human heart, that very few men, who have no property, have any judgment of their own. They talk and vote as they are directed by some man of property, who has attached their minds to his interest.

Upon my word, sir, I have long thought an army, a piece of clockwork and to be governed only by principles and maxims, as fixed as any in mechanics, and by all that I have read in the history of mankind, and in authors, who have speculated upon society and government, I am much inclined to think, a government must manage a society in the same manner; and that this is machinery too.

Harrington[5] has shown that power always follows property. This I believe to be as infallible a maxim, in politics, as, that action and re-action are equal, is in mechanics. Nay I believe we may advance one step farther and affirm that the balance of power in a society, accompanies the balance of property in land. The only possible way then of preserving the balance of power on the side of equal liberty and public virtue, is to make the acquisition of land easy to every member of society; to make a division of the land into small quantities, so that the multitude may be possessed of landed estates. If the multitude is possessed of the balance of real estate, the multitude will have the balance of power, and in that case the multitude will take care of the liberty, virtue, and interest of the multitude in all acts of government.

I believe these principles have been felt, if not understood, in the Massachusetts Bay [colony], from the beginning; and therefore I should think that wisdom and policy would dictate, in these times, to be very cautious of making alterations. Our people have never been very rigid in scrutinizing into the qualifications of voters, and I presume they will not now begin to be so. But I would not advise them to make any alteration in the laws, at present, respecting the qualifications of voters.

Your idea, that those laws, which affect the lives and personal liberty of all, or which inflict corporal punishment, affect those, who are not qualified to vote, as well as those who are, is just. But, so they do women, as well as men, children as well as adults. What reason should there be, for excluding a man of twenty years, eleven months and twenty-seven days old, from a vote when you admit one, who is twenty-one? The reason is, you must fix upon some period in life, when the understanding and will of men in general is fit to be trusted by the public. Will not the same reason justify the state in fixing upon some certain quantity of property as a qualification?

The same reasoning, which will induce you to admit all men, who have no property, to vote, with those who have, for those laws, which affect the person will prove that you ought to admit women and children.... Generally speaking, women and children have as good judgment, and as independent minds, as those men who are wholly destitute of property—these last being to all intents and purposes as much dependent upon others, who will please to feed, clothe, and employ them, as women are upon their husbands, or children on their parents.

---

[5] James Harrington (1611–1677) was an English political theorist whose republican ideals were influential in the resistance to the Stuart monarchy.

As to your idea, of proportioning the votes of men in money matters, to the property they hold, it is utterly impracticable. There is no possible way of ascertaining, at any one time, how much every man in a community is worth; and if there was, so fluctuating is trade and property, that this state of it, would change in half an hour. The property of the whole community is shifting every hour, and no record can be kept of the changes.

Society can be governed only by general rules. Government cannot accommodate itself to every particular case, as it happens, nor to the circumstances of particular persons. It must establish general, comprehensive regulations for cases and persons. The only question is, which general rule will accommodate most cases and most persons?

Depend upon it, sir, it is dangerous to open so fruitful a source of controversy and altercation, as would be opened by attempting to alter the qualifications of voters. There will be no end of it. New claims will arise. Women will demand a vote. Lads from 12 to 21 will think their rights not enough attended to, and every man, who has not a farthing, will demand an equal voice with any other in all acts of state. It tends to confound and destroy all distinctions, and prostrate all ranks, to one common level.

DOCUMENT 23

## Thoughts on Government

John Adams

April 1776

*The first half of 1776—a no man's land between inclusion in the British empire and American independence—provided a fertile environment for the cultivation of new ideas as well as the grafting of traditional practices to new circumstances. Like Thomas Paine's* Common Sense *or Abigail Adams's startling suggestion that members of Congress "remember the ladies," John Adams's* Thoughts on Government *revealed an optimistic sense of possibility.*

*But Adams was not optimistic about all things. His understanding of human nature made him wary that people might use government to promote their own interests at the expense of others and bolster their own power to the detriment of others. How best to account for people's capacity for vice when constructing governments designed to protect individuals' rights and promote their virtue?*

*This question weighed on William Hooper (1742–1790) and John Penn (1740–1788), Continental Congress delegates from North Carolina, when they asked Adams to share his thoughts. The letters he wrote in response helped form the basis of his* Thoughts on Government, *which appeared as a pamphlet in Philadelphia and, months later, in Boston. Adams's insights, including the importance of dividing power within a government, would help to shape numerous constitutions, including his 1779 draft of the 1780 plan for government in Massachusetts and the federal Constitution sent to the states for ratification in 1787.*

SOURCE: John Adams, *Thoughts on Government*.... (Philadelphia: John Dunlap, 1776), in Charles Francis Adams, ed., *The Works of John Adams*, 10 vols. (Boston: Little, Brown and Co., 1850–56), 4:193–200. http://oll.libertyfund.org/titles/adams-the-works-of-john-adams-10-vols

---

If I was equal to the task of forming a plan for the government of a colony, I should be flattered with your request, and very happy to comply with it; because, as the divine science of politics is the science of social happiness, and the blessings of society depend entirely on the constitutions of government, which are generally institutions that last for many generations, there can be no employment more agreeable to a benevolent mind than a research after the best.

Pope[1] flattered tyrants too much when he said,
"For forms of government let fools contest,
That which is best administered is best."[2]

Nothing can be more fallacious than this. But poets read history to collect flowers, not fruits; they attend to fanciful images, not the effects of social institutions. Nothing is more certain, from the history of nations and nature of man, than that some forms of government are better fitted for being well administered than others.

We ought to consider what is the end of government, before we determine which is the best form. Upon this point all speculative politicians will agree, that the happiness of society is the end of government, as all divines and moral philosophers will agree that the happiness of the individual is the end of man. From this principle it will follow, that the form of government which communicates ease, comfort, security, or in one word, happiness, to the greatest number of persons, and in the greatest degree, is the best.

All sober inquirers after truth, ancient and modern, pagan and Christian, have declared that the happiness of man, as well as his dignity, consists in virtue. Confucius,[3] Zoroaster,[4] Socrates,[5] Mahomet,[6] not to mention authorities really sacred, have agreed in this.

If there is a form of government, then, whose principle and foundation is virtue, will not every sober man acknowledge it better calculated to promote the general happiness than any other form?

Fear is the foundation of most governments; but it is so sordid and brutal a passion, and renders men in whose breasts it predominates so stupid and miserable, that Americans will not be likely to approve of any political institution which is founded on it.

Honor is truly sacred, but holds a lower rank in the scale of moral

---

[1] Alexander Pope (1688–1744) was an English poet.
[2] Pope, *An Essay on Man: Epistle III* (London: J. Wilford, 1733), 54.
[3] Confucius (551 B.C.–479 B.C.) was a Chinese philosopher.
[4] Zoroaster (who lived to age 77 at some point between ca. 1500 B.C. and ca. 1000 B.C.) was a Persian prophet.
[5] Socrates (ca. 470 B.C.–399 B.C.) was a Greek philosopher.
[6] Muhammad (ca. 570–632) was an Arabian prophet and the founder of Islam.

excellence than virtue. Indeed, the former is but a part of the latter, and consequently has not equal pretensions to support a frame of government productive of human happiness.

The foundation of every government is some principle or passion in the minds of the people. The noblest principles and most generous affections in our nature, then, have the fairest chance to support the noblest and most generous models of government.

A man must be indifferent to the sneers of modern Englishmen, to mention in their company the names of Sidney,[7] Harrington,[8] Locke,[9] Milton,[10] Nedham,[11] Neville,[12] Burnet,[13] and Hoadly.[14] No small fortitude is necessary to confess that one has read them. The wretched condition of this country, however, for ten or fifteen years past, has frequently reminded me of their principles and reasonings. They will convince any candid mind, that there is no good government but what is republican. That the only valuable part of the British constitution is so; because the very definition of a republic is "an empire of laws, and not of men." That, as a republic is the best of governments, so that particular arrangement of the powers of society, or, in other words, that form of government which is best contrived to secure an impartial and exact execution of the laws, is the best of republics.

Of republics there is an inexhaustible variety, because the possible combinations of the powers of society are capable of innumerable variations.

As good government is an empire of laws, how shall your laws be made? In a large society, inhabiting an extensive country, it is impossible that the whole should assemble to make laws. The first necessary step, then, is to depute power from the many to a few of the most wise and good. But by what rules shall you choose your representatives? Agree upon the number and

---

[7] Algernon Sidney (1623–1683) was an English politician and political theorist.
[8] James Harrington (1611–1677) was an English political theorist.
[9] John Locke (1632–1704) was an English philosopher.
[10] John Milton (1608–1674) was an English poet and civil servant.
[11] Marchamont Nedham (1620–1678) was a pamphleteer during the English Civil War (1642–1651).
[12] Henry Neville (1620–1694) was an English politician and author.
[13] Gilbert Burnet (1643–1715) was a Scottish historian, philosopher, and Protestant clergyman who served as bishop of Salisbury (1689–1715).
[14] Benjamin Hoadly (1676–1761) was an English Protestant clergyman who served as bishop of Bangor (1715–1721), Hereford (1721–1723), Salisbury (1723–1734), and Winchester (1734–1761).

qualifications of persons who shall have the benefit of choosing, or annex this privilege to the inhabitants of a certain extent of ground.

The principal difficulty lies, and the greatest care should be employed, in constituting this representative assembly. It should be in miniature an exact portrait of the people at large. It should think, feel, reason, and act like them. That it may be the interest of this assembly to do strict justice at all times, it should be an equal representation, or, in other words, equal interests among the people should have equal interests in it. Great care should be taken to effect this, and to prevent unfair, partial, and corrupt elections. Such regulations, however, may be better made in times of greater tranquility than the present; and they will spring up themselves naturally, when all the powers of government come to be in the hands of the people's friends. At present, it will be safest to proceed in all established modes, to which the people have been familiarized by habit.

A representation of the people in one assembly being obtained, a question arises, whether all the powers of government, legislative, executive, and judicial, shall be left in this body? I think a people cannot be long free, nor ever happy, whose government is in one assembly. My reasons for this opinion are as follows:

1. A single assembly is liable to all the vices, follies, and frailties of an individual; subject to fits of humor, starts of passion, flights of enthusiasm, partialities, or prejudice, and consequently productive of hasty results and absurd judgments. And all these errors ought to be corrected and defects supplied by some controlling power.

2. A single assembly is apt to be avaricious, and in time will not scruple to exempt itself from burdens, which it will lay, without compunction, on its constituents.

3. A single assembly is apt to grow ambitious, and after a time will not hesitate to vote itself perpetual....

4. A representative assembly, although extremely well qualified, and absolutely necessary, as a branch of the legislative, is unfit to exercise the executive power, for want of two essential properties, secrecy and dispatch.

5. A representative assembly is still less qualified for the judicial power, because it is too numerous, too slow, and too little skilled in the laws.

6. Because a single assembly, possessed of all the powers of government, would make arbitrary laws for their own interest, execute all laws arbitrarily for their own interest, and adjudge all controversies in their own favor.

But shall the whole power of legislation rest in one assembly? Most of the foregoing reasons apply equally to prove that the legislative power ought to be more complex; to which we may add, that if the legislative power is wholly in one assembly, and the executive in another, or in a single person, these two powers will oppose and encroach upon each other, until the contest shall end in war, and the whole power, legislative and executive, be usurped by the strongest.

The judicial power, in such case, could not mediate, or hold the balance between the two contending powers, because the legislative would undermine it. And this shows the necessity, too, of giving the executive power a negative upon the legislative, otherwise this will be continually encroaching upon that.

To avoid these dangers, let a distinct assembly be constituted, as a mediator between the two extreme branches of the legislature, that which represents the people, and that which is vested with the executive power.

Let the representative assembly then elect by ballot, from among themselves or their constituents, or both, a distinct assembly, which, for the sake of perspicuity, we will call a council. It may consist of any number you please, say twenty or thirty, and should have a free and independent exercise of its judgment, and consequently a negative voice in the legislature.

These two bodies, thus constituted, and made integral parts of the legislature, let them unite, and by joint ballot choose a governor, who, after being stripped of most of those badges of domination, called prerogatives, should have a free and independent exercise of his judgment, and be made also an integral part of the legislature. This, I know, is liable to objections; and, if you please, you may make him only president of the council, as in Connecticut. But as the governor is to be invested with the executive power, with consent of council, I think he ought to have a negative upon the legislative. If he is annually elective, as he ought to be, he will always have so much reverence and affection for the people, their representatives and counselors, that, although you give him an independent exercise of his judgment, he will seldom use it in opposition to the two houses, except in cases the public utility of which would be conspicuous; and some such cases would happen.

In the present exigency of American affairs, when, by an act of Parliament, we are put out of the royal protection, and consequently discharged from our allegiance, and it has become necessary to assume government for our immediate security, the governor, lieutenant governor, secretary, treasurer, commissary, [and] attorney general, should be chosen by joint ballot of both houses. And these and all other elections, especially of representatives and counselors, should be annual, there not being in the whole circle of the sciences a maxim more infallible than this, "where annual elections end, there slavery begins."

These great men, in this respect, should be, once a year,

"Like bubbles on the sea of matter borne,

They rise, they break, and to that sea return."[15]

This will teach them the great political virtues of humility, patience, and moderation, without which every man in power becomes a ravenous beast of prey.

This mode of constituting the great offices of state will answer very well for the present; but if by experiment it should be found inconvenient, the legislature may, at its leisure, devise other methods of creating them, by elections of the people at large, as in Connecticut, or it may enlarge the term for which they shall be chosen to seven years, or three years, or for life, or make any other alterations which the society shall find productive of its ease, its safety, its freedom, or, in one word, its happiness.

A rotation of all offices, as well as of representatives and counselors, has many advocates, and is contended for with many plausible arguments. It would be attended, no doubt, with many advantages; and if the society has a sufficient number of suitable characters to supply the great number of vacancies which would be made by such a rotation, I can see no objection to it. These persons may be allowed to serve for three years, and then be excluded three years, or for any longer or shorter term.

Any seven or nine of the legislative council may be made a quorum, for doing business as a privy council, to advise the governor in the exercise of the executive branch of power, and in all acts of state.

The governor should have the command of the militia and of all your armies. The power of pardons should be with the governor and council.

Judges, justices, and all other officers, civil and military, should be nominated and appointed by the governor, with the advice and consent of council, unless you choose to have a government more popular; if you do, all officers, civil and military, may be chosen by joint ballot of both houses; or, in order to preserve the independence and importance of each house, by ballot of one house, concurred in by the other. Sheriffs should be chosen by the freeholders[16] of counties; so should registers of deeds and clerks of counties.

All officers should have commissions, under the hand of the governor and seal of the colony.

---

[15] Pope, *An Essay on Man*, 40.

[16] Property owners.

The dignity and stability of government in all its branches, the morals of the people, and every blessing of society depend so much upon an upright and skillful administration of justice, that the judicial power ought to be distinct from both the legislative and executive, and independent upon both, that so it may be a check upon both, as both should be checks upon that. The judges, therefore, should be always men of learning and experience in the laws, of exemplary morals, great patience, calmness, coolness, and attention. Their minds should not be distracted with jarring interests; they should not be dependent upon any man, or body of men. To these ends, they should hold estates for life in their offices; or, in other words, their commissions should be during good behavior, and their salaries ascertained and established by law. For misbehavior, the grand inquest of the colony, the house of representatives, should impeach them before the governor and council, where they should have time and opportunity to make their defense; but, if convicted, should be removed from their offices, and subjected to such other punishment as shall be thought proper.

A militia law, requiring all men, or with very few exceptions besides cases of conscience, to be provided with arms and ammunition, to be trained at certain seasons; and requiring counties, towns, or other small districts, to be provided with public stocks of ammunition and entrenching utensils, and with some settled plans for transporting provisions after the militia, when marched to defend their country against sudden invasions; and requiring certain districts to be provided with field-pieces, companies of matrosses,[17] and perhaps some regiments of light horse,[18] is always a wise institution, and, in the present circumstances of our country, indispensable.

Laws for the liberal education of youth, especially of the lower class of people, are so extremely wise and useful, that, to a humane and generous mind, no expense for this purpose would be thought extravagant.

The very mention of sumptuary laws[19] will excite a smile. Whether our countrymen have wisdom and virtue enough to submit to them, I know not; but the happiness of the people might be greatly promoted by them, and a revenue saved sufficient to carry on this war forever. Frugality is a great revenue, besides curing us of vanities, levities, and fopperies, which are real antidotes to all great, manly, and warlike virtues....

---

[17] Artillerists.
[18] Lightly armed and lightly armored cavalry.
[19] Laws relating to consumption, especially laws that impose taxes on luxuries or vices.

A constitution founded on these principles introduces knowledge among the people, and inspires them with a conscious dignity becoming freemen; a general emulation takes place, which causes good humor, sociability, good manners, and good morals to be general. That elevation of sentiment inspired by such a government, makes the common people brave and enterprising. That ambition which is inspired by it makes them sober, industrious, and frugal. You will find among them some elegance, perhaps, but more solidity; a little pleasure, but a great deal of business; some politeness, but more civility. If you compare such a country with the regions of domination, whether monarchical or aristocratical, you will fancy yourself in Arcadia[20] or Elysium....[21]

---

[20] Utopia.
[21] Heaven.

DOCUMENT 24

# Virginia Declaration of Rights

George Mason

*June 12, 1776*

The Virginia Declaration of Rights, authored principally by George Mason (1725–1792), stands as one of the most elegant positive statements of the political philosophy of the American Revolution. Written to accompany Virginia's new constitution (authored mostly by Mason), which would be ratified on June 29, the Declaration of Rights accepted independence from Great Britain as not only a fact but also an opportunity to establish the principles on which Virginia's government would (and would not) be based. It borrowed liberally from the concepts that had animated England's Glorious Revolution of 1688–89, especially John Locke's social contract theory and the 1689 English Bill of Rights, but it rejected monarchy and aristocracy by insisting that "all power is vested in . . . the people."

Mason's Declaration delineated people's natural and civil rights as well as the structural features most likely to enable the new Virginia government to uphold them. It influenced several other important texts, including the Declaration of Independence and the 1791 Bill of Rights. The fact that the 1787 Constitution did not originally include such a statement contributed to Mason's decision to oppose its ratification. The addition of the Bill of Rights in the form of the first ten amendments to the Constitution, just one year prior to Mason's death, stands as his most lasting legacy. Thomas Jefferson (1743–1826) remembered him as a man "of the first order of greatness."

SOURCE: Francis Newton Thorpe, ed., *The Federal and State Constitutions, Colonial Charters, and Other Organic Laws....*, 7 vols. (Washington, D.C.: Government Printing Office, 1909), 7:3812–14. http://oll.libertyfund.org/titles/thorpe-the-federal-and-state-constitutions-7-vols

---

A declaration of rights made by the representatives of the good people of Virginia, assembled in full and free convention; which rights do pertain to them and their posterity, as the basis and foundation of government.

SECTION 1. That all men are by nature equally free and independent, and have certain inherent rights, of which, when they enter into a state of society, they cannot, by any compact, deprive or divest their posterity; namely, the enjoyment of life and liberty, with the means of acquiring and possessing property, and pursuing and obtaining happiness and safety.

SEC. 2. That all power is vested in, and consequently derived from, the people; that magistrates are their trustees and servants, and at all times amenable to them.

SEC. 3. That government is, or ought to be, instituted for the common benefit, protection, and security of the people, nation, or community; of all the various modes and forms of government, that is best which is capable of producing the greatest degree of happiness and safety, and is most effectually secured against the danger of maladministration; and that, when any government shall be found inadequate or contrary to these purposes, a majority of the community hath an indubitable, inalienable, and indefeasible right to reform, alter, or abolish it, in such manner as shall be judged most conducive to the public weal.[1]

SEC. 4. That no man, or set of men, are entitled to exclusive or separate emoluments or privileges from the community, but in consideration of public services; which, not being descendible, neither ought the offices of magistrate, legislator, or judge to be hereditary.

SEC. 5. That the legislative and executive powers of the state should be separate and distinct from the judiciary; and that the members of the two first may be restrained from oppression, by feeling and participating the burdens of the people, they should, at fixed periods, be reduced to a private station, return into that body from which they were originally taken, and the vacancies be supplied by frequent, certain, and regular elections, in which all, or any part of the former members, to be again eligible, or ineligible, as the laws shall direct.

SEC. 6. That elections of members to serve as representatives of the people, in assembly, ought to be free; and that all men, having sufficient evidence of permanent common interest with, and attachment to, the community, have the right of suffrage, and cannot be taxed or deprived of their property for public uses, without their own consent, or that of their representatives so elected, nor bound by any law to which they have not, in like manner, assembled, for the public good.

SEC. 7. That all power of suspending laws, or the execution of laws, by any authority, without consent of the representatives of the people, is injurious to their rights, and ought not to be exercised.

---

[1] Well-being, prosperity, or happiness.

SEC. 8. That in all capital or criminal prosecutions a man has a right to demand the cause and nature of his accusation, to be confronted with the accusers and witnesses, to call for evidence in his favor, and to a speedy trial by an impartial jury of twelve men of his vicinage,[2] without whose unanimous consent he cannot be found guilty; nor can he be compelled to give evidence against himself; that no man be deprived of his liberty, except by the law of the land or the judgment of his peers.

SEC. 9. That excessive bail ought not to be required, nor excessive fines imposed, nor cruel and unusual punishments inflicted.

SEC. 10. That general warrants, whereby an officer or messenger may be commanded to search suspected places without evidence of a fact committed, or to seize any person or persons not named, or whose offence is not particularly described and supported by evidence; are grievous and oppressive, and ought not to be granted.

SEC. 11. That in controversies respecting property, and in suits between man and man, the ancient trial by jury is preferable to any other, and ought to be held sacred.

SEC. 12. That the freedom of the press is one of the greatest bulwarks of liberty, and can never be restrained but by despotic governments.

SEC. 13. That a well-regulated militia, composed of the body of the people, trained to arms, is the proper, natural, and safe defense of a free state; that standing armies, in time of peace, should be avoided, as dangerous to liberty; and that in all cases the military should be under strict subordination to, and governed by, the civil power.

SEC. 14. That the people have a right to uniform government; and, therefore, that no government separate from, or independent of the government of Virginia, ought to be erected or established within the limits thereof.

SEC. 15. That no free government, or the blessings of liberty, can be preserved to any people, but by a firm adherence to justice, moderation, temperance, frugality, and virtue, and by frequent recurrence to fundamental principles.

SEC. 16. That religion, or the duty which we owe to our Creator, and the manner of discharging it, can be directed only by reason and conviction, not by force or violence; and therefore all men are equally entitled to the free exercise of religion, according to the dictates of conscience; and that it is the mutual duty of all to practice Christian forbearance, love, and charity towards each other.

---

[2] Neighborhood or community.

DOCUMENT 25

# Draft of The Declaration of Independence

Thomas Jefferson

July 2–4, 1776

Acting on instructions from the Virginia Convention, on June 7, 1776, Richard Henry Lee (1732–1794) stood before his fellow members of the Continental Congress to propose a resolution "that these United Colonies are, and of right ought to be, free and independent states." After John Adams (1735–1826) of Massachusetts seconded the motion, debate raged for two full days. Finally, Congress decided to table Lee's resolution for three weeks in order to allow delegates to receive instructions from their legislatures. In the meantime, in the event that the resolution should pass, it appointed a committee to draft a declaration of independence. The committee consisted of Adams, Roger Sherman (1721–1793) of Connecticut, Robert R. Livingston (1746–1814) of New York, Benjamin Franklin (1706–1790) of Pennsylvania, and Virginia delegate Thomas Jefferson (1743–1826).

Jefferson thought that Adams should take the lead in composing a draft, but Adams disagreed. As he later recalled, he insisted that Jefferson accept the task for three reasons: "Reason first, you are a Virginian, and a Virginian ought to appear at the head of this business. Reason second, I am obnoxious, suspected, and unpopular. You are very much otherwise. Reason third, you can write ten times better than I can." Adams appreciated not only Jefferson's "happy talent for composition" but also his status as the committee's only southerner. New England delegates stood firmly behind independence. Adams himself had pushed the idea so insistently that he sensed the annoyance of certain delegates, who believed that Massachusetts, which had borne the brunt of British sanctions and gunfire, stood to gain the most from separation from Great Britain. If a popular delegate from Virginia championed independence, then maybe wavering delegates from the middle colonies and South Carolina would too.

Accepting the task, Jefferson got to work in his rented rooms at the house of Jacob Graff (1727–1780), a Philadelphia bricklayer. For nearly three weeks Jefferson worked through a succession of drafts. He wrote, revised, and sought feedback from Adams, Franklin, and finally the entire committee.

The Declaration, he later wrote, aimed "to be an expression of the American mind." It sought "not to find out new principles, or new arguments, never before thought of... but to place before mankind the common sense of the subject, in terms so plain and firm as to command their assent." Not everyone assented, however. John Dickinson (1732–1808), a member of Congress who had labored mightily in opposition to British imperial policies (Documents 4 and 18), could not bring himself to vote for independence. Considering it too much, too soon, and too sure to further inflame a war already raging out of control, he marveled at his peers' willingness to "brave the storm in a skiff made of paper."

On July 2, once Congress voted in favor of Lee's resolution, it turned its attention to Jefferson's draft. In Jefferson's notes on the debate over the Declaration, he provided a brief account of how his draft was amended; he then transcribed the draft he had submitted to Congress to show how it had been changed. The text below includes Jefferson's explanatory note and underlines, as Jefferson did, the parts of the Declaration deleted by Congress. In Jefferson's original transcription, the words and phrases inserted by Congress are displayed in the margin; here they are italicized and placed within curly brackets in the body of the text.

SOURCE: H. A. Washington, ed., *The Writings of Thomas Jefferson*, 9 vols. (Washington, D.C.: Taylor and Maury, 1853–54), 1:19–26. https://catalog.hathitrust.org/Record/000365325

---

... Congress proceeded the same day [*July 2*] to consider the Declaration of Independence, which had been reported and laid on the table the Friday preceding, and on Monday referred to a committee of the whole. The pusillanimous idea that we had friends in England worth keeping terms with, still haunted the minds of many. For this reason, those passages which conveyed censures on the people of England were struck out, lest they should give them offense. The clause too, reprobating the enslaving the inhabitants of Africa, was struck out in complaisance[1] to South Carolina and Georgia, who had never attempted to restrain the importation of slaves, and who, on the contrary, still wished to continue it. Our northern brethren also, I believe, felt a little tender under those censures; for though their people have very few slaves themselves, yet they had been pretty considerable carriers of them to others. The debates, having taken up the greater parts of the 2rd, 3rd, and 4th days of July, were, in the evening of the last, closed; the Declaration was reported by the committee, agreed to by the House, and signed

---

[1] In order to comply with the wishes of.

by every member present,[2] except Mr. Dickinson.[3] As the sentiments of men are known not only by what they receive, but what they reject also, I will state the form of the Declaration as originally reported. The parts struck out by Congress shall be distinguished by a black line drawn under them; and those inserted by them shall be placed in the margin or in a concurrent column(s).

## A Declaration by the Representatives of the United States of America, in <u>General</u> Congress assembled

When, in the course of human events, it becomes necessary for one people to dissolve the political bands which have connected them with another, and to assume among the powers of the earth the separate and equal station to which the laws of nature and of nature's God entitle them, a decent respect to the opinions of mankind requires that they should declare the causes which impel them to the separation.

We hold these truths to be self evident: that all men are created equal; that they are endowed by their creator with {*certain*} <u>inherent and</u> inalienable rights; that among these are life, liberty and the pursuit of happiness; that to secure these rights, governments are instituted among men, deriving their just powers from the consent of the governed; that whenever any form of government becomes destructive of these ends, it is the right of the people to alter or to abolish it, and to institute new government, laying its foundation on such principles, and organizing its powers in such form, as to them shall seem most likely to effect their safety and happiness. Prudence, indeed, will dictate that governments long established should not be changed for light and transient causes; and accordingly all experience hath shown that mankind are more disposed to suffer while evils are sufferable, than to right themselves by abolishing the forms to which they are accustomed. But when a long train of abuses and usurpations, <u>begun at a distinguished period and</u> pursuing invariably the same object, evinces[4] a design to reduce them under absolute despotism, it is their right, it is their duty to throw off such

---

[2] Jefferson's memory deceived him. Although the Continental Congress approved the text of the Declaration of Independence on July 4, the official parchment copy was not signed by delegates until August 1776.

[3] John Dickinson (1732–1808), one of Pennsylvania's delegates to the Continental Congress, withheld his signature because he still hoped for reconciliation with Great Britain.

[4] Reveals, demonstrates, makes evident.

government, and to provide new guards for their future security. Such has been the patient sufferance of these colonies; and such is now the necessity which constrains them to {alter} expunge their former systems of government. The history of the present king of Great Britain is a history of {repeated} unremitting injuries and usurpations, among which appears no solitary fact to contradict the uniform tenor of the rest but all have {all having} in direct object the establishment of an absolute tyranny over these states. To prove this let facts be submitted to a candid world for the truth of which we pledge a faith yet unsullied by falsehood.

 He has refused his assent to laws the most wholesome and necessary for the public good.

 He has forbidden his governors to pass laws of immediate and pressing importance, unless suspended in their operation till his assent should be obtained; and, when so suspended, he has utterly neglected to attend to them.

 He has refused to pass other laws for the accommodation of large districts of people, unless those people would relinquish the right of representation in the legislature, a right inestimable to them and formidable to the tyrants only.

 He has called together legislative bodies at places unusual, uncomfortable, and distant from the depository of their public records, for the sole purpose of fatiguing them into compliance with his measures.

 He has dissolved representative houses repeatedly and continually for opposing with manly firmness his invasions on the rights of the people.

 He has refused for a long time after such dissolutions to cause others to be elected, whereby the legislative powers, incapable of annihilation, have returned to the people at large for their exercise, the state remaining, in the meantime, exposed to all the dangers of invasion from without and convulsions within.

 He has endeavored to prevent the population of these states; for that purpose obstructing the laws for naturalization of foreigners, refusing to pass others to encourage their migrations hither, and raising the conditions of new appropriations of lands.

 He has {obstructed} suffered the administration of justice totally to cease in some of these states {by} refusing his assent to laws for establishing judiciary powers.

 He has made our judges dependent on his will alone for the tenure of their offices, and the amount and payment of their salaries.

 He has erected a multitude of new offices by a self assumed power and sent hither swarms of new officers to harass our people and eat our their substance.

He has kept among us in times of peace standing armies and ships of war without the consent of our legislatures.

He has affected to render the military independent of, and superior to, the civil power.

He has combined with others to subject us to a jurisdiction foreign to our constitutions and unacknowledged by our laws, giving his assent to their acts of pretended legislation for quartering large bodies of armed troops among us; for protecting them by a mock trial from punishment for any murders which they should commit on the inhabitants of these states; for cutting off our trade with all parts of the world; for imposing taxes on us without our consent; for depriving us {*in many cases*} of the benefits of trial by jury; for transporting us beyond seas to be tried for pretended offences; for abolishing the free system of English laws in a neighboring province,[5] establishing therein an arbitrary government, and enlarging its boundaries, so as to render it at once an example and fit instrument for introducing the same absolute rule into these {*colonies*} states; for taking away our charters, abolishing our most valuable laws, and altering fundamentally the forms of our governments; for suspending our own legislatures, and declaring themselves invested with power to legislate for us in all cases whatsoever.

He has abdicated government here {*by declaring us out of his protection and waging war against us.*} withdrawing his governors, and declaring us out of his allegiance and protection.

He has plundered our seas, ravaged our coasts, burnt our towns, and destroyed the lives of our people.

He is at this time transporting large armies of foreign mercenaries to complete the works of death, desolation and tyranny already begun with circumstances of cruelty and perfidy[6] {*scarcely paralleled in the most barbarous ages, and totally*} unworthy the head of a civilized nation.

He has constrained our fellow citizens taken captive on the high seas, to bear arms against their country, to become the executioners of their friends and brethren, or to fall themselves by their hands.

He has {*excited domestic insurrections among us, and has*} endeavored to bring on the inhabitants of our frontiers the merciless Indian savages, whose known rule of warfare is an undistinguished destruction of all ages, sexes, and conditions of existence.

---

[5] Canada.
[6] Treachery, deceitfulness, untrustworthiness.

He has incited treasonable insurrections of our fellow citizens, with the allurements of forfeiture and confiscation of our property.

He has waged cruel war against human nature itself, violating its most sacred rights of life and liberty in the persons of a distant people who never offended him, captivating and carrying them into slavery in another hemisphere or to incur miserable death in their transportation thither. This piratical warfare, the opprobrium of INFIDEL powers, is the warfare of the CHRISTIAN king of Great Britain. Determined to keep open a market where MEN should be bought and sold, he has prostituted his negative for suppressing every legislative attempt to prohibit or to restrain this execrable commerce. And that this assemblage of horrors might want no fact of distinguished die,[7] he is now exciting those very people to rise in arms among us, and to purchase that liberty of which he has deprived them, by murdering the people on whom he also obtruded them: thus paying off former crimes committed against the LIBERTIES of one people, with crimes which he urges them to commit against the LIVES of another.

In every stage of these oppressions we have petitioned for redress in the most humble terms: our repeated petitions have been answered only by repeated injuries.

A prince whose character is thus marked by every act which may define a tyrant is unfit to be the ruler of a {*free*} people who mean to be free. Future ages will scarcely believe that the hardiness of one man adventured, within the short compass of twelve years only, to lay a foundation so broad and so undisguised for tyranny over a people fostered and fixed in principles of freedom.

Nor have we been wanting in attentions to our British brethren. We have warned them from time to time of attempts by their legislature to extend {*an unwarrantable*} a jurisdiction over {*us*} these our states. We have reminded them of the circumstances of our emigration and settlement here, no one of which could warrant so strange a pretension: that these were effected at the expense of our own blood and treasure, unassisted by the wealth or the strength of Great Britain: that in constituting indeed our several forms of government, we had adopted one common king, thereby laying a foundation for perpetual league and amity with them: but that submission to their parliament was no part of our constitution, nor ever in idea, if history may be credited: and, we {*have*} appealed to their native justice and magnanimity and {*we have conjured them by*} as well as to the ties of our common kindred

---

[7] A stamp used to certify government documents.

to disavow these usurpations which {*would inevitably*} were likely to interrupt our connection and correspondence. They too have been deaf to the voice of justice and of consanguinity, and when occasions have been given them, by the regular course of their laws, of removing from their councils the disturbers of our harmony, they have, by their free election, re-established them in power. At this very time too, they are permitting their chief magistrate to send over not only soldiers of our common blood, but Scotch and foreign mercenaries to invade and destroy us. These facts have given the last stab to agonizing affection, and manly spirit bids us to renounce forever these unfeeling brethren. We must endeavor to forget our former love for them, and to hold them as we hold the rest of mankind, enemies in war, in peace friends. We might have been a free and a great people together; but a communication of grandeur and of freedom, it seems, is below their dignity. Be it so, since they will have it. The road to happiness and to glory is open to us too. We will tread it apart from them, and {*We must therefore*} acquiesce in the necessity which denounces our eternal separation {*and hold them as we hold the rest of mankind, enemies in war, in peace friends.*}!

Editor: *The two final paragraphs, in their original and amended forms, were placed by Jefferson in two parallel columns. The conclusion of the Declaration as he submitted it appeared in the left column and the text as altered by Congress appeared in the right column.*

[*Jefferson's draft*]
We, therefore, the representatives of the United States of America in General Congress assembled, do in the name, and by the authority of the good people of these states reject and renounce all allegiance and subjection to the kings of Great Britain and all others who may hereafter claim by, through or under them; we utterly dissolve all political connection which may heretofore have subsisted between us and the people or parliament of Great Britain: and finally we do assert and declare these colonies to be free and independent states, and that as free and

[*Congress's final version*]
We, therefore, the representatives of the United States of America in General Congress assembled, appealing to the supreme judge of the world for the rectitude of our intentions, do in the name, and by the authority of the good people of these colonies, solemnly publish and declare, that these united colonies are, and of right ought to be free and independent states; that they are absolved from all allegiance to the British crown, and that all political connection between them and the state of Great Britain is, and ought to be, totally dissolved; and

independent states, they have full power to levy war, conclude peace, contract alliances, establish commerce, and to do all other acts and things which independent states may of right do.

And for the support of this declaration, we mutually pledge to each other our lives, our fortunes, and our sacred honor.

that as free and independent states, they have full power to levy war, conclude peace, contract alliances, establish commerce and to do all other acts and things which independent states may of right do.

And for the support of this declaration, with a firm reliance on the protection of divine providence, we mutually pledge to each other our lives, our fortunes, and our sacred honor.

DOCUMENT 26

# Celebrations of American Independence in Boston and Watertown, Massachusetts

*The American Gazette*

*July 18, 1776*

News of the Continental Congress's July 2 approval of Richard Henry Lee's resolution to separate from Great Britain—together with its July 4 passage of the Declaration of Independence—traveled by sail and on horseback. As a result, it took about two weeks for people in and around Boston to learn that the crisis within the British empire had been transformed (at least in the eyes of American Patriots) into a war between Great Britain and the sovereign United States. This newspaper account of their reactions highlights events organized by elected officials to celebrate independence as well as more spontaneous displays of the people's support for Congress's decisions.

SOURCE: *The American Gazette, or the Constitutional Journal* (Salem, Mass.), July 23, 1776.

---

## WATERTOWN, JULY 22 . . . .

Thursday last,[1] pursuant to the orders of the honorable council, was proclaimed, from the balcony of the State House in Boston, the DECLARATION of the AMERICAN CONGRESS, absolving the United Colonies from their allegiance to the British crown, and declaring them FREE and INDEPENDENT STATES. There were present on the occasion, in the council chamber, the committee of council, a number of the honorable House of Representatives, the magistrates, ministers, selectmen, and other gentlemen of Boston and the neighboring towns; also the committee of officers of the Continental regiments stationed in Boston, and other officers. Two of those regiments were under arms in King Street, formed into three lines on the north side of the street, and in thirteen divisions; and a detachment from the Massachusetts Regiment of Artillery, with two pieces of cannon, was

---

[1] July 18, 1776.

on their right wing. At one o'clock the Declaration was proclaimed by the sheriff of the county of Suffolk,[2] which was received with great joy expressed by three huzzahs from the concourse of people assembled on the occasion. After which, on a signal given, thirteen pieces of cannon were fired at the fort on Fort Hill, the forts at Dorchester Neck, the Castle, the Nantasket, and Point Alderton, likewise discharged their cannon. Then the detachment of artillery fired their cannon thirteen times, which was followed by the two regiments giving their fire from the thirteen divisions in succession. These firings corresponded to the number of the American states united. The ceremony was closed with a proper collation[3] to the gentlemen in the council chamber; during which the following toasts were given by the president of the council,[4] and heartily pledged by the company:

1. Prosperity and perpetuity to the United States of America.
2. The American Congress.
3. The general court of the state of Massachusetts Bay.
4. General WASHINGTON, and success to the army of the United States.
5. The downfall of tyrants and tyranny.
6. The universal prevalence of civil and religious liberty.
7. The friends of the United States in all quarters of the globe.

The bells of the town were rung on the occasion; and undissembled[5] festivity cheered and brightened every face.

On the same day a number of the members of the council (who were prevented attending the ceremony at Boston, on account of the small pox being there), together with those of the hon[orable] House of Representatives who were in town, and a number of other gentlemen, assembled at the council chamber in this town, where the said Declaration was also proclaimed by the secretary, from one of the windows; after which, the gentlemen present

---

[2] William Greenleaf (1725–1803) served as sheriff of Suffolk County, which included Boston, from 1775 to 1780.
[3] A light meal.
[4] James Warren (1726–1808), husband of writer Mercy Otis Warren (1728–1814), served as president of the Massachusetts Provincial Congress (and its executive council) from 1776 to 1780.
[5] Genuine, undisguised.

partook of a decent collation prepared on the occasion, and drank a number of constitutional toasts, and then retired.

We hear that on Thursday last every king's arms[6] in Boston, and every sign with any resemblance of it, whether lion and crown, pestle and mortar and crown, heart and crown, etc., together with every sign that belonged to a Tory was taken down, and made a general conflagration of in King Street.

The king's arms, in this town, was on Saturday last,[7] also defaced.

---

[6] These symbols of royal authority often inspired the names of—and appeared on the signs of—colonial taverns.
[7] July 20, 1776.

DOCUMENT 27

# The American Crisis
"Common Sense" (Thomas Paine)
*December 23, 1776*

Although it was easy to celebrate independence, the British army made it difficult for Americans to secure it. By the end of 1776, Jefferson's pen seemed mightier than Washington's sword. The year's military campaign began propitiously when in March artillery pieces dragged by Henry Knox's men to Dorchester Heights caused the Redcoats to withdraw from Boston. Fortunes reversed, however, when the British attacked in New York. Washington met them on Long Island, withdrew to Manhattan, retreated to White Plains, and eventually allowed the enemy to push him south through New Jersey and across the Delaware River to Pennsylvania.

At a time when the Continental army—and the American people—needed a lesson in perseverance, Thomas Paine (1737–1809) could speak from experience. Prior to the stunning success of Common Sense, he had lived a life of obscurity and setbacks. Before moving to America from England in late 1774, he had failed at his father's trade of corset-making. He had also failed as a teacher, tax collector, and shopkeeper. Now, however, his writing had earned him his status as a leading American revolutionary and motivator of his adopted countrymen.

The American Crisis appeared throughout the war in multiple installments, both in pamphlet form and on the pages of newspapers, mostly in 1776 and 1777. Signed with the penname "Common Sense," Paine leveraged his earlier success to gain attention for this series, which aimed to reinforce the resolve of Patriots while chastening Loyalists. George Washington ordered that copies of this first installment of the series, which appeared shortly before the December 26 Battle of Trenton, be distributed to every brigade and read aloud to the soldiers of the Continental Army.

SOURCE: Moncure Daniel Conway, ed., *The Writings of Thomas Paine*, 4 vols. (New York: G. P. Putnam's Sons, 1894–96), 1:170–79. http://oll.libertyfund.org/titles/paine-the-writings-of-thomas-paine-4-vols

THESE are the times that try men's souls. The summer soldier and the sunshine patriot will, in this crisis, shrink from the service of their country; but he that stands it *now*, deserves the love and thanks of man and woman. Tyranny, like hell, is not easily conquered; yet we have this consolation with us, that the harder the conflict, the more glorious the triumph. What we obtain too cheap, we esteem to lightly: it is dearness only that gives everything its value. Heaven knows how to put a proper price upon its goods; and it would be strange indeed if so celestial an article as FREEDOM should not be highly rated. Britain, with an army to enforce her tyranny, has declared that she has a right (*not only to* TAX but) "to BIND *us in* ALL CASES WHATSOEVER,"[1] and if being *bound in that manner,* is not slavery, then is there not such a thing as slavery upon earth. Even the expression is impious; for so unlimited a power can belong only to God....

I have as little superstition in me as any man living, but my secret opinion has ever been, and still is, that God Almighty will not give up a people to military destruction, or leave them, unsupported, to perish, who have so earnestly and so repeatedly sought to avoid the calamities of war, by every decent method which wisdom could invent. Neither have I so much of the infidel in me, as to suppose that He has relinquished the government of the world, and given us up to the care of devils; and as I do not, I cannot see on what grounds the king of Britain can look up to heaven for help against us: a common murderer, a highwayman,[2] or a housebreaker,[3] has as good a pretense as he.

It is surprising to see how rapidly a panic will sometimes run through a country.... Yet panics, in some cases, have their uses; they produce as much good as hurt. Their duration is always short; the mind soon grows through them, and acquires a firmer habit than before. But their peculiar advantage is, that they are the touchstones of sincerity and hypocrisy, and bring things and men to light, which might otherwise have lain forever undiscovered.... They sift out the hidden thoughts of man, and hold them up in public to the world. Many a disguised Tory has lately shown his head....

... Why is it that the enemy have left the New England provinces, and made these middle ones the seat of war? The answer is easy: New England

---

[1] The March 1766 Declaratory Act had insisted that Parliament possessed authority to impose its will on American colonists "in all cases whatsoever."
[2] A thief who steals from travelers.
[3] A thief who breaks into and then steals items from a house.

is not infested with Tories, and we are. I have been tender in raising the cry against these men, and used numberless arguments to show them their danger, but it will not do to sacrifice a world either to their folly or their baseness. The period is now arrived, in which either they or we must change our sentiments, or one or both must fall. And what is a Tory? Good God! What is he? I should not be afraid to go with a hundred Whigs against a thousand Tories, were they to attempt to get into arms. Every Tory is a coward; for servile, slavish, self-interested fear is the foundation of Toryism; and a man under such influence, though he may be cruel, never can be brave.

But, before the line of irrecoverable separation be drawn between us let us reason the matter together: Your conduct is an invitation to the enemy, yet not one in a thousand of you has heart enough to join him. Howe[4] is as much deceived by you as the American cause is injured by you. He expects you will all take up arms, and flock to his standard, with muskets on your shoulders. Your opinions are of no use to him, unless you support him personally, for it is soldiers, and not Tories, that he wants.

... I consider Howe as the greatest enemy the Tories have. He is bringing a war into their country, which, had it not been for him and partly for themselves, they had been clear of. Should he now be expelled, I wish with all the devotion of a Christian, that the names of Whig and Tory may never more be mentioned; but should the Tories give him encouragement to come, or assistance if he come, I as sincerely wish that our next year's arms may expel them from the continent, and the Congress appropriate their possessions to the relief of those who have suffered in well-doing. A single successful battle next year will settle the whole. America could carry on a two-year war by the confiscation of the property of disaffected persons, and be made happy by their expulsion. Say not that this is revenge, call it rather the soft resentment of a suffering people, who, having no object in view but the good of all, have staked their own all upon a seemingly doubtful event. Yet it is folly to argue against determined hardness; eloquence may strike the ear, and the language of sorrow draw forth the tear of compassion, but nothing can reach the heart that is steeled with prejudice.

Quitting this class of men, I turn with the warm ardor of a friend to those who have nobly stood, and are yet determined to stand the matter out. I call not upon a few, but upon all; not on this state or that state, but on every state. Up and help us; lay your shoulders to the wheel; better have too much force

---

[4] General William Howe (1729–1814) was commander-in-chief of British forces in North America (1775–1778).

than too little, when so great an object is at stake. Let it be told to the future world, that in the depth of winter, when nothing but hope and virtue could survive, that the city and the country, alarmed at one common danger, came forth to meet and to repulse it. Say not that thousands are gone, turn out your tens of thousands; throw not the burden of the day upon Providence, but "show your faith by your works,"[5] that God may bless you. It matters not where you live, or what rank of life you hold, the evil or the blessing will reach you all. The far and the near, the home counties and the back, the rich and the poor, will suffer or rejoice alike. The heart that feels not now, is dead; the blood of his children will curse his cowardice, who shrinks back at a time when a little might have saved the whole, and made them happy. I love the man that can smile in trouble, that can gather strength from distress, and grow brave by reflection. It is the business of little minds to shrink; but he whose heart is firm, and whose conscience approves his conduct, will pursue his principles until death. My own line of reasoning is to myself as straight and clear as a ray of light. Not all the treasures of the world, so far as I believe, could have induced me to support an offensive war, for I think it murder; but if a thief breaks into my house, burns and destroys my property, and kills or threatens to kill me, or those that are in it, and to "bind me in all cases whatsoever" to his absolute will, am I to suffer it? What signifies it to me, whether he who does it is a king or a common man; my countryman or not my countryman; whether it be done by an individual villain, or an army of them? If we reason to the root of things we shall find no difference; neither can any just cause be assigned why we should punish in the one case and pardon in the other. Let them call me rebel ... I feel no concern from it; but I should suffer the misery of devils, were I to make a whore of my soul by swearing allegiance to one whose character is that of a sottish,[6] stupid, stubborn, worthless, brutish man. I conceive likewise a horrid idea in receiving mercy from a being, who, at the last day shall be shrieking to the rocks and mountains to cover him, and fleeing with terror from the orphan, the widow, and the slain of America.

There are cases which cannot be overdone by language, and this is one. There are persons, too, who see not the full extent of the evil which threatens them; they solace themselves with hopes that the enemy, if he succeed, will be merciful. It is the madness of folly, to expect mercy from those who have refused to do justice; and even mercy, where conquest is the object, is

---

[5] See James 2:18.
[6] Drunken and/or foolish.

only a trick of war; the cunning of the fox is as murderous as the violence of the wolf, and we ought to guard equally against both. Howe's first object is, partly by threats and partly by promises, to terrify or seduce the people to deliver up their arms and receive mercy. The ministry recommended the same plan to Gage, and this is what the Tories call making their peace, "a peace which passes all understanding"[7] indeed! A peace, which would be the immediate forerunner of a worse ruin than any we have yet thought of.... And were any one state to give up its arms, that state must be garrisoned by all Howe's army of Britons and Hessians to preserve it from the anger of the rest. Mutual fear is the principal link in the chain of mutual love, and woe be to that state that breaks the compact. Howe is mercifully inviting you to barbarous destruction, and men must be either rogues or fools that will not see it. I dwell not upon the vapors of imagination: I bring reason to your ears, and, in language as plain as A, B, C, hold up truth to your eyes.

... By perseverance and fortitude we have the prospect of a glorious issue; by cowardice and submission, the sad choice of a variety of evils—a ravaged country—a depopulated city—habitations without safety, and slavery without hope—our homes turned into barracks and bawdyhouses for Hessians,[8] and a future race to provide for, whose fathers we shall doubt of. Look on this picture and weep over it! And if there yet remains one thoughtless wretch who believes it not, let him suffer it unlamented.

COMMON SENSE

---

[7] See Philippians 4:6.
[8] Approximately 30,000 men from Hesse-Kassel and other German regions were ordered by their governments to reinforce the British army. Frequently mischaracterized as mercenaries, it was not the Hessians but instead their governments that profited from their service.

DOCUMENT 28

# Massachusetts Antislavery Petition

Prince Hall, et al.

January 13, 1777

The ideas of the American Revolution could not be contained—a fact made clear by this 1777 petition signed by Prince Hall (ca. 1735–1807), a free black man, and seven other African Americans in behalf of people in Massachusetts who remained enslaved. Hall's appeal made clear his awareness of the central tenets of the Declaration of Independence: it was sent to the state's legislature less than six months after the Declaration insisted that "all men are created equal, that they are endowed by their Creator with certain unalienable rights," and that "to secure these rights, governments are instituted by men."

Although the Massachusetts legislature ignored the petition, the inconsistency between slavery and America's founding principles did not go unnoticed. Vermont abolished slavery in its 1777 constitution, while New Hampshire's 1783 frame of government—which declared that "all men are born equal and independent" with natural rights to the enjoyment and defense of "life and liberty"—preceded a decline in slavery so steep that in 1800 only eight slaves were counted in the census. Meanwhile, a 1783 court case ended slavery in Massachusetts. Pennsylvania adopted a gradual emancipation law in 1780, as did Connecticut and Rhode Island in 1784, New York in 1799, and New Jersey in 1804.

On the national level, Thomas Jefferson proposed for the Ordinance of 1784 a clause banning slavery in all land west of the Appalachians and east of the Mississippi River. The provision failed by a single vote in the Confederation Congress, setting the stage for the eventual expansion of slavery into the future states of Kentucky, Tennessee, Alabama, and Mississippi—and presumably Louisiana, Missouri, and Texas. "Thus we see the fate of millions unborn hanging on the tongue of one man," Jefferson observed, "and heaven was silent in that awful moment."

SOURCE: "To the Honorable Counsel & House of [Representa]tives of the State of Massachusetts Bay in General Court assembled," *Collections of the Massachusetts Historical Society*, 5th ser., 3 (1877): 436–37. https://babel.hathitrust.org/cgi/pt?id=njp.32101076467586;view=1up;seq=454

The petition of a great number of blacks detained in a state of slavery in the bowels of a free and Christian country humbly shows that your petitioners apprehend that they have in common with all other men a natural and unalienable right to that freedom which the Great Parent of the Universe has bestowed equally on all mankind and which they have never forfeited by any compact or agreement whatever—but they were unjustly dragged by the hand of cruel power from their dearest friends and some of them even torn from the embraces of their tender parents—from a populous, pleasant, and plentiful country, and in violation of laws of nature and of nations and in defiance of all the tender feelings of humanity brought here to be sold like beasts of burden and like them condemned to slavery for life—among a people professing the mild religion of Jesus, a people not insensible of the secrets of rational being nor without spirit to resent the unjust endeavors of others to reduce them to a state of bondage and subjection. Your honors need not be informed that a life of slavery like that of your petitioners, deprived of every social privilege, of everything requisite to render life tolerable, is far worse than nonexistence.

In imitation of the laudable example of the good people of these states your petitioners have long and patiently waited the event of petition after petition by them presented to the legislative body of this state and cannot but with grief reflect that their success has been but too similar. They cannot but express their astonishment that it has never been considered that every principle from which America has acted in the course of their unhappy difficulties with Great Britain pleads stronger than a thousand arguments in favor of your petitioners. They therefore humbly beseech your honors to give this petition its due weight and consideration and cause an act of the legislature to be passed whereby they may be restored to the enjoyments of that which is the natural right of all men—and their children who were born in this land of liberty may not be held as slaves after they arrive at the age of twenty-one years. So may the inhabitants of this state [be] no longer chargeable with the inconsistency of acting themselves the part which they condemn and oppose in others. Be prospered in the present glorious struggle for liberty....

DOCUMENT 29

# The Continentals Encounter Civilians

Private Hugh McDonald

*December 1776–April 1777*

While Thomas Jefferson and Thomas Paine sought to secure Americans' support for independence through their words, it fell upon the members of the Continental Army to win hearts and minds through their deeds. This was no small task given the diversity of opinion regarding the American Revolution. Further complicating matters, the army's new, young, and sometimes undisciplined soldiers were often poorly fed and supplied. Under these circumstances, how could the Continental Army convince American citizens—who had been raised to fear armies as instruments of oppression—that it deserved support as a defender of their lives, liberty, and property?

The recollections of Hugh McDonald (born in Scotland ca. 1762), who at age fourteen enlisted as a Continental Army private, shed light on this question. In 1774 McDonald settled in North Carolina with his father, who cast his lot with the Loyalists. They fought Patriots at the February 1776 Battle of Moore's Creek Bridge. Defeated, captured, and then released, they returned home. Four months later, as Continental cavalrymen approached their farm, McDonald's father threatened to kill him if he aided the rebels, but that's what he ended up doing. Afraid to return home, he joined the Continental Army's North Carolina brigade, eventually serving under Brigadier General Francis Nash (ca. 1742–1777). Nash led his North Carolina soldiers at the 1777 battles of Brandywine (September 11) and Germantown (October 4), where he was shot in the head and endured the mangling of his leg by a cannonball. He died on October 7.

SOURCE: "Memoir by Hugh McDonald [Extract]," *Colonial and State Records of North Carolina* 11 (1895): 833–34, 835–36. https://archive.org/details/afj9245.0001.001.umich.edu/page/833

---

... We received orders to march to the north and join the grand camp, commanded by Washington.... We marched from Wilmington,[1] under the

---

[1] An important port town on North Carolina's southern coastline.

command of Gen. Frank Nash, and proceeded to the Roanoke River and encamped about a mile and a half from the town of Halifax....[2] There we remained about three weeks, when [*in late December 1776*] we received orders to turn back and go and meet the British... and prevent them from getting into the State of Georgia.... On our march, we lay on the south side of Contentnea Creek,[3] where there were living an old man and woman who had a number of geese about the house. The next morning about twenty of their geese were missing. They came to the camp inquiring about them, but getting no information among the tents, they went to the general, who said he could do nothing unless they produced the guilty. On his giving them ten dollars,[4] however, they went away satisfied; and I am very sure I got some of them [*the geese*] to eat. Being a sleepy-headed boy, I always went to sleep as soon as the fires were made, and having done so now, about midnight a Mr. John Turner,[5] a messmate of mine, tried to awaken me, which he found difficult to do, but being a strong man, he lifted me up and began sticking pins in my rump until I was fully awake, when he said: "Damn you, go to the kettle and see what you'll find there." I went and found fowl, fresh and fat. I did not understand it that night, but did when the old folks came next morning inquiring about their geese. The general, after paying them, gave the men strict orders to be honest or he would punish the least offense of that kind with severity....

[*Around April 1777*] we... crossed the James River at the town of Richmond, where there were fishers, and having gotten leave there also to draw the seine,[6] every man took as many fish as he wanted. While passing through the town a shoemaker stood in his door and cried, "Hurrah for King George," of which no one took any notice; but after halting in a wood a little distance beyond, where we cooked and ate our fish, the shoemaker came to us and began again to hurrah for King George. When the general and his aids mounted and started, he still followed them, hurrahing for King George, upon which the general ordered him to be taken back to the river and ducked. We brought a long rope, tied it about his middle and seesawed him backwards and forwards until we had him nearly drowned, but every time he got his head above water he would cry for King George. The general having then

---

[2] A North Carolina town about twelve miles south of the Virginia border.
[3] A tributary of the Neuse River in northeastern North Carolina.
[4] In 1777, ten dollars was about six weeks' wages for a Continental Army private.
[5] John Turner (ca. 1755–1825) would rise to the rank of sergeant in the North Carolina brigade.
[6] Net used to capture fish.

ordered him to be tarred and feathered, a feather bed was taken from his own house, where were his wife and four likely daughters crying and beseeching their father to hold his tongue, but still he would not. We tore the bed open and knocked the top out of a tar barrel into which we plunged him headlong. He was then drawn out by the heels and rolled in the feathers until he was a sight, but still he would hurrah for King George. The general then ordered him drummed out of the west end of the town and told him expressly that if he plagued him any more in that way he would have him shot. So we saw no more of the shoemaker.

DOCUMENT 30

# Generals Gates and Burgoyne on the Murder of Jane McCrea

*September 2–6, 1777*

Great Britain's northern campaign of 1777 began with promise for the Redcoats but ended with humiliation. Masterminded by Lieutenant General John Burgoyne (1722–1792), the plan was to isolate rebellious New England by taking control of the Hudson River, Lake George, and Lake Champlain, allowing the British to command the corridor between New York City and Quebec.

After the July 5 capture of Fort Ticonderoga, Britain's fortunes began to falter. A concerted Patriot effort to slow Burgoyne's march south by destroying bridges, diverting streams, and downing trees across roads meant that the main element of his army advanced only about a mile each day. August witnessed the failure of the siege of Fort Stanwix and the defeat of British-allied Hessians near Bennington, Vermont. At battles near Saratoga, New York, on September 19 and October 7, Burgoyne resolved first to dig in and then finally to admit defeat.

Yet the campaign of 1777 taught Burgoyne that winning Americans' hearts and minds could be even more difficult than winning battles. Burgoyne's Native American allies did less than he hoped to assist him militarily and more than he feared to alienate civilians. This was especially true after reports emerged of the July 26 or 27 murder of young Jane McCrea (1752–1777). The daughter of a New Jersey Presbyterian minister, after her mother's death she moved to live with her brother near Saratoga. Here she accepted a marriage proposal from Lieutenant David Jones, a Loyalist serving in Burgoyne's army. Accounts of her death vary. Most agree that she had arrived near Fort Edward, abandoned by American troops, in order to rendezvous with her fiancé, when she fell victim to the tomahawk of a British-allied Huron named Wyandot Panther. Americans charged that Redcoats were paying Native Americans for Patriot scalps. Did McCrea's Loyalist scalp look any different?

Reports of McCrea's murder at the hands of Britain's "savage" partners outraged Americans. One depicted the "hell-like cruelties" of Redcoats' Indian allies who, operating in front of British regulars, "butchered the poor innocent girl, and scalped her in the sight of those very men who are continually preaching... the forbearance of their more than Christian king." Major General Horatio Gates

(1727–1806), realizing the story's value, sent a letter to Burgoyne that baited a response. It appeared in seventeen of America's nineteen active newspapers. Burgoyne's reply, which acknowledged his pardoning of McCrea's killer, appeared alongside Gates's message in about half of these publications, nearly all of which favored the cause of independence.

SOURCE: *Pennsylvania Evening Post* (Philadelphia), September 16, 1777.

## Major General Horatio Gates to Lieutenant General John Burgoyne, September 2, 1777

Last night I had the honor to receive your excellency's letter of the first instant.[1] I am astonished you should mention inhumanity, or threaten retaliation. Nothing happened in the action at Bennington[2] but what is common when works are carried by assault.

That the savages of America should in their warfare mangle and scalp the unhappy prisoners who fall into their hands, is neither new nor extraordinary, but that the famous Lieutenant General Burgoyne, in whom the fine gentleman is united with the soldier and the scholar, should hire the savages of America to scalp Europeans and the descendants of Europeans; nay more, that he should pay a price for each scalp so barbarously taken, is more than will be believed in Europe, until authenticated facts shall, in every Gazette, convince mankind of the truth of the horrid tale. Miss McCrea, a young lady lovely to the sight, of virtuous character and amiable disposition, engaged to be married to an officer in your army, was, with other women and children, taken out of a house near Fort Edward, carried into the woods, and there scalped and mangled in the most shocking manner. Two parents, with their six children, were all treated with the same inhumanity, while quietly residing in their once happy and peaceful dwelling.[3] The miserable fate of Miss McCrea was particularly aggravated by her being dressed to receive her

---

[1] September 1, 1777.

[2] This August 16, 1777 battle, which took place in New York about ten miles from Bennington, Vermont, resulted in an American victory in which about two-thirds of Burgoyne's troops were killed or captured.

[3] On July 25 or 26, 1777, not far from Fort Edward near Argyle, New York, a group of Native Americans reportedly descended on the farm of John and Eva Allen, scalping them and their three children as well as three enslaved people and Eva's unmarried sister, Catherine Kilmer.

promised husband, but met her murderer employed by you. Upwards of one hundred men, women, and children have perished by the hands of ruffians, to whom, it is asserted, you have paid the price of blood.

Enclosed are letters from your wounded officers, prisoners in my hands. By them you will be informed of the generosity of their conquerors. Such money, clothing, attendants, and other necessaries which your excellency pleases to send to the prisoners, shall be faithfully delivered. The late Colonel Baum's[4] servant is at Bennington and would have come to your excellency's camp, but when I offered him a flag,[5] he was afraid to run the risk of being scalped, and declined going.

When I know what surgeon and attendants your excellency is desirous of sending to Bennington, I shall dispatch an officer to your lines, to conduct them to my camp.

## Lieutenant General John Burgoyne to Major General Horatio Gates, September 6, 1777

I received your letter of the second instant,[6] and in consequence of your compliance with my proposal of sending a surgeon to visit the wounded officers in your hands, and some servants to carry money and necessaries to their masters, and to remain with them, I have now to desire the favor of you to dispatch the officer you design with a drum and a flag of truce, so that he may arrive at Stillwater about noon, on the ninth, and he shall be met there by the persons he is to conduct, accompanied also by a drum and flag of truce. I trust, sir, that it is understood between us that the surgeon shall have safe conduct to my outposts, when his visit shall be made, and he shall request it, and you may be assured on my part, that your officer shall meet with security and civility.

I have hesitated, sir, upon answering the other paragraphs of your letter. I disdain to justify myself against the rhapsodies of fiction and calumny, which, from the first of this contest, it has been an unvaried American policy to propagate.... I am induced to deviate from this general rule, in the

---

[4] Lieutenant Colonel Friedrich Baum (1727–1777) of Brunswick died at the Battle of Bennington.
[5] A white flag of truce, which, according to the rules of war, would have assured him safe passage.
[6] September 2, 1777.

present instance, lest my silence should be construed an acknowledgment of the truth of your allegations, and a pretense be thence taken for exercising future barbarities by the American troops.

Upon this motive, and upon this only, I condescend to inform you that I would not be conscious of the acts you presume to impute to me, for the whole continent of America, though the wealth of worlds were in its bowels, and a paradise upon its surface.

It has happened that all my transactions with the Indian nations, last year and this, have been open, clearly heard, distinctly understood, accurately minuted, by very numerous and, in many parts, very unprejudiced audiences. So diametrically opposite to truth is your assertion that I have paid a price for scalps that one of the first regulations established by me at the great council in May, and repeated, and enforced, and invariably adhered to since, was, that the Indians should receive compensation for prisoners, because it would prevent cruelties, and that not only such compensation should be withheld, but strict account demanded for scalps. These pledges of conquest, for such you well know they will ever esteem them, were solemnly and peremptorily[7] prohibited to be taken from the wounded and even the dying, and the persons of aged men, women, children, and prisoners were pronounced sacred even in assaults.

In regard to Miss McCrea, her fall wanted not of the tragic display you have labored to give it, to make it as sincerely abhorred and lamented by me as it can be by the tenderest of her friends. The fact was no premeditated barbarity. On the contrary, two chiefs, who had brought her off for the purpose of security, not of violence to her person, disputed which should be her guard; and in a fit of savage passion in the one from whose hands she was snatched, the unhappy woman became the victim. Upon the first intelligence of this event, I obliged the Indians to deliver the murderer into my hands; and though to have punished him by our laws or principles of justice, would have been perhaps unprecedented, he certainly should have suffered an ignominious[8] death, had I not been convinced by circumstances and observation, beyond the possibility of a doubt, that a pardon under the terms which I prescribed, and they accepted, would be more efficacious than an execution to prevent similar mischiefs.

---

[7] In a manner commanding unquestioning obedience.
[8] Shameful, disgraceful, and dishonorable.

The above instance excepted, your intelligence respecting cruelties of the Indians is false.

You seem to threaten me with European publications, which affects me as little as any other threats you could make; but in regard to American publications, whether your charge against me, which I acquit you of believing, was penned *from* a Gazette, or *for* a Gazette, I desire, and demand from you as a man of honor, that should it appear in print at all, this answer may follow it.

DOCUMENT 31

# Articles of Confederation

*Proposed by Congress on November 15, 1777*
*Ratified on March 1, 1781*

First conceived in 1776, revised and sent for approval to the thirteen states in 1777, and finally ratified in 1781, the Articles of Confederation might best be understood as a testimonial of the former colonies' desire for autonomy and disdain for British imperial rule.

This plan of government reflected nearly all the grievances of 1760–1776. Hostility to executive authority, cultivated by the colonies' royal governors, resulted in a president elected by and answerable to the legislature. Opposition to Parliament's attempts to raise revenue without representation caused the Continental Congress to ensure that, under the Articles, the national government had no direct power to tax. The Articles required a supermajority of nine states for many decisions; amendments to this first constitution required the states' unanimous consent. Although twelve states had ratified the Articles by February 1779, Maryland's jealousy of Virginia's western land claims caused it to withhold its approval of this constitution for two additional years. In the meantime, the Continental Congress operated under the Articles as its de facto charter.

In some respects, the Articles functioned precisely as designed by providing a framework for the United States to act as one in terms of foreign policy while safeguarding states' independence in most domestic matters. Under the Articles, the United States achieved victory in the War for Independence and saw states cede sometimes-overlapping western land claims to the national government. Yet many people, especially veterans of the Continental Army, had come to view the Articles as too feeble to enable a sufficient defense of Americans' liberty.

Although only five states sent delegates to the September 1786 Annapolis Convention, their representatives succeeded in calling for a Constitutional Convention to discuss improving the Articles. The following year delegates from all the states except Rhode Island gathered in the Pennsylvania State House, where, with George Washington presiding, thirty-six-year-old James Madison led a bold effort between May and September to draft an entirely new Constitution.

SOURCE: Charles Tansill, ed., *Documents Illustrative of the Formation of the Union of the United States* (Washington, DC: Government Printing Office, 1927), 27–37. https://archive.org/details/documentsillustroolibr/page/26

---

Articles of Confederation and perpetual Union between the states of New Hampshire, Massachusetts-bay, Rhode Island and Providence Plantations, Connecticut, New York, New Jersey, Pennsylvania, Delaware, Maryland, Virginia, North Carolina, South Carolina and Georgia.

**Article I.** The style of this confederacy shall be "The United States of America."

**Article II.** Each state retains its sovereignty, freedom, and independence, and every power, jurisdiction, and right, which is not by this confederation expressly delegated to the United States, in Congress assembled.

**Article III.** The said states hereby severally enter into a firm league of friendship with each other, for their common defense, the security of their liberties, and their mutual and general welfare, binding themselves to assist each other, against all force offered to, or attacks made upon them, or any of them, on account of religion, sovereignty, trade, or any other pretense whatever....

**Article V.** For the most convenient management of the general interests of the United States, delegates shall be annually appointed in such manner as the legislatures of each state shall direct, to meet in Congress on the first Monday in November, in every year, with a power reserved to each state to recall its delegates, or any of them, at any time within the year, and to send others in their stead for the remainder of the year.

No state shall be represented in Congress by less than two, nor more than seven members; and no person shall be capable of being a delegate for more than three years in any term of six years; nor shall any person, being a delegate, be capable of holding any office under the United States, for which he, or another for his benefit, receives any salary, fees, or emolument of any kind.

Each state shall maintain its own delegates in a meeting of the states, and while they act as members of the committee of the states.

In determining questions in the United States in Congress assembled, each state shall have one vote....

**Article VI.** No state, without the consent of the United States in Congress assembled, shall send any embassy to, or receive any embassy from, or enter into any conference, agreement, alliance, or treaty with any king, prince, or state; nor shall any person holding any office of profit or trust under the United States, or any of them, accept any present, emolument, office, or title of any kind whatever from any king, prince, or foreign state; nor shall the United States in Congress assembled, or any of them, grant any title of nobility.

No two or more states shall enter into any treaty, confederation, or alliance whatever between them, without the consent of the United States in Congress assembled, specifying accurately the purposes for which the same is to be entered into, and how long it shall continue....

No vessel of war shall be kept up in time of peace by any state, except such number only, as shall be deemed necessary by the United States in Congress assembled, for the defense of such state, or its trade; nor shall any body of forces be kept up by any state in time of peace, except such number only, as in the judgment of the United States in Congress assembled, shall be deemed requisite to garrison the forts necessary for the defense of such state; but every state shall always keep up a well-regulated and disciplined militia, sufficiently armed and accoutered,[1] and shall provide and constantly have ready for use, in public stores, a due number of field pieces and tents, and a proper quantity of arms, ammunition, and camp equipage.

No state shall engage in any war without the consent of the United States in Congress assembled, unless such state be actually invaded by enemies....

**Article VIII.** All charges of war, and all other expenses that shall be incurred for the common defense or general welfare, and allowed by the United States in Congress assembled, shall be defrayed out of a common treasury, which shall be supplied by the several states in proportion to the value of all land within each state, granted or surveyed for any person, as such land and the buildings and improvements thereon shall be estimated according to such mode as the United States in Congress assembled, shall from time to time direct and appoint.

The taxes for paying that proportion shall be laid and levied by the authority and direction of the legislatures of the several states within the time agreed upon by the United States in Congress assembled.

**Article IX.** The United States, in Congress assembled, shall have the sole and exclusive right and power of determining on peace and war, except in the cases mentioned in the sixth article—of sending and receiving ambassadors—entering into treaties and alliances....

The United States, in Congress assembled, shall have authority to... ascertain the necessary sums of money to be raised for the service of the

---

[1] Provided with the appropriate attire and equipment.

United States, and to appropriate and apply the same for defraying the public expenses—to borrow money, or emit bills on the credit of the United States, transmitting every half-year to the respective states an account of the sums of money so borrowed or emitted—to build and equip a navy—to agree upon the number of land forces, and to make requisitions from each state for its quota, in proportion to the number of white inhabitants in such state; which requisition shall be binding, and thereupon the legislature of each state shall appoint the regimental officers, raise the men and clothe, arm, and equip them in a solid-like manner, at the expense of the United States....

The United States, in Congress assembled, shall never engage in a war, nor grant letters of marque[2] or reprisal in time of peace, nor enter into any treaties or alliances, nor coin money, nor regulate the value thereof, nor ascertain the sums and expenses necessary for the defense and welfare of the United States, or any of them, nor emit bills, nor borrow money on the credit of the United States, nor appropriate money, nor agree upon the number of vessels of war, to be built or purchased, or the number of land or sea forces to be raised, nor appoint a commander in chief of the army or navy, unless nine states assent to the same: nor shall a question on any other point, except for adjourning from day to day be determined, unless by the votes of the majority of the United States in Congress assembled....

**Article XIII.** Every state shall abide by the determination of the United States in Congress assembled, on all questions which by this confederation are submitted to them. And the Articles of this Confederation shall be inviolably observed by every state, and the union shall be perpetual; nor shall any alteration at any time hereafter be made in any of them; unless such alteration be agreed to in a Congress of the United States, and be afterwards confirmed by the legislatures of every state....

---

[2] Licenses to capture the ships of another nation—that is, to act as privateer and commit government-sanctioned piracy.

DOCUMENT 32

# Foraging for Valley Forge

Private Joseph Plumb Martin
*December 1777–April 1778*

George Washington's failure to prevent the British army from seizing Philadelphia guided his decision to make Valley Forge the site of the Continental Army's 1777–1778 winter encampment. Less than twenty miles from the captured capital, it was close enough to curtail British movement in the Pennsylvania countryside but distant enough to diminish the chances his army would fall victim to a surprise attack. Its ridgelines and streams made it easily defensible, and its relative remoteness from settled areas saved any one group of civilians from the burden of living beside an army that, on arrival, had about 12,000 men. The neat rows of log huts ordered built by Washington contained nearly as many people as Charleston—the fourth largest city in the United States.

Although fifth in size, Valley Forge ranked first in terms of hunger. While an excellent harvest satisfied the appetites of most Americans, the Continental Army's poor logistics meant that soldiers learned to content themselves, as Private Joseph Plumb Martin (1760–1850) wryly remembered, with meals consisting of "a leg of nothing and no turnips."

Not long after his arrival at Valley Forge, this seventeen-year-old soldier found himself assigned to the quartermaster, who made him a member of a foraging party based twenty miles to the west of the encampment. Here it was his duty to engage in what he described as the "plundering" of civilians' corn, livestock, and other provisions so that soldiers back at Valley Forge could spend fewer nights eating flour and water baked into "firecake." For Martin, who first enlisted in 1776 as a 15-year-old from Milford, Connecticut, interacting with Pennsylvanians and serving at the start of the supply chain made this a plum assignment. "We fared much better than I had ever done in the army before," he later recollected, for "we had very good provisions all winter and generally enough of them."

During the course of the war Martin rose to the rank of sergeant. He fought at numerous battles, including Monmouth and Yorktown, before his discharge from the army in 1783. He later helped establish the town of Prospect, Maine, where he married, had five children, wrote his Revolutionary War memoir, and lived until the age of 89.

SOURCE: [Joseph Plumb Martin,] *A Narrative of Some of the Adventures, Dangers, and Sufferings of a Revolutionary Soldier....* (Hallowell, Maine: Glazier, Masters & Co., 1830), 75–83. https://books.google.com/books?id=ZbdcAAAAcAAJ

---

The army... marched for the Valley Forge in order to take up our winter quarters. We were now in a truly forlorn condition—no clothing, no provisions, and as disheartened as need be. We arrived, however, at our destination a few days before Christmas. Our prospect was indeed dreary. In our miserable condition, to go into the wild woods and build us habitations to *stay* (not to *live*) in, in such a weak, starved, and naked condition, was appalling in the highest degree, especially to New Englanders, unaccustomed to such kind of hardships at home. However, there was no remedy—no alternative but this or dispersion. But dispersion, I believe, was not thought of—at least, I did not think of it. We had engaged in the defense of our injured country and were willing, nay, we were determined to persevere as long as such hardships were not altogether intolerable.... But we were now absolutely in danger of perishing, and that too, in the midst of a plentiful country. We then had but little, and often nothing to eat for days together; but now we had nothing and saw no likelihood of any betterment of our condition. Had there fallen deep snows (and it was the time of year to expect them) or even heavy and long rainstorms, the whole army must inevitably have perished. Or had the enemy, strong and well provided as he then was, thought fit to pursue us, our poor emaciated carcasses must have "strewed the plain." But a kind and holy Providence took more notice and better care of us than did the country in whose service we were wearing away our lives by piecemeal.

We arrived at the Valley Forge in the evening. It was dark; there was no water to be found, and I was perishing with thirst, I searched for water till I was weary, and came to my tent without finding any. Fatigue and thirst, joined with hunger, almost made me desperate. I felt at that instant as if I would have taken victuals or drink from the best friend I had on earth by force. I am not writing fiction, all are sober realities. Just after I arrived at my tent, two soldiers, whom I did not know, passed by. They had some water in their canteens which they told me they had found a good distance off, but could not direct me to the place as it was very dark. I tried to beg a draught of water from them but they were as rigid as Arabs. At length I persuaded them to sell me a drink for three pence, Pennsylvania currency, which was every cent of property I could then call my own; so great was the necessity I was then reduced to.

I lay here two nights and one day, and had not a morsel of anything to eat all the time, save half of a small pumpkin, which I cooked by placing it upon a rock, the skin side uppermost, and making a fire upon it. By the time it was heat through I devoured it with as keen an appetite as I should a pie made of it at some other time.

The second evening after our arrival here I was warned to be ready for a two days command. I never heard a summons to duty with so much disgust before or since, as I did that. How I could endure two days more fatigue without nourishment of some sort I could not tell, for I heard nothing said about "provisions." However, in the morning at roll call I was obliged to comply. I went to the parade where I found a considerable number, ordered upon the same business, whatever it was. We were ordered to go to the quartermaster general and receive from him our final orders. We accordingly repaired to his quarters, which was about three miles from camp; here we understood that our destiny was to go into the country on a foraging expedition, which was nothing more nor less than to procure provisions from the inhabitants for the men in the army and forage for the poor perishing cattle belonging to it, at the point of the bayonet. We stayed at the quartermaster general's quarters till some time in the afternoon, during which time a beef creature was butchered for us. I well remember the fine stuff it was; it was quite transparent. I thought at the time what an excellent lantern it would make. I was, notwithstanding, very glad to get some of it, bad as it looked.... We were then divided into several parties and sent off upon our expedition.

Our party consisted of a lieutenant, a sergeant, a corporal and eighteen privates. We marched till night when we halted and took up our quarters at a large farmhouse. The lieutenant, attended by his waiter, took up his quarters for the night in the hall with the people of the house, we were put into the kitchen; we had a snug room and a comfortable fire, and we began to think about cooking some of our *fat* beef. One of the men proposed to the landlady to sell her a shirt for some sauce. She very readily took the shirt, which was worth a dollar at least. She might have given us a mess of sauce, for I think she would not have suffered poverty by so doing, as she seemed to have a plenty of *all* things. After we had received the sauce, we went to work to cook our suppers. By the time it was eatable the family had gone to rest. We saw where the woman went into the cellar, and, she having left us a candle, we took it into our heads that little good cider would not make our supper relish any the worse; so some of the men took the water pail and drew it full of excellent cider, which did not fail to raise our spirits considerably. Before we lay down the man who sold the shirt, having observed that the landlady had flung it into a closet, took a notion to repossess it again. We marched off early in the morning before the people of the house were stirring, consequently did not know or see the woman's chagrin at having been overreached by the soldiers.

This day we arrived at Milltown, or Downingtown, a small village halfway between Philadelphia and Lancaster, which was to be our quarters for the winter. It was dark when we had finished our day's march. There was a commissary and a wagon master general to regulate the conduct of the wagoners and direct their motions. The next day after our arrival at this place we were put into a small house in which was only one room, in the center of the village. We were immediately furnished with rations of good and wholesome beef and flour, built us up some births to sleep in, and filled them with straw, and felt as happy as any other pigs that were no better off than ourselves....

The first expedition I undertook in my new vocation, was a foraging cruise. I was ordered off into the country in a party consisting of a corporal and six men. What our success was I do not now remember; but I well remember the transactions of the party in the latter part of the journey. We were returning to our quarters on Christmas afternoon, when we met three ladies, one a young married woman with an infant in her arms, the other two were maidens... [or at least] they passed for such. They were all comely, particularly one of them; she was handsome. They immediately fell into familiar discourse with us—were very inquisitive like the rest of the sex—asked us a thousand questions respecting our business, where we had been and where going, etc. After we had satisfied their curiosity, or at least had endeavored to do so, they told us that they (that is, the two youngest) lived a little way on our road in a house which they described, desired us to call in and rest ourselves a few minutes, and said they would return as soon as they had seen their sister and babe safe[ly] home.

As for myself, I was very unwell, occasioned by a violent cold I had recently taken, and I was very glad to stop a short time to rest my bones. Accordingly, we stopped at the house described by the young ladies, and in a few minutes they returned as full of chat as they were when we met them in the road. After a little more information respecting our business, they proposed to us to visit one of their neighbors, against whom it seemed they had a grudge, and upon whom they wished to wreak their vengeance through our agency. To oblige the ladies we undertook to obey their injunctions. They very readily agreed to be our guides as the way lay across fields and pastures full of bushes. The distance was about half a mile.... The girls went with us until we came in sight of the house. We concluded we could do no less than fulfill our engagements with them, so we went into the house, the people of which, appeared to be genuine Pennsylvania farmers, and very fine folks.

We all now began to relent, and after telling them our business, we concluded that if they would give us a canteen (which held about a quart) full of whiskey and some bread and cheese, we would depart without any further exactions. To get rid of us, doubtless, the man of the house gave us our canteen of whiskey, and the good woman gave us a fine loaf of wheaten flour bread and the whole of a small cheese, and we raised the siege and departed. I was several times afterwards at this house, and was always well treated. I believe the people did not recollect me, and I was glad they did not, for when I saw them I had always a twinge or two of conscience for thus dissembling with them at the instigation of persons who certainly were no better than they should be, or they would not have employed strangers to glut their vengeance upon innocent people; innocent at least as it respected us. But after all, it turned much in their favor. It was in our power to take cattle or horses, hay, or any other produce from them; but we felt that we had done wrong in listening to the tattle of malicious neighbors, and for that cause we refrained from meddling with any property of theirs ever after. So that good came to them out of intended evil.

After we had received our bread, cheese, and whiskey, we struck across the fields into the highway again. It was now nearly sunset, and as soon as we had got into the road, the youngest of the girls, and handsomest and chattiest, overtook us again, riding on horseback with a gallant.[1] As soon as she came up with us, "O here is my little captain again," said she. (It appeared it was our corporal that attracted her attention.) "I am glad to see you again." The young man, her sweetheart, did not seem to wish her to be quite so familiar with her "little captain," and urged on his horse as fast as possible. But female policy is generally too subtle for the male's, and she exhibited a proof of it, for they had scarcely passed us when she slid from the horse upon her feet, into the road, with a shriek as though some frightful accident had happened to her. There was nothing handy to serve as a horseblock, so the "little captain" must take her in his arms and set her upon her horse again, much, I suppose, to their mutual satisfaction—but not so to her gallant, who, as I thought, looked rather grum....[2]

---

[1] A suitor or boyfriend.
[2] Grim, glum, stern, surly, sour.

I shall not relate all the minute transactions which passed while I was on this foraging party, as it would swell my narrative to too large a size. I will, however, give the reader a brief account of some of my movements that I may not leave him entirely ignorant how I spent my time. We fared much better than I had ever done in the army before, or ever did afterwards. We had very good provisions all winter and generally enough of them. Some of us were constantly in the country with the wagons; we went out by turns and had no one to control us. Our lieutenant scarcely ever saw us or we him; our sergeant never went out with us once, all the time we were there, nor our corporal *but* once, and that was when he was the "little captain." When we were in the country we were pretty sure to fare well, for the inhabitants were remarkably kind to us. We had no guards to keep; our only duty was to help load the wagons with hay, corn, meal, or whatever they were to take off, and when they were thus loaded, to keep them company till they arrived at the commissary's, at Milltown. From thence the articles, whatever they were, were carried to camp in other vehicles, under other guards.

I do not remember that during the time I was employed in this business, which was from Christmas to the latter part of April, ever to have met with the least resistance from the inhabitants, take what we would from their barns, mills, corncribs, or stalls; but when we came to their stables, then look out for the women. Take what horse you would, it was one or the other's "pony" and they had no other to ride to church; and when we had got possession of a horse we were sure to have half a dozen or more women pressing upon us, until by some means or other, if possible, they would slip the bridle from the horse's head, and then we might catch him again if we could. They would take no more notice of a charged bayonet than a blind horse would of a cocked pistol. It would answer no purpose to threaten to kill them with the bayonet or musket; they knew as well as we did that we would not put our threats in execution, and when they had thus liberated a horse (which happened but seldom) they would laugh at us and ask us why we did not do as we threatened, kill them, and then they would generally ask us into their houses and treat us with as much kindness as though nothing had happened.

The women of Pennsylvania, taken in general, are certainly very worthy characters; it is but justice, as far as I am concerned, for me to say, that I was always well treated both by them and the men, especially the Friends or Quakers, in every part of the state through which I passed, and that was the greater part of what was then inhabited. But the southern ladies had a queer idea of the Yankees (as they always called the New Englanders). They seemed to think that they were a people quite different from themselves, as

# King George III
*Allan Ramsay, 1762*

SOURCE: Courtesy of the Indianapolis Museum of Art at Newfields.

PATRIOT KING: Scottish artist Allan Ramsay's 1762 portrait captured the new monarch in his coronation robes and at the height of his popularity in America. When he assumed the throne at age twenty-two, Great Britain seemed poised for victory in war against France, which was ruled by a monarch with almost absolute power. The British monarch's standing as a champion of liberty, together with his duty to share power with Parliament, led Boston minister Andrew Eliot in 1765 to describe Britain's balanced constitution as "the glory of Britons, and the envy of foreigners." George III retained his popularity even after the post-war Imperial Crisis led Americans to oppose the actions of Parliament. In 1766, the New York General Assembly commissioned an equestrian statue of the king to recognize "the innumerable and singular benefits" this "most gracious sovereign" had bestowed. The statue was erected in Manhattan in 1770, but by 1776 the tide of opinion turned against the king. His statue was toppled, chopped into pieces, and melted into 42,000 musket balls for the Continental Army.

# "This is the Place to affix the Stamp"
## October 24, 1765

SOURCE: *The Pennsylvania Journal and Weekly Advertiser,* October 24, 1765 Library of Congress, LC-USZ62-242.

OVER MY DEAD BODY: Philadelphia's *Pennsylvania Journal and Weekly Advertiser* published this protest against the Stamp Act on October 24, 1765. The law, set to go into effect on November 1, mandated that everything from newspapers and legal documents to playing cards be printed on taxed paper embossed with an official seal. Noting that not a single member of the British Parliament had been elected by Americans, colonists demanded "no taxation without representation." Taxation by a government to which Americans had not consented, they insisted, was theft. The *Pennsylvania Journal* printed this skull-and-crossbones warning on the bottom right corner of its first page.

# "An Attempt to Land a Bishop in America"

## 1768

SOURCE: *Political Register* (London), 1768, Library of Congress, LC-DIG-ppmsca-13637.

"LIBERTY & FREEDOM OF CONSCIENCE": Published in London's *Political Register*, this satirical engraving mocked colonists opposed to the appointment of a North American Anglican bishop. Many who learned of Archbishop of Canterbury Thomas Secker's ambition to establish an American bishopric, however, considered it a serious threat to their freedom and the autonomy of their churches. Congregationalists especially feared falling under the control of the Church of England. Boston minister Jonathan Mayhew warned of a British plot "to root out all New England churches." Although no bishop ever arrived during the colonial period, this 1768 cartoon depicts a bishop fleeing a New England mob, members of which carry books by philosophers John Locke and Algernon Sidney as well as a banner demanding "Liberty and Freedom of Conscience." One member of the Calvinist crowd has hurled a copy of the works of John Calvin at the head of the bishop, who pleads "Lord, now lettest thou thy Servant depart in Peace."

# The Bloody Massacre
*Paul Revere, 1770*

SOURCE: Paul Revere, "The Bloody Massacre Perpetrated in King Street, Boston, on March 5th 1770 by a party of the 29thRegt.," Library of Congress, LC-DIG-ppmsca-01657.

PROPAGANDA WORTH 1,000 WORDS: This engraving by Paul Revere (1735–1818) distorts key facts. It was the Redcoats, not the civilians, who had their backs against the wall. No one alleged that Captain Thomas Preston, their commanding officer, raised his sword to command a neatly aligned group of soldiers to fire their weapons. The Redcoats' facial expressions suggest hard-hearted determination; those in the crowd appear sad and shocked, and one man holds up his hand as if to plead for mercy. Revere largely copied this depiction from another engraving, "The Fruits of Arbitrary Power, or the Bloody Massacre," by Henry Pelham. Revere's engraving was advertised for sale a week earlier than Pelham's and became the iconic image of the "massacre." One difference is that Revere labeled the customhouse, seen at right, "Butcher's Hall." At the bottom he also added a poem, the first two lines of which read "Unhappy Boston! see thy Sons deplore, Thy hallow'd walks besmear'd with guiltless Gore."

D

# The Bedford Battle Flag
*c. 1720*

SOURCE: The Bedford Flag is located at the Bedford Library in Bedford, Massachusetts.

"CONQUER OR DIE": This flag, reportedly carried at the Battle of Concord by minuteman Nathaniel Page of Bedford, Massachusetts, testifies to the deep roots of the New England militia tradition. Previously carried by Page's father, uncle, and grandfather, it dates to around 1720 and is recognized as the oldest extant flag in the United States. Featuring a sword-wielding arm emerging from a cloud of gun smoke, the design includes three cannonballs and the Latin motto "VINCE AUT MORIRE" ("CONQUER OR DIE"). Page, a member of the select minutemen component of the Bedford militia, recounted to his grandson how he carried the flag to Concord's North Bridge on April 19, 1775. It may have helped inspire the famous first lines of the poem "Concord Hymn" (1837) by Ralph Waldo Emerson: "By the rude bridge that arched the flood, / Their flag to April's breeze unfurled, / Here once the embattled farmers stood, / And fired the shot heard round the world."

E

# Representation of the terrible fire at New York
*c. 1778*

SOURCE: André Basset, *Political Register* (London), "Representation du feu terrible a Nouvelle Yorck," Library of Congress, LC-DIG-ppmsca-19163.

UP IN FLAMES: On September 15, 1776, Redcoats captured New York. Six days later, an inferno consumed much of America's second-largest city, destroying hundreds of buildings and complicating British plans to turn Manhattan island into a base for military operations and a refuge for Loyalists. A London newspaper blamed the fire on Patriot arsonists and noted "that the first incendiary who fell into the hands of the troops was a *woman*, provided with matches and combustibles." As was the case with her male counterparts, punishment was swift, "for without ceremony, she was tossed into the flames" by the soldiers. This engraving by Frenchman André Basset only hints at the scope of destruction.

# Count de Rochambeau

## 1780

SOURCE: "Count de Rochambeau: French General of the Land Forces in America Reviewing the French Troops," 1780, Library of Congress, LC-DIG-ppmsca-40856.

SATIRE: This British cartoon exploited anti-French stereotypes to downplay the value of Rochambeau and his army to the cause of American independence. The unknown artist portrayed Rochambeau standing before a mere six soldiers and one flag-bearing officer—far fewer than his 5500-man army. Portrayed with huge noses, spindly legs, shirts with exaggerated ruffles, and backpacks that look like powder puffs, these Frenchmen vaguely resemble poodles and seem simultaneously ugly and effeminate. These details, along with the almost impossibly long pigtails of Rochambeau and his officer, aimed to make the French objects for mockery. In 1781 at Yorktown, where the Continental Army, Rochambeau's troops, and the fleet of Admiral de Grasse surrounded the British and forced their surrender, the French and their American allies had the last laugh.

# George Washington
*Jean-Antoine Houdon, 1784*

SOURCE: Detroit Publishing Co. *Houdon's statue of Washington*, [Between 1905 and 1920], Library of Congress, LC-DIG-det-4a18652.

CINCINNATUS: After America's victory in the War for Independence, Washington's decision to resign as commander-in-chief of the Continental Army and return to private life inspired people to liken him to Cincinnatus, a Roman warrior-statesman revered for winning victory in war and then giving up almost unlimited power. In 1784, Virginia's General Assembly commissioned Frenchman Jean-Antoine Houdon to sculpt this statue of the Revolutionary War hero. Houdon depicted Washington returning to Mount Vernon on Christmas Eve, 1783. Still wearing his uniform, Washington holds a civilian's cane. His sword is put away in its scabbard. Behind him is a plow, suggesting his resumption of life as a planter. His left hand rests on a *fasces*—a Roman Republican symbol of strength through unity. The fasces is composed of 13 rods—one for each state.

indeed they were in many respects. I could mention many things and ways in which they differed, but it is of no consequence; they were clever and that is sufficient. I will, however, mention one little incident, just to show what their conceptions were of us.

I happened once to be with some wagons, one of which was detached from the party. I went with this team as its guard; we stopped at a house, the mistress of which and the wagoner were acquainted. (These foraging teams all belonged in the neighborhood of our quarters.) She had a pretty little female child about four years old. The teamster was praising the child, extolling its gentleness and quietness, when the mother observed that it had been quite cross and crying all day. "I have been threatening," said she, "to give her to the Yankees." "Take care," said the wagoner, "how you speak of the Yankees, I have one of them here with me." "La!" said the woman, "is he a Yankee? I thought he was a Pennsylvanian. I don't see any difference between him and other people."

I have before said that I should not narrate all the little affairs which transpired while I was on this foraging party. But if I pass them all over in silence the reader may perhaps think that I had nothing to do all winter, or at least, that I *did* nothing, when in truth it was quite the reverse. Our duty was hard, but generally not altogether unpleasant. I had to travel far and near, in cold and in storms, by day and by night, and at all times to run the *risk* of abuse, if not of injury, from the inhabitants, when *plundering* them of their property (for I could not, while in the very act of taking their cattle, hay, corn, and grain from them against their wills, consider it a whit better than plundering—sheer privateering). But I will give them the credit of never receiving the least abuse or injury from an individual during the whole time I was employed in this business. I doubt whether the people of New England would have borne it as patiently, their "steady habits"[3] to the contrary notwithstanding.

---

[3] Connecticut was known as "the land of steady habits."

DOCUMENT 33

# Envisioning an African American Regiment

Lieutenant Colonel John Laurens

*February 2, 1778*

Born into the South Carolina aristocracy, John Laurens (1754–1782) devoted his brief adulthood to the struggle for liberty. The eldest son of Henry Laurens (1724–1792), president of the Continental Congress from 1777 to 1778, he was a lieutenant colonel in the Continental Army who served as George Washington's aide-de-camp. He gained a reputation for bravery at the battles of Brandywine and Germantown, where a musket ball grazed his shoulder, as well as at Monmouth, where his horse was shot out from under him.

Motivated by a strong opposition to slavery as well as a desire for a field command, Laurens proposed to his father enlisting the able-bodied male slaves who would have been part of his inheritance to form the core of a regiment he would lead into battle. Military service, he wrote to his father on January 14, 1778, "would advance those who are unjustly deprived of the rights of mankind to a state which would be a proper gradation between abject slavery and perfect liberty," preparing them for freedom after the war.

His father, while not dismissing the idea, raised concerns. Would the former slaves view life in the army—away from loved ones and exposed to mortal danger—as an improvement? Would they run away? Would the plan survive likely opposition in South Carolina and elsewhere? In his February 2 response to his father, Laurens helped to answer these objections.

In the spring of 1779, as the British invaded South Carolina, the Continental Congress acquiesced to the enlistment of African Americans. The government of South Carolina, however, blocked the plan. Laurens persisted, but became a prisoner of war when captured by the British in May 1780; then, upon his release at the end of the year, he received an appointment to serve as an American diplomat in France. He returned to the United States in time to lead a battalion at Yorktown in October 1781. While the British surrender there brought an end to major hostilities, in August 1782 Laurens suffered mortal wounds when he led a group of infantrymen into a British ambush at the Battle of the Combahee River near Beaufort, South Carolina. Neither Laurens nor his plan to raise a regiment of African Americans survived the War for Independence.

SOURCE: John Laurens to Henry Laurens, February 2, 1778, in William Gilmore Simms, ed., *The Army Correspondence of Colonel John Lauren in the Years 1777–8* (New York: John B. Moreau, 1867), 114–18. https://archive.org/details/armylaurensyearoojohnrich/page/114

## John Laurens to Henry Laurens | Valley Forge, Penn., February 2, 1778

The more I reflect upon the difficulties and delays which are likely to attend the completing [of] our Continental regiments, the more anxiously is my mind bent upon the scheme, which I lately communicated to you. The obstacles to the execution of it had presented themselves to me, but by no means appeared insurmountable. I was aware of having that monstrous popular prejudice, open-mouthed against me, of undertaking to transform beings almost irrational, into well-disciplined soldiers, of being obliged to combat the arguments, and perhaps the intrigues, of interested persons. But zeal for the public service, and an ardent desire to assert the rights of humanity, determined me to engage in this arduous business, with the sanction of your consent. My own perseverance, aided by the countenance of a few virtuous men, will, I hope, enable me to accomplish it.

You seem to think, my dear father, that men reconciled by long habit to the miseries of their condition, would prefer their ignominious[1] bonds to the untasted sweets of liberty, especially when offered upon the terms which I propose.

I confess, indeed, that the minds of this unhappy species must be debased by a servitude, from which they can hope for no relief but death, and that every motive to action but fear, must be nearly extinguished in them. But do you think they are so perfectly molded to their state as to be insensible that a better exists? Will the galling comparison between themselves and their masters leave them unenlightened in this respect? Can their self-love be so totally annihilated as not frequently to induce ardent wishes for a change?

You will accuse me, perhaps, my dearest friend, of consulting my own feelings too much; but I am tempted to believe that this trampled people have so much human left in them, as to be capable of aspiring to the rights of men by noble exertions, if some friend to mankind would point the road, and give them a prospect of success. If I am mistaken in this, I would avail myself, even of their weakness, and, conquering one fear by another, produce

---

[1] Humiliating, shameful, embarrassing.

equal good to the public. You will ask in this view, how do you consult the benefit of the slaves? I answer, that like other men, they are the creatures of habit. Their cowardly ideas will be gradually effaced, and they will be modified anew. Their being rescued from a state of perpetual humiliation, and being advanced, as it were, in the scale of being, will compensate the dangers incident to their new state.

The hope that will spring in each man's mind, respecting his own escape, will prevent his being miserable. Those who fall in battle will not lose much; those who survive will obtain their reward. Habits of subordination, patience under fatigues, sufferings and privations of every kind, are soldierly qualifications, which these men possess in an eminent degree.

Upon the whole, my dearest friend and father, I hope that my plan for serving my country and the oppressed negro race will not appear to you the chimera of a young mind, deceived by a false appearance of moral beauty, but a laudable sacrifice of private interest, to justice and the public good.

You say, that my resources would be small, on account of the proportion of women and children. I do not know whether I am right, for I speak from impulse, and have not reasoned upon the matter. I say, although my plan is at once to give freedom to the negroes, and gain soldiers to the states, in case of concurrence, I should sacrifice the former interest, and therefore would change the women and children for able-bodied men. The more of these I could obtain, the better; but forty might be a good foundation to begin upon.

It is a pity that some such plan as I propose could not be more extensively executed by public authority. A well-chosen body of 5,000 black men, properly officered, to act as light troops, in addition to our present establishment, might give us decisive success in the next campaign.

I have long deplored the wretched state of these men, and considered in their history, the bloody wars excited in Africa, to furnish America with slaves—the groans of despairing multitudes, toiling for the luxuries of merciless tyrants.

I have had the pleasure of conversing with you, sometimes, upon the means of restoring them to their rights. When can it be better done, than when their enfranchisement may be made conducive to the public good, and be modified, as not to overpower their weak minds?

You ask, what is the general's opinion, upon this subject? He is convinced, that the numerous tribes of blacks in the southern parts of the continent, offer a resource to us that should not be neglected. With respect to my particular plan, he only objects to it, with the arguments of pity for a man who would be less rich than he might be.

I am obliged, my dearest friend and father, to take my leave for the present; you will excuse whatever exceptionable may have escaped in the course of my letter, and accept the assurance of filial love, and respect....

DOCUMENT 34

# List of Prints to Illustrate British Cruelties

Benjamin Franklin and the Marquis de Lafayette

ca. May 1779

Although the British military won numerous battles during the War for Independence, it experienced great difficulty winning over the hearts and minds of American civilians. One reason was that it tended to employ all the weapons at its disposal—such as its warships' cannons, which pounded American seaports when more surgical strikes could have minimized collateral damage. The heavy-handed behavior of British soldiers, who often demonstrated little sympathy for civilians in their path, alienated Americans as well. Continental soldiers such as Hugh McDonald (born ca. 1762) and Joseph Plumb Martin (1760–1850) generally did their best to treat civilians as "us." Meanwhile, British frustrations mounted as the war dragged on, increasingly causing Redcoats as well as their Loyalist and Indian allies to disregard noncombatants, such as Jane McCrea (1752–1777), as "them."

The Continental Congress sought to exploit this British disadvantage when it asked Benjamin Franklin (1706–1790), its emissary in Paris, to create and have published an illustrated book, primarily intended for children, highlighting British wartime cruelties. Franklin reached out to the Marquis de Lafayette (1757–1834), who had returned to France after two years with the Continental Army, for help deciding on which British actions to focus. Working together, they composed this list of atrocities to become the subjects of illustrations. Franklin enumerated the first eighteen, Lafayette the six that followed, and then Franklin added the final two. Although their book was never published, their efforts help to emphasize the ways in which protracted warfare in North America undermined British objectives.

SOURCE: Franklin and Lafayette's List of Prints to Illustrate British Cruelties [ca. May 1779], *Founders Online*, National Archives, http://founders.archives.gov/documents/Franklin/01-29-02-0477.

LIST OF PRINTS TO ILLUSTRATE BRITISH CRUELTIES 159

1. The Burning of Charlesto[w]n (Date)[1]
   A fine town by the waterside, being a port, but without any defense.
   A spire rising among the houses, belonging to the house of worship.
   A belfry belonging to the town house all in flames.
   The inhabitants had all left it.
2. The Burning of Falmouth (Date Nov. 1775)[2]
   A fine town and port, but without defense.
   Ships firing hot shot, and throwing bombs and carcasses into the town; English colors.
   The houses partly in flames.
   Sailors with torches setting fire to others.
   The inhabitants flying out of it carrying off the sick and aged.
   Women with children in their arms.
   Some killed as they go off, and lying on the ground.
3. The Burning of Norfolk[3]
   Fine town and port, several churches.
   Town house.
   Inhabitants flying as above, and ships firing.
4. The Burning of Bedford[4]
5. The Burning of Esopus[5]
6. The Cannonading of Bristol[6]
7. ——— of Stoningtown people flying, etc.[7]

   } all defenseless Places.—

8. The putting prisoners to death in cold blood after having surrendered their arms, and demanded quarter—Baylor's troop.[8]

---

[1] Charlestown, Mass., was burned on June 17, 1775, during the Battle of Bunker Hill.
[2] Falmouth (now Portland, Maine) was actually burned on October 18, 1775.
[3] On January 1, 1776, British warships shelled Norfolk, Va.; sailors landed to torch specific buildings. Many residents of Norfolk were Loyalists who had been driven away by the Patriot troops who occupied the city; these Patriot forces, believing that Norfolk could not be defended against future British occupation, later burned much of what had remained after the British attack.
[4] A British expeditionary force burned Bedford village, incorporated in 1787 into the town of New Bedford, Mass., on September 5 and 6, 1778.
[5] Kingston (or Esopus), N.Y., was burned on October 16, 1777.
[6] British warships bombarded Bristol, R.I., on October 7, 1775. On May 25, 1778, 500 British and Hessian troops attacked the town and burned about thirty homes and other structures.
[7] Stonington, Conn., was attacked by the frigate H.M.S. *Rose* on August 30, 1775.
[8] On the night of September 28, 1778, British soldiers serving under Major General Charles "No-Flint" Grey (1729–1807) bayonetted about one hundred members of

9. Prisoners dying in their jails, with hunger, cold, and want of fresh air.
10. Dunmore's hiring the negroes to murder their masters' families[9]
    A large house.
    Blacks armed with guns and hangers.[10]
    Master and his sons on the ground dead,
    Wife and daughters lifted up in the arms of the negroes as they are carrying off.
11. Savages killing and scalping the frontier farmers and their families, women and children, English officers mixed with the savages, and giving them orders and encouraging them.
12. Governor Tonyn sitting in state, a table before him, his soldiers and savages bringing in scalps of the Georgia people, and presenting them. Money on the table with which he pays for them.[11]
13. The commanding officer at Niagara, receiving in like manner the scalps of the Wyoming families.[12]
14. The king of England, giving audience to his secretary [of] war, who presents him a schedule entitled Acc[oun]t of Scalps, which he receives very graciously.
15. American prisoners, put on board men of war, and whips to make them fight against their countrymen and relations.
16. Americans put on board ships in irons to be carried to the East Indies, and Senegal, where they died with misery and the unwholesomeness of the climate.[13]

---

the 3rd Regiment of Continental Light Dragoons, commanded by Colonel George Baylor (1752–1784), as they slept near modern-day River Vale, N.J.

[9] On November 7, 1775, John Murray, 4th Earl of Dunmore (1730–1809), royal governor of Virginia, signed a proclamation offering freedom to slaves of Patriots who joined the British army.

[10] Metal hooks.

[11] General Patrick Tonyn (1725–1804) served as British governor of East Florida (1774–1783). A January 17, 1777 letter had informed Franklin that, "at the instigation" of Tonyn, Cherokee and Creek warriors had "in one day taken seven hundred scalps from the inoffensive frontier families of the Carolinas and Georgia."

[12] The July 3, 1778, Wyoming Massacre resulted in the loss of about 300 Pennsylvania settlers' lives at the hands of Loyalist and Iroquois forces under the command of Colonel John Butler (1728–1796) of Fort Niagara. The victorious Loyalists and Iroquois burned Patriots' houses and allegedly scalped prisoners and retreating opponents.

[13] On May 8, 1779, Franklin wrote to Antoine de Sartine (1729–1801), the French naval secretary (1774–1780), about American prisoners of war forced to serve in the

17. Burning the wounded with straw at the Crooked Billet, small place in Pennsylvania.[14]
18. Prisoners killed and roasted for a great festival where the Canadian Indians are eating American flesh, Colonel Butler[15] an[d] English officer sitting at table.
19. British officers who being prisoners on parole are well received in the best American families, and take that opportunity of corrupting negroes and engaging them to desert from the house, to rob, and even to murder their masters.
20. American officers who, as they arrive in the British camp, are insulted by an enraged soldiery—their money, their cockades, their sword, and all their clothes are taken away from them.
21. A dirty prison ship where American officers are confined without being at liberty to take the air, and so crowded that they can live but a few days—British officers come to laugh at them and insult at their miseries.
22. British officers plundering with their own hands farm houses, abusing the old people of the house, insulting the young landlady, and frightening the children.
23. An honorable Captain Corning last spring in the house of a gentleman called Mr. West at White Marsh, rushing in the room where Miss West and another young lady were sleeping at two o'clock in the morning—the captain and soldiers jump to the beds of the two ladies, and with fixed bayonets upon their breasts make several inquiries, and laugh at their dreadful situation in the most abusive manner.[16]

---

British navy as well as others "sent as slaves to Africa."

[14] After the American defeat at the May 1, 1778, Battle of Crooked Billet, British and Loyalist forces reportedly murdered prisoners of war. Andrew Long (ca. 1730–1812), a Bucks County justice of the peace, took statements from five witnesses who reported "savage barbarity in its utmost exertion of cruelty" including the intentional burning alive of the wounded.

[15] Colonel John Butler, Loyalist commander of Fort Niagara, mentioned in note 12.

[16] Although Lafayette here referred to a specific instance in which British soldiers assaulted American women, Washington's wartime correspondence, which contains numerous references to redcoat attacks on American women and girls, makes clear that such crimes were not uncommon. In August 1776, for example, British General Lord Rawdon (Francis Rawdon-Hastings, 1st Marquess of Hastings, 1754–1826) described "the fair nymphs" of Staten Island, N.Y., as "fresh meat" that made

24. Another right honorable captain going out on a detachment an[d] killing defenseless people.
25. General Gage's perfidy to the inhab[i]t[ant]s of Boston.
26. Counterfeiting the paper money.

---

his "healthy and spirited" soldiers "as riotous as satyrs. A girl cannot step into the bushes to pluck a rose without running the most imminent risk of being ravished, and they are so little accustomed to these vigorous methods that they don't bear them with the proper resignation, and of consequence we have the most entertaining courts-martial every day."

DOCUMENT 35

# Redcoats in South Carolina

Eliza Wilkinson

June 1779

The October 1777 surrender of General John Burgoyne (1722–1792) at Saratoga shattered Britain's northern strategy, which had aimed to isolate New England. It also emboldened the French, who in 1778 joined the war as America's ally. This prompted General Henry Clinton (1730–1795), who after the resignation of William Howe (1729–1814) in 1777 had become the British commander-in-chief, to withdraw from Philadelphia and consolidate his forces in New York and the Caribbean.

Beginning in December 1778, when Redcoats captured Savannah, a war that had started in the North and spread to the middle states shifted to the South. The belief that Loyalism remained strong in Georgia and the Carolinas constituted a central premise of the British southern strategy. Britain also hoped that the prevalence of slavery in the region would cause southerners to think twice before taking up arms and thereby inviting instability.

The account of Eliza Yonge Wilkinson (1757–1818), a twenty-two-year-old widow who fled inland to her sister's plantation after Redcoats attacked Beaufort in 1779, underscores the limits of these presumptions—especially when the behavior of British troops made enemies instead of friends. Already highly hostile to Great Britain, Wilkinson grew increasingly bitter in the months that followed her June 1779 encounter with British forces. In addition to their 1780 capture of Charleston, Redcoats would burn her parents' house and kill several of their slaves. Meanwhile, one of her brothers lost his life fighting for independence. After the war, Wilkinson remarried and had four children. A granddaughter, Caroline Gilman, published her letters.

SOURCE: Caroline Gilman, ed., *Letters of Eliza Wilkinson* (New York: S. Colman, 1839), 24, 27–31. https://archive.org/details/lettersofelizawioowilk/page/24

---

All this time we had not seen the face of an enemy, not an open one—for I believe private ones were daily about. One night, however, upwards of sixty dreaded Redcoats, commanded by Major Graham,[1] passed our gate, in order to surprise Lieutenant Morton Wilkinson[2] at his own house, where they understood he had a party of men. A negro wench was their informer, and also their conductor; but (thank heaven) somehow or other they failed in their attempt, and repassed our avenue early in the morning, but made a halt at the head of it, and wanted to come up; but a negro fellow, whom they had got at a neighbor's not far from us to go as far as the ferry with them, dissuaded them from it, by saying it was not worth while, for it was only a plantation belonging to an old decrepit gentleman, who did not live there; so they took his word for it, and proceeded on. You may think how much we were alarmed when we heard this, which we did the next morning; and how many blessings the negro had from us for his consideration and pity....

Well, now comes the day of terror—the 3d of June. (I shall never love the anniversary of that day.) In the morning, fifteen or sixteen horsemen rode up to the house; we were greatly terrified, thinking them the enemy, but from their behavior, were agreeably deceived, and found them friends. They sat a while on their horses, talking to us; and then rode off, except two, who tarried a minute or two longer, and then followed the rest, who had nearly reached the gate. One of the said two [*fell from his horse*].... We saw him, and sent a boy to tell him, if he was hurt, to come up to the house, and we could endeavor to do something for him. He and his companion accordingly came up; he looked very pale, and bled much; his gun, somehow in the fall, had given him a bad wound behind the ear, from whence the blood flowed down his neck and bosom plentifully. We were greatly alarmed on seeing him in this situation, and had gathered around him, some with one thing, some with another, in order to give him assistance. We were very busy examining the wound, when a negro girl ran in, exclaiming, "Oh! The king's people are coming; it must be them, for they are all in red." Upon this cry, the two men that were with us snatched up their guns, mounted their horses, and made off; but had not got many yards from the house, before the enemy discharged a pistol at them. Terrified almost to death as I was, I was still anxious for my friends' safety; I tremblingly flew to the window, to see if the shot had proved fatal. When, seeing them both safe, "Thank heaven," said I, "they've got off without hurt!" I'd hardly uttered this, when I heard the horses of the inhuman

---

[1] Major Colin Graham (ca. 1725–1799) led the British Army's 16th Regiment of Foot Light Infantry Company.
[2] Lieutenant Morton Wilkinson (ca. 1742–1799).

Britons coming in such a furious manner, that they seemed to tear up the earth, and the riders at the same time bellowing out the most horrid curses imaginable; oaths and imprecations which chilled my whole frame. Surely, thought I, such horrid language denotes nothing less than death; but I'd no time for thought—they were up to the house—entered with drawn swords and pistols in their hands; indeed, they rushed in, in the most furious manner, crying out, "Where's these rebel bastards?" (Pretty language to ladies from the *once famed Britons!*) That was the first salutation! The moment they espied us, off went our caps. (I always heard say none but women pulled caps!)[3] And for what, think you? Why, only to get a paltry stone-and-wax pin, which kept them on our heads; at the same time uttering the most abusive language imaginable, and making as if they'd hew us to pieces with their swords. But it's not in my power to describe the scene: it was terrible to the last degree; and, what augmented it, they had several armed negroes with them, who threatened and abused us greatly. They then began to plunder the house of everything they thought valuable or worth taking; our trunks were split to pieces, and each mean, pitiful wretch crammed his bosom with the contents, which were our apparel, etc., etc., etc.

    I ventured to speak to the inhuman monster who had my clothes. I represented to him the times were such we could not replace what they'd taken from us, and begged him to spare me only a suit or two; but I got nothing but a hearty curse for my pains; nay, so far was his callous heart from relenting, that, casting his eyes towards my shoes, "I want them buckles," said he, and immediately knelt at my feet to take them out, which, while he was busy about, a brother villain, whose enormous mouth extended from ear to ear, bawled out "Shares there, I say; shares." So they divided my buckles between them. The other wretches were employed in the same manner; they took my sister's earrings from her ears; hers, and Miss Samuells's buckles; they demanded her ring from her finger; she pleaded for it, told them it was her wedding ring, and begged they'd let her keep it; but they still demanded it, and, presenting a pistol at her, swore if she did not deliver it immediately, they'd fire. She gave it to them, and, after bundling up all their booty, they mounted their horses. But such despicable figures! Each wretch's bosom stuffed so full, they appeared to be all afflicted with some dropsical disorder.[4]

---

[3] Pulled caps: an eighteenth-century expression meaning to quarrel like women, who would pull each other's caps off in a dispute.
[4] Dropsical disorder: edema, a condition in which excess fluids collect in the bodily tissue or cavities.

Had a party of rebels (as they called us) appeared, we should soon have seen their circumference lessen.

They took care to tell us, when they were going away, that they had favored us a great deal—that we might thank our stars it was no worse. But I had forgot to tell you, that, upon their first entering the house, one of them gave my arm such a violent grasp, that he left the print of his thumb and three fingers, in black and blue, which was to be seen, very plainly, for several days after. I showed it to one of our officers, who dined with us, as a specimen of British cruelty. If they call this *favor*, what must their cruelties be? It must want a name. To be brief, after a few words more, they rode off, and glad was I. "Good riddance of bad rubbish," and indeed such rubbish was I never in company with before.... After they were gone, I began to be sensible of the danger I'd been in, and the thoughts of the vile men seemed worse (if possible) than their presence; for they came so suddenly up to the house, that I'd no time for thought.... But when they were gone, and I had time to consider, I trembled so with terror, that I could not support myself. I went into the room, threw myself on the bed, and gave way to a violent burst of grief, which seemed to be some relief to my full-swollen heart.

For an hour or two I indulged the most melancholy reflections. The whole world appeared to me as a theater, where nothing was acted but cruelty, bloodshed, and oppression; where neither age nor sex escaped the horrors of injustice and violence; where the lives and property of the innocent and inoffensive were in continual danger, and lawless power ranged at large.

DOCUMENT 36

# "To the Traitor General Arnold"

"Plain Truth"
September 25, 1781

It is no exaggeration to assert that Benedict Arnold (1741–1801) transformed himself from national hero to national pariah more quickly than any other American before or since. Prior to his treasonous September 1780 attempt to sell West Point, the pivotal Hudson River fortress entrusted to him by Washington, to the British, this native of Norwich, Connecticut, had earned the esteem of his countrymen. He had suffered wounds to his left leg during the 1775 Battle of Quebec, the 1777 Battle of Ridgefield, and the climactic 1777 Battle of Saratoga.

In 1778, after the British withdrew from Philadelphia, Washington had placed the recuperating Arnold in command of the divided city. Here he met and married Margaret "Peggy" Shippen (1760–1804), a young woman with numerous Loyalist connections. After a delayed promotion followed by being court-martialed for corruption as Philadelphia's administrator, Major General Arnold soon demonstrated that, although a brilliant tactician and battlefield commander, his greatest talent was feeling sorry for himself.

Arnold's scheme to sell West Point to the British in exchange for £20,000 and a commission in the British Army failed when Major John André, a Redcoat spy to whom he had entrusted documents related to the plot, was captured by three militiamen. They sent word both to West Point and to George Washington, who was en route to visit Arnold and inspect his Hudson Highland fortifications. His treason exposed, Arnold fled down the Hudson and sought refuge on a British warship. The news dismayed Washington. "Arnold," he declared, "has betrayed us!... Whom can we trust now?"

A year later, a writer using the pen name "Plain Truth" addressed this open letter to Arnold. In no uncertain terms it excoriated the turncoat for both his treason and his subsequent actions as a British brigadier general. Arnold, who had helped lead the invasion of Virginia in the first half of 1781, by early September had turned his attention to an assault on Connecticut's coastline. His men captured Fort Griswold, slaughtering American troops after their surrender, and set fire to New London, the port town just twelve miles from the place of his birth.

SOURCE: "Plain Truth," "To the Traytor General Arnold," *Pennsylvania Packet* (Philadelphia), September 25, 1781.

---

Is there not stored in heaven's wrath, some red hot thunder bolts to come hurling down with dreadful vengeance upon the unaccountable miscreant wretch, whose serpentine soul betrays his country, and sets the place of his nativity in flames?

## TO THE TRAITOR GENERAL ARNOLD

READ and tremble at the above awful question! Light as you may think of it, there is a tremendous Judge.

Your actions are so infamous, that if General Clinton[1] had employed the devil and all his imps to have raked hell for a complete villain, they could not have found your equal.

When I consider you as a man mounting rapidly to the highest pitch of honor, all on a sudden descending from that pinnacle of glory to the mean lucrative traitor: I am indeed surprised. But, as if your crimes were not yet sufficient, when I find you slaughtering your countrymen, and carrying on the ravages and devastations of the war with a degree of inveteracy never before heard of; I stand confounded and shocked at the thoughts of such a viper ever being brought into the world. And as if you were determined to outdo the furies of the infernal regions; you have, contrary to what human nature could be supposed capable of, set New London, the neighborhood of your nativity, in flames, while you murdered its inhabitants and your most intimate acquaintances.

To make up your measure of iniquity, and to hand your name down to posterity, as the most consummate demon that ever existed; there is only a few crimes more for you to commit, viz.[2] to rip open the womb which gave such a rancorous serpent birth, to imbrue your hands in the blood of your dearest connections, then tear out the heart of your patron and protector General Clinton, and to close the scene lay violent hands on your own life.

I took up my pen with an intent to show a reflective glass, wherein you

---

[1] General Henry Clinton (1730–1795) served as commander-in-chief of British forces in North America (1778–1782).
[2] Abbreviation for videlicet, which means 'namely.'

might at one view behold your actions; but soon found such a horrid ugly deformity in the outlines of your picture, that I was frightened at the sight, so the mirror dropped and broke to pieces each of which discovered you to be a gigantic overgrown monster, of such a variety of shapes, all over ulcerated, that it is in vain to attempt to describe them.

DOCUMENT 37

# Account of the British Surrender at Yorktown

Dr. James Thacher

*October 19, 1781*

By early 1781 it had become clear that Britain's southern campaign had produced only mixed results. Initial successes in Georgia and South Carolina were answered in October 1780 by Patriot militiamen at Kings Mountain, just south of the North Carolina border, and then again in January 1781 at the Battle of Cowpens, deep in the South Carolina backcountry, where Continentals under the command of Brigadier General Daniel Morgan (1736–1802) vanquished British and Loyalist troops serving under Lieutenant Colonel Banastre Tarleton (1754–1833). In March at Guilford Court House in North Carolina, Lieutenant General Charles Cornwallis (1738–1805) won a "victory" that left one-quarter of his Redcoats wounded, missing, or dead. Back in London, Whig war critic Charles James Fox (1749–1806) roared in the House of Commons that "another such victory would ruin the British army!"

Cornwallis drove north into Virginia, raiding farms and skirmishing intermittently with Continentals commanded by the Marquis de Lafayette (1757–1834) until General Henry Clinton (1730–1795), British commander-in-chief for North America, ordered Cornwallis to fortify a port as a base for naval operations. Lafayette felt bewildered when Cornwallis withdrew to Yorktown on the Virginia Peninsula, exposing his army to possible capture. When George Washington (1732–1799) received news that a French fleet under Admiral de Grasse (1722–1788) had set sail for the Chesapeake, he and French Lieutenant General Rochambeau (1725–1807) decided to march their armies from the vicinity of New York City all the way to Virginia. Leaving behind a small rear detachment to conceal their departure, their combined forces joined Lafayette at Yorktown in mid-September. Cornwallis soon discovered that he was outnumbered and also surrounded—both on land and at sea. After a three-week siege, Cornwallis accepted the inevitable and agreed to capitulate.

Dr. James Thacher (1754–1844), a Massachusetts physician who served as a surgeon in the Continental Army, recorded in his diary a thorough account of the surrender ceremony, but three details seem to have escaped his notice. First, when humiliated British troops filed between the columns of French and American soldiers, they turned their heads toward the French to avert the eyes of the Americans. Noting this, Lafayette ordered his fifes and drums to play "Yankee Doodle." The tune, originally embraced by Redcoats to mock their American counterparts, now caused them to turn their heads to acknowledge the ragtag army that had helped secure their defeat.

Second, while Thacher noted Cornwallis's conspicuous absence from the ceremony, he failed to witness the subtle but symbolically important maneuvers of the ranking British, French, and American officers. Cornwallis's second in command, Brigadier General Charles O'Hara (1740–1802), first attempted to surrender his sword to Rochambeau. Understanding this as an insult to an American army fighting for the recognition of its nation's independence, Rochambeau pointed toward Washington. But the Continental commander-in-chief also refused O'Hara's sword, directing instead that it be given to Major General Benjamin Lincoln (1733–1810), his own second in command. When Lincoln accepted O'Hara's sword, young America reinforced its equality among nations on the world's stage.

A third detail is more difficult to substantiate. As Redcoats threw down their weapons, the British military band reportedly played a tune called "The World Turned Upside Down."

SOURCE: James Thacher, *A Military Journal during the American Revolutionary War, from 1775 to 1783*.... (Boston: Richardson and Lord, 1823), 345–48. https://archive.org/details/militaryjournaloothac/page/344

---

This is to us a most glorious day, but to the English one of bitter chagrin and disappointment. Preparations are now making to receive as captives, that vindictive, haughty commander, and that victorious army, who by their robberies and murders have so long been a scourge to our brethren of the southern states. Being on horseback, I anticipate a full share of satisfaction in viewing the various movements in the interesting scene.

The stipulated terms of capitulation are similar to those granted to General Lincoln at Charleston the last year.[1] The captive troops are to march out with shouldered arms, colors cased, and drums beating a British or German

---

[1] General Henry Clinton (1730–1795), British commander-in-chief for North America, had denied Major General Benjamin Lincoln the traditional honors of war when, on May 12, 1780, Lincoln surrendered after the Siege of Charleston. Allowing the defeated army to surrender with flags flying was seen as a gesture of respect and an acknowledgment of its valor.

march, and to ground their arms at a place assigned for the purpose. The officers are allowed their side arms and private property, and the generals and such officers as desire it, are to go on parole to England or New York. The marines and seamen of the king's ships are prisoners of war to the navy of France, and the land forces to the United States. All military and artillery stores to be delivered up unimpaired. The royal prisoners to be sent into the interior of Virginia, Maryland, and Pennsylvania in regiments, to have rations allowed them equal to the American soldiers, and to have their officers near them. Lord Cornwallis to man and dispatch the Bonetta sloop of war with dispatches to Sir Henry Clinton at New York without being searched, the vessel to be returned and the hands accounted for.

At about twelve o'clock, the combined army was arranged and drawn up in two lines extending more than a mile in length. The Americans were drawn up in a line on the right side of the road, and the French occupied the left. At the head of the former the great American commander, mounted on his noble courser,[2] took his station, attended by his aides. At the head of the latter was posted the excellent Count Rochambeau and his suite. The French troops, in complete uniform, displayed a martial and noble appearance, their band of music, of which the timbrel[3] formed a part, is a delightful novelty, and produced while marching to the ground a most enchanting effect. The Americans, though not all in uniform nor their dress so neat, yet exhibited an erect soldierly air, and every countenance beamed with satisfaction and joy. The concourse of spectators from the country was prodigious, in point of numbers probably equal to the military, but universal silence and order prevailed.

It was about two o'clock when the captive army advanced through the line formed for their reception. Every eye was prepared to gaze on Lord Cornwallis, the object of peculiar interest and solicitude; but he disappointed our anxious expectations; pretending indisposition, he made General O'Hara his substitute as the leader of his army. This officer was followed by the conquered troops in a slow and solemn step, with shouldered arms, colors cased, and drums beating a British march. Having arrived at the head of the line, General O'Hara, elegantly mounted, advanced to his excellency, the commander-in-chief, taking off his hat, and apologized for the non-appearance of Earl Cornwallis. With his usual dignity and politeness his excellency pointed to Major General Lincoln for directions, by whom

---

[2] A swift, strong horse—in this case, Washington's horse, "Nelson" (1763–1790).
[3] A tambourine or similar percussion instrument.

the British army was conducted into a spacious field where it was intended they should ground their arms.

The royal troops, while marching through the line formed by the allied army, exhibited a decent and neat appearance, as respects arms and clothing, for their commander opened his store and directed every soldier to be furnished with a new suit complete, prior to the capitulation. But in their line of march we remarked a disorderly and un-soldierly conduct; their step was irregular and their ranks frequently broken.

But it was in the field when they came to the last act of the drama, that the spirit and pride of the British soldier was put to the severest test—here their mortification could not be concealed. Some of the platoon officers appeared to be exceedingly chagrined when giving the word "ground arms," and I am a witness that they performed this duty in a very un-officer-like manner, and that many of the soldiers manifested a sullen temper, throwing their arms on the pile with violence, as if determined to render them useless. This irregularity, however, was checked by the authority of General Lincoln. After having grounded their arms and divested themselves of their accouterments, the captive troops were conducted back to Yorktown and guarded by our troops until they could be removed to the place of their destination.

The British troops that were stationed at Gloucester surrendered at the same time, and in the same manner to the command of the Duke de Lauzun.[4]

This must be a very interesting and gratifying transaction to General Lincoln, who having himself been obliged to surrender an army to a haughty foe the last year, has now assigned him the pleasing duty of giving laws to a conquered army in return, and of reflecting that the terms which were imposed on him are adopted as a basis of the surrender in the present instance. It is a very gratifying circumstance that every degree of harmony, confidence, and friendly intercourse subsisted between the American and French troops during the campaign, no contest except an emulous spirit to excel in exploits and enterprise against the common enemy, and a desire to be celebrated in the annals of history for an ardent love of great and heroic actions.

We are not to be surprised that the pride of the British officers is humbled on this occasion, as they have always entertained an exalted opinion of their own military prowess, and affected to view the Americans as a contemptible, undisciplined rabble. But there is no display of magnanimity when a great commander shrinks from the inevitable misfortunes of war, and when

---

[4] Armand Louis de Gontaut (1747–1793), Duc de Lauzun, was a brigadier general in the French army.

it is considered that Lord Cornwallis has frequently appeared in splendid triumph at the head of his army by which he is almost adored, we conceive it incumbent on him cheerfully to participate in their misfortunes and degradations, however humiliating; but it is said he gives himself up entirely to vexation and despair.

DOCUMENT 38

# Notes on the State of Virginia
Thomas Jefferson
1781–1784

At the conclusion of the 1787 Constitutional Convention, a woman reportedly asked Benjamin Franklin (1706–1790) whether the United States would have a monarchy or a republic. "A republic," he replied, but only "if you can keep it."

Franklin's belief that the liberty of the American people hinged not only on their form of government but also on their character was shared by Thomas Jefferson (1743–1826), who between 1781 and 1784 wrote and revised a book, privately printed in 1785 and published in 1787, titled Notes on the State of Virginia. Inspired by a series of questions posed by a French diplomat, Jefferson's Notes considered everything from agriculture to zoology. What he wrote in response to queries regarding Virginia's culture and economy helps to capture his mixed feelings about the ability of Virginians and other Americans to successfully carry out their experiment in self-government.

In "Manners" (Query XVIII), Jefferson considered the ways in which the institution of slavery harmed the enslaved as well as their masters. He had seen firsthand the obvious injustices that slavery inflicted on African Americans. He also perceived its ill effects on the work ethic and capacity for citizenship of white people. One of his first public acts had been to sponsor a 1769 measure, rejected by the Virginia House of Burgesses, to make it legal for masters to emancipate their slaves. In 1778 he succeeded in banning the importation of enslaved Africans to Virginia. In 1779, however, his proposal for gradual emancipation in his state failed to win support. Complicating his opposition to slavery was his worry, expressed in Query XVIII, that African Americans would have difficulty forgiving those who had once exploited them, as well as his suspicion, recorded elsewhere in his Notes, that former slaves could never rise to the level of their former masters.

If slavery caused Jefferson to fear America's future, he found reasons for hope in his section on "Manufactures" (Query XIX). Unlike in Europe, where a scarcity of land forced the populace into positions of dependence as urban wage laborers, America remained a nation composed largely of farmers who owned their own land and worked as their own bosses. Therefore they enjoyed an independence *of mind and means, making possible their participation in politics as virtuous citizens seeking the common good instead of selfish gain.*

SOURCE: Thomas Jefferson, *Notes on the State of Virginia* (London: John Stockdale, 1787), 270–75. https://archive.org/details/notesonstateofvi1787jeff/page/270

---

### Query XVIII: The particular customs and manners that may happen to be received in that state?

It is difficult to determine on the standard by which the manners of a nation may be tried, whether *catholic,* or *particular.* It is more difficult for a native to bring to that standard the manners of his own nation, familiarized to him by habit. There must doubtless be an unhappy influence on the manners of our people produced by the existence of slavery among us. The whole commerce between master and slave is a perpetual exercise of the most boisterous passions, the most unremitting despotism on the one part, and degrading submissions on the other. Our children see this, and learn to imitate it; for man is an imitative animal. This quality is the germ of all education in him. From his cradle to his grave he is learning to do what he sees others do. If a parent could find no motive either in his philanthropy or his self-love, for restraining the intemperance of passion towards his slave, it should always be a sufficient one that his child is present. But generally it is not sufficient. The parent storms, the child looks on, catches the lineaments[1] of wrath, puts on the same airs in the circle of smaller slaves, gives a loose to his worst of passions, and thus nursed, educated, and daily exercised in tyranny, cannot but be stamped by it with odious peculiarities. The man must be a prodigy who can retain his manners and morals undepraved by such circumstances. And with what execration[2] should the statesman be loaded, who permitting one half the citizens thus to trample on the rights of the other, transforms those into despots, and these into enemies, destroys the morals of the one part, and the *amor patriae*[3] of the other. For if a slave can have a country in this world, it must be any other in preference to that in which he is born to live and labor for another: in which he must lock up the faculties of his nature, contribute as far as depends on his individual endeavors to the evanishment[4] of the

---

[1] Distinctive features or details of facial or bodily expression.
[2] Curse, jinx, hex.
[3] *Latin*: love of country, patriotism.
[4] Disappearance.

human race, or entail[5] his own miserable condition on the endless generations proceeding from him. With the morals of the people, their industry also is destroyed. For in a warm climate, no man will labor for himself who can make another labor for him. This is so true, that of the proprietors of slaves a very small proportion indeed are ever seen to labor. And can the liberties of a nation be thought secure when we have removed their only firm basis, a conviction in the minds of the people that these liberties are of the gift of God? That they are not to be violated but with his wrath? Indeed I tremble for my country when I reflect that God is just: that his justice cannot sleep for ever: that considering numbers, nature, and natural means only, a revolution of the wheel of fortune, an exchange of situation, is among possible events: that it may become probable by supernatural interference! The Almighty has no attribute which can take side with us in such a contest. But it is impossible to be temperate and to pursue this subject through the various considerations of policy, of morals, of history natural and civil. We must be contented to hope they will force their way into everyone's mind. I think a change already perceptible, since the origin of the present revolution. The spirit of the master is abating, that of the slave rising from the dust, his condition mollifying, the way I hope preparing, under the auspices of heaven, for a total emancipation, and that this is disposed, in the order of events, to be with the consent of the masters, rather than by their extirpation.[6]

## Query XIX: The present state of manufactures, commerce, interior and exterior trade?

We never had an interior trade of any importance. Our exterior commerce has suffered very much from the beginning of the present contest. During this time we have manufactured within our families the most necessary articles of clothing. Those of cotton will bear some comparison with the same kinds of manufacture in Europe; but those of wool, flax, and hemp are very coarse, unsightly, and unpleasant; and such is our attachment to agriculture, and such our preference for foreign manufactures, that be it wise or unwise, our people will certainly return as soon as they can, to the raising of raw materials, and exchanging them for finer manufactures than they are able to execute themselves.

The political economists of Europe have established it as a principle that

---

[5] Impose.
[6] Extermination.

every state should endeavor to manufacture for itself; and this principle, like many others, we transfer to America, without calculating the difference of circumstance which should often produce a difference of result. In Europe the lands are either cultivated, or locked up against the cultivator. Manufacture must therefore be resorted to of necessity not of choice, to support the surplus of their people. But we have an immensity of land courting the industry of the husbandman. Is it best then that all our citizens should be employed in its improvement, or that one half should be called off from that to exercise manufactures and handicraft arts for the other? Those who labor in the earth are the chosen people of God, if ever he had a chosen people, whose breasts he has made his peculiar deposit for substantial and genuine virtue. It is the focus[7] in which he keeps alive that sacred fire, which otherwise might escape from the face of the earth. Corruption of morals in the mass of cultivators is a phenomenon of which no age nor nation has furnished an example. It is the mark set on those, who not looking up to heaven, to their own soil and industry, as does the husbandman, for their subsistence, depend for it on the casualties and caprice of customers. Dependence begets subservience and venality, suffocates the germ of virtue, and prepares fit tools for the designs of ambition. This, the natural progress and consequence of the arts, has sometimes perhaps been retarded by accidental circumstances: but, generally speaking, the proportion which the aggregate of the other classes of citizens bears in any state to that of its husbandmen, is the proportion of its unsound to its healthy parts, and is a good enough barometer whereby to measure its degree of corruption. While we have land to labor then, let us never wish to see our citizens occupied at a workbench, or twirling a distaff. Carpenters, masons, smiths, are wanting in husbandry; but, for the general operations of manufacture, let our workshops remain in Europe. It is better to carry provisions and materials to workmen there, than bring them to the provisions and materials, and with them their manners and principles. The loss by the transportation of commodities across the Atlantic will be made up in happiness and permanence of government. The mobs of great cities add just so much to the support of pure government, as sores do to the strength of the human body. It is the manners and spirit of a people which preserve a republic in vigor. A degeneracy in these is a canker[8] which soon eats to the heart of its laws and constitution.

---

[7] *Latin*: domestic hearth, fireplace.
[8] Cancer.

DOCUMENT 39

# The Newburgh Address

George Washington
March 15, 1783

Most Americans cheered the Continental Army's victory at Yorktown and the subsequent peace negotiations at Paris. But the fact that the war might soon end caused some army officers to grumble. Most had not been paid in months. Some had not been paid in years. If this was how the Continental Congress, which teetered on the brink of insolvency, treated them during a war, how would it treat them once the army disbanded? Many doubted the Congress's 1780 promise that officers would receive a pension of half pay for life. Once the war was over, would their country forget all they had sacrificed in behalf of independence?

Encamped just north of West Point near Newburgh, New York, some of these officers fantasized about dispensing with Congress and crowning George Washington (1732–1799) as king. In 1782, when Lieutenant Colonel Lewis Nicola (1717–1807) suggested the idea to Washington, the commander-in-chief shot it down, insisting that nothing during the entire war had given him "more painful sensations" than Nicola's proposal. Months later, did an alternative plan, which would come to be known as the Newburgh conspiracy, begin to take shape? Evidence suggests that a small number of officers (including Major General Alexander McDougall [1732–1786]) teamed up with a small number of civilian officials (including Alexander Hamilton [1755/57–1804], then a member of Congress, as well as superintendent of finance Robert Morris [1734–1806] and his assistant, Gouverneur Morris [1752–1816]) to contemplate the creation of a crisis that could lead to a central government with greater powers to tax American citizens and compensate those who had fought in the Revolution. Maybe the army would march west and leave the United States undefended. Or maybe, at war's end, the army would refuse to disband and march to the next meeting of Congress, weapons in hand, to demand action.

The conspiracy, whatever its exact nature or motivation, was exposed when Washington learned of two anonymous letters circulating among his officers. The first announced a mass meeting on March 11, 1783. The second disparaged an ungrateful "country that tramples on your rights, disdains your cries, and insults your distresses." He responded by canceling the March 11 meeting, informing

*Congress, sending a pointed letter to Hamilton announcing his determination to "rescue" his officers "from plunging themselves into a gulf of civil horror," and calling for a new meeting of his officers on March 15. Here, he made a surprise appearance and delivered a speech condemning any attempt to undermine civilian control of American government.*

SOURCE: George Washington to Officers of the Army, March 15, 1783, *Founders Online*, National Archives. http://founders.archives.gov/documents/Washington/99-01-02-10840.

---

By an anonymous summons, an attempt has been made to convene you together—how inconsistent with the rules of propriety! how unmilitary! and how subversive of all order and discipline—let the good sense of the army decide.

In the moment of this summons, another anonymous production was sent into circulation; addressed more to the feelings and passions, than to the reason and judgment of the army. The author of the piece, is entitled to much credit for the goodness of his pen; and I could wish he had as much credit for the rectitude of his heart—for, as men see through different optics, and are induced by the reflecting faculties of the mind, to use different means to attain the same end; the author of the address, should have had more charity, than to mark for suspicion, the man who should recommend moderation and longer forbearance—or, in other words, who should not think as he thinks, and act as he advises. But he had another plan in view, in which candor and liberality of sentiment, regard to justice, and love of country, have no part; and he was right, to insinuate the darkest suspicion, to effect the blackest designs.

That the address is drawn with great art, and is designed to answer the most insidious purposes. That it is calculated to impress the mind, with an idea of premeditated injustice in the sovereign power of the United States, and rouse all those resentments which must unavoidably flow from such a belief. That the secret mover of this scheme (whoever he may be) intended to take advantage of the passions, while they were warmed by the recollection of past distresses, without giving time for cool, deliberative thinking, and that composure of mind which is so necessary to give dignity and stability to measures, is rendered too obvious, by the mode of conducting the business, to need other proof than a reverence to the proceeding.

Thus much, gentlemen, I have thought it incumbent on me to observe to you, to show upon what principles I opposed the irregular and hasty meeting which was proposed to have been held on Tuesday last; and not because

I wanted a disposition to give you every opportunity, consistent with your honor, and the dignity of the army, to make known your grievances. If my conduct heretofore, has not evinced to you, that I have been a faithful friend to the army, my declaration of it at this time w[oul]d be equally unavailing and improper. But as I was among the first who embarked in the cause of our common country—as I have never left your side one moment, but when called from you, on public duty—as I have been the constant companion and witness of your distresses, and not among the last to feel, and acknowledge your merits—as I have ever considered my own military reputation as inseparably connected with that of the army—as my heart has ever expanded with joy, when I have heard its praises—and my indignation has arisen, when the mouth of detraction has been opened against it—it can *scarcely be supposed*, at this late stage of the war, that I am indifferent to its interests.

But—how are they to be promoted? The way is plain, says the anonymous addresser. If war continues, remove into the unsettled country—there establish yourselves, and leave an ungrateful country to defend itself. But who are they to defend? Our wives, our children, our farms and other property, which we leave behind us. Or, in this state of hostile separation, are we to take the two first (the latter cannot be removed) to perish in a wilderness, with hunger, cold, and nakedness? If peace takes place, never sheath your sword, says he, until you have obtained full and ample justice. This dreadful alternative, of either deserting our country in the extremest hour of her distress, or turning our army against it (which is the apparent object, unless Congress can be compelled into an instant compliance), has something so shocking in it, that humanity revolts at the idea. My God! What can this writer have in view, by recommending such measures? Can he be a friend to the army? Can he be a friend to this country? Rather, is he not an insidious foe? Some emissary, perhaps, from New York,[1] plotting the ruin of both, by sowing the seeds of discord and separation between the civil and military powers of the continent? And what a compliment does he pay to our understandings, when he recommends measures, in either alternative, impracticable in their nature?

But here, gentlemen, I will drop the curtain; because it w[oul]d be as imprudent in me to assign my reasons for this opinion, as it would be insulting to your conception, to suppose you stood in need of them. A moment's reflection will convince every dispassionate mind of the physical impossibility of carrying either proposal into execution.

---

[1] The British had occupied Manhattan since September 1776. They withdrew in November 1783.

There might, gentlemen, be an impropriety in my taking notice, in this address to you, of an anonymous production—but the manner in which that performance has been introduced to the army—the effect it was intended to have, together with some other circumstances, will amply justify my observations on the tendency of that writing. With respect to the advice given by the author—to suspect the man, who shall recommend moderate measures and longer forbearance—I spurn it—as every man, who regards that liberty, and reveres that justice for which we contend, undoubtedly must. For if men are to be precluded from offering their sentiments on a matter, which may involve the most serious and alarming consequences, that can invite the consideration of mankind; reason is of no use to us—the freedom of speech may be taken away—and dumb and silent we may be led, like sheep, to the slaughter.

I cannot, in justice to my own belief, and what I have great reason to conceive is the intention of Congress, conclude this address, without giving it as my decided opinion, that that humble body, entertain exalted sentiments of the services of the army; and, from a full conviction of its merits and sufferings, will do it complete justice. That their endeavors, to discover and establish funds for this purpose, have been unwearied, and will not cease, until they have succeeded, I have not a doubt. But, like all other large bodies, where there is a variety of different interests to reconcile, their deliberations are slow. Why, then, should we distrust them? And, in consequence of that distrust, adopt measures, which may cast a shade over that glory which has been so justly acquired; and tarnish the reputation of an army which is celebrated through all Europe, for its fortitude and patriotism? And for what is this done? To bring the object we seek for nearer? No! Most certainly, in my opinion, it will cast it at a greater distance.

For myself (and I take no merit in giving the assurance, being induced to it from principles of gratitude, veracity, and justice), a grateful sense of the confidence you have ever placed in me—a recollection of the cheerful assistance, and prompt obedience I have experienced from you, under every vicissitude[2] of fortune, and the sincere affection I feel for an army, I have so long had the honor to command, will oblige me to declare, in this public and solemn manner, that, in the attainment of complete justice for all your toils and dangers, and in the gratification of every wish, so far as may be done consistently with the great duty I owe my country, and those powers we are bound to respect, you may freely command my services to the utmost of my abilities.

---

[2] A change of circumstances—usually for the worse.

While I give you these assurances, and pledge myself in the most unequivocal manner, to exert whatever ability I am possessed of, in your favor—let me entreat you, gentlemen, on your part, not to take any measures, which, viewed in the calm light of reason, will lessen the dignity, and sully the glory you have hitherto maintained. Let me request you to rely on the plighted faith of your country, and place a full confidence in the purity of the intentions of Congress; that, previous to your dissolution as an Army they will cause all your acc[oun]ts to be fairly liquidated, as directed in their resolutions, which were published to you two days ago—and that they will adopt the most effectual measures in their power, to render ample justice to you, for your faithful and meritorious services. And let me conjure you, in the name of our common country—as you value your own sacred honor—as you respect the rights of humanity, and as you regard the military and national character of America, to express your utmost horror and detestation of the man who wishes, under any specious pretenses, to overturn the liberties of our country, and who wickedly attempts to open the floodgates of civil discord, and deluge our rising empire in blood.

By thus determining—and thus acting, you will pursue the plain and direct road to the attainment of your wishes. You will defeat the insidious designs of our enemies, who are compelled to resort from open force to secret artifice. You will give one more distinguished proof of unexampled patriotism and patient virtue, rising superior to the pressure of the most complicated sufferings; and you will, by the dignity of your conduct, afford occasion for posterity to say, when speaking of the glorious example you have exhibited to mankind, "had this day been wanting, the world had never seen the last stage of perfection to which human nature is capable of attaining."

DOCUMENT 40

# An Officer's Account of Washington's Remarks

Captain Samuel Shaw

April 1783

George Washington's March 15, 1783, speech confronting the Newburgh conspiracy (Document 39) made clear his belief that his officers' whispers possessed the potential to snatch defeat from the jaws of victory. After the army's success at Yorktown, the War for Independence was as good as won—so long as the army didn't subvert the liberty for which the war had been fought in the first place. As Washington understood, if the Continental Army acted in defiance of Congress, then the American Revolution—like so many previous wars and revolutions—could end in military dictatorship.

The impression Washington's speech made on his officers comes through clearly in the account of Captain Samuel Shaw (1754–1794), who was present for the meeting. Aide-de-camp from 1779 to 1783 to Major General Henry Knox (1750–1806), Shaw wrote about Washington's performance the following month. According to Shaw, it was not only Washington's prepared remarks but also the officers' regard for Washington as a man and a leader that put an end to any thoughts of disobedience. A particularly emotional moment, Shaw noted, was when Washington, while reading to his officers a letter from a member of Congress, paused to reach into his pocket and retrieve his spectacles. Only Washington's closest aides had seen him wear them, probably because eyeglasses, in the eighteenth century, were viewed as a sign of old age and infirmity. As Shaw recounted, Washington "put them on, observing at the same time, that he had grown gray in their service, and now found himself growing blind." This declaration, Shaw wrote, "moisten[ed] every eye" in the room. Others portrayed the battle-hardened veterans sobbing openly as a result of Washington's statement.

At no other point did Washington seem so big to his officers, who at this juncture felt so small. Washington had led the army almost since the beginning of the Revolution. One of the richest men in America, he had more to lose than almost anyone. He had exposed himself to every hardship. Horses had been shot out from under him. Musket balls had whistled past his ears. He had served— and sacrificed—while refusing a salary. Yet here they were, grumbling about pay and pensions. Although historians debate the extent to which the Newburgh *conspiracy posed a real threat, none dispute that Washington's forceful remarks put an end to any possibility that hushed discussions at the Continental Army's last encampment might coalesce into a challenge to elected representatives' control of American government.*

SOURCE: *The Journals of Major Samuel Shaw...*, ed. Josiah Quincy (Boston: Wm. Crosby and H. P. Nichols, 1847), 103–5. https://archive.org/details/journalsofmajorsooshaw/page/102

---

The meeting of the officers was in itself exceedingly respectable, the matters they were called to deliberate upon were of the most serious nature, and the unexpected attendance of the commander-in-chief heightened the solemnity of the scene. Every eye was fixed upon the illustrious man, and attention to their beloved general held the assembly mute. He opened the meeting by apologizing for his appearance there, which was by no means his intention when he published the order which directed them to assemble. But the diligence used in circulating the anonymous pieces rendered it necessary that he should give his sentiments to the army on the nature and tendency of them, and determined him to avail himself of the present opportunity; and, in order to do it with greater perspicuity,[1] he had committed his thoughts to writing, which, with the indulgence of his brother officers, he would take the liberty of reading to them. It is needless for me to say anything of this production; *it speaks for itself.* After he had concluded his address, he said that, as a corroborating testimony of the good disposition in Congress towards the army, he would communicate to them a letter[2] received from a worthy member of that body, and one who on all occasions had ever proved himself their fast friend. This was an exceedingly sensible letter; and, while it pointed out the difficulties and embarrassments of Congress, it held up very forcibly the idea that the army should, at all events, be generously dealt with. One circumstance in reading this letter must not be omitted. His excellency, after reading the first paragraph, made a short pause, took out his spectacles, and begged the indulgence of his audience while he put them on, observing at the same time, that he had grown gray in their service, and now found himself growing blind. There was something so natural, so unaffected, in this appeal,

---

[1] Clarity, precision, intelligibility.
[2] Joseph Jones to George Washington, February 27, 1783, available at *Founders Online*, National Archives, https://founders.archives.gov/documents/Washington/99-01-02-10732.

as rendered it superior to the most studied oratory; it forced its way to the heart, and you might see sensibility moisten every eye. The general, having finished, took leave of the assembly....

I cannot dismiss this subject without observing, that it is happy for America that she has a patriot army, and equally so that a Washington is its leader. I rejoice in the opportunities I have had of seeing this great man in a variety of situations—calm and intrepid where the battle raged, patient and persevering under the pressure of misfortune, moderate and possessing himself in the full career of victory. Great as these qualifications deservedly render him, he never appeared to me more truly so, than at the assembly we have been speaking of. On other occasions he has been supported by the exertions of an army and the countenance of his friends; but in this he stood single and alone. There was no saying where the passions of an army, which were not a little inflamed, might lead; but it was generally allowed that longer forbearance was dangerous, and moderation had ceased to be a virtue. Under these circumstances he appeared, not at the head of his troops, but as it were in opposition to them; and for a dreadful moment the interests of the army and its general seemed to be in competition! He spoke—every doubt was dispelled, and the tide of patriotism rolled again in its wonted[3] course. Illustrious man! What he says of the army may with equal justice be applied to his own character. Had this day been wanting, the world had never seen the last stage of perfection to which human nature is capable of attaining.

---

[3] Usual, habitual.

DOCUMENT 41

# Circular Letter to the States

George Washington

*June 8–21, 1783*

The government brought forth by the Articles of Confederation (Document 31) worked just as designed. Unfortunately, it was not really designed to work as a government. Everything remained voluntary. Congress provided a forum for discussion and debate, but it had no power to tax (unless one counts draining paper money of its value through the act of printing more of it) and it had no power to compel the thirteen states to provide it with funds or comply with its decisions. These restrictions made sense given Americans' experience with British imperial rule, but sometimes government power possesses a greater potential to secure liberty than to threaten it. Drafted in 1777 and finally ratified in 1781, the Articles reflected the Spirit of '76 more than the requirements of a costly eight-year War for Independence.

No one better understood the inadequacies of the Articles than General George Washington (1732–1799), whose army had suffered almost continuously from a lack of pay and provisions. As Washington knew too well, the inability of a near-bankrupt Congress to compensate his officers—in the past, present, and, as many worried, in the future—led to the near mutinous Newburgh conspiracy (Documents 39 and 40). In March 1783 he had defused that powder keg, in part, by promising to continue his efforts to secure justice for the officers and soldiers of the Continental army.

Here, in a "circular letter" addressed to the governor of each state, Washington made good on that promise. Making the most of America's victory in the War for Independence as an occasion not only for celebration but also as an opportunity to warn of possible future difficulties, Washington made clear his desire for a more muscular alternative to the status quo of the Articles of Confederation.

SOURCE: George Washington to the States, June 8–21, 1783, *Founders Online*, National Archives, https://founders.archives.gov/documents/Washington/99-01-02-11404.

The great object, for which I had the honor to hold an appointment in the service of my country being accomplished, I am now preparing to resign it into the hands of Congress, and to return to that domestic retirement; which it is well known I left with the greatest reluctance, a retirement for which I have never ceased to sigh through a long and painful absence, and in which (remote from the noise and trouble of the world) I meditate to pass the remainder of life, in a state of undisturbed repose. But before I carry this resolution into effect, I think is a duty incumbent on me, to make this my last official communication; to congratulate you on the glorious events which Heaven has been pleased to produce in our favor; to offer my sentiments respecting some important subjects which appear to me to be intimately connected with the tranquility of the United States; to take my leave of your excellency as a public character; and to give my final blessing to that country, in whose service I have spent the prime of my life, for whose sake I have consumed so many anxious days and watchful nights, and whose happiness, being extremely dear to me, will always constitute no inconsiderable part of my own....

The citizens of America, placed in the most enviable condition, as the sole lords and proprietors of a vast tract of continent, comprehending all the various soils and climates of the world and abounding with all the necessaries and conveniences of life, are now, by the late satisfactory pacification, acknowledged to be possessed of absolute freedom and independency. They are from this period to be considered as the actors, on a most conspicuous theater, which seems to be peculiarly designated by Providence for the display of human greatness and felicity. Here they are not only surrounded with everything which can contribute to the completion of private and domestic enjoyment, but Heaven has crowned all its other blessings by giving a fairer opportunity for political happiness, than any other nation has ever been favored with. Nothing can illustrate these observations more forcibly than a recollection of the happy conjuncture of times and circumstances under which our republic assumed its rank among the nations. The foundation of our empire was not laid in the gloomy age of ignorance and superstition, but at an epoch when the rights of mankind were better understood and more clearly defined, than at any former period....

Such is our situation, and such are our prospects; but notwithstanding the cup of blessing is thus reached out to us; notwithstanding happiness is ours if we have a disposition to seize the occasion and make it our own. Yet it appears to me there is an option still left to the United States of America; that it is in their choice and depends upon their conduct, whether they will be respectable and prosperous or contemptible and miserable as a nation. This is the time of their political probation; this is the moment when the eyes of the whole world are turned upon them. This is the moment to establish or ruin their national character forever. This is the favorable moment to give such a tone to our federal government, as will enable it to answer the ends of its institution—or this may be the ill-fated moment for relaxing the powers of the Union, annihilating the cement of the Confederation, and exposing us to become the sport of European politics, which may play one state against another, to prevent their growing importance, and to serve their own interested purposes. For, according to the system of policy the states shall adopt at this moment, they will stand or fall, and by their confirmation or lapse, it is yet to be decided whether the Revolution must ultimately be considered as a blessing or a curse; a blessing or a curse, not to the present age alone, for with our fate will the destiny of unborn millions be involved.

With this conviction of the importance of the present crisis, silence in me would be a crime. I will therefore speak to your excellency the language of freedom and sincerity without disguise. I am aware, however, that those who differ from me in political sentiment may perhaps remark I am stepping out of the proper line of my duty, and they may possibly ascribe to arrogance or ostentation what I know is alone the result of the purest intention. But the rectitude of my own heart, which disdains such unworthy motives; the part I have hitherto acted in life; the determination I have formed of not taking any share in public business hereafter; the ardent desire I feel and shall continue to manifest of quietly enjoying, in private life, after all the toils of war, the benefits of a wise and liberal government, will, I flatter myself, sooner or later convince my countrymen that I could have no sinister views in delivering, with so little reserve, the opinions contained in this address.

There are four things, which I humbly conceive are essential to the well-being, I may venture to say, to the existence, of the United States as an independent power:

First. An indissoluble union of the states under one federal head.

Secondly. A sacred regard to public justice.

Thirdly. The adoption of a proper peace establishment—and

Fourthly. The prevalence of that pacific and friendly disposition among the people of the United States, which will induce them to forget their local prejudices and policies; to make those mutual concessions which are requisite to the general prosperity; and, in some instances, to sacrifice their individual advantages to the interest of the community.

These are the pillars on which the glorious fabric of our independency and national character must be supported. Liberty is the basis—and whoever would dare to sap the foundation, or overturn the structure, under whatever specious pretexts he may attempt it, will merit the bitterest execration and the severest punishments which can be inflicted by his injured country.

On the three first articles I will make a few observations, leaving the last to the good sense and serious consideration of those immediately concerned.

Under the first head, although it may not be necessary or proper for me ... to enter into a particular disquisition of the principles of the Union and to take up the great question which has been frequently agitated, whether it be expedient and requisite for the states to delegate a larger proportion of power to Congress, or not; yet it will be a part of my duty, and that of every true patriot, to assert without reserve and to insist upon the following positions. That, unless the states will suffer Congress to exercise those prerogatives they are undoubtedly invested with by the constitution, everything must very rapidly tend to anarchy and confusion. That it is indispensible to the happiness of the individual states that there should be lodged somewhere a supreme power to regulate and govern the general concerns of the confederated republic, without which the Union cannot be of long duration. That there must be a faithful and pointed compliance, on the part of every state, with the late proposals and demands of Congress, or the most fatal consequences will ensue; that whatever measures have a tendency to dissolve the Union, or contribute to violate or lessen the sovereign authority, ought to be considered as hostile to the liberty and independency of America, and the authors of them treated accordingly. And last, that unless we can be enabled, by the concurrence of the states, to participate of the fruits of the Revolution, and enjoy the essential benefits of civil society, under a form of government so free and uncorrupted, so happily guarded against the danger of oppression, as has been devised and adopted by the Articles of Confederation, it will be a subject of regret that so much blood and treasure have been lavished for no purpose, that so many sufferings have been encountered without a compensation, and that so many sacrifices have been made in vain.

Many other considerations might here be adduced to prove, that, without an entire conformity to the spirit of the Union, we cannot exist as an independent power. It will be sufficient for my purpose, to mention but one or two, which seem to me of the greatest importance. It is only in our united character, as an empire, that our independence is acknowledged, that our power can be regarded, or our credit supported among foreign nations. The treaties of the European powers with the United States of America will have no validity on a dissolution of the Union. We shall be left nearly in a state of nature; or we may find, by our own unhappy experience, that there is a natural and necessary progression from the extreme of anarchy to the extreme of tyranny, and that arbitrary power is most easily established on the ruins of liberty abused to licentiousness.

As to the second article, which respects the performance of public justice, Congress have, in their late address to the United States, almost exhausted the subject; they have explained their ideas so fully, and have enforced the obligations the states are under, to render complete justice to all the public creditors, with so much dignity and energy, that, in my opinion, no real friend to the honor and independency of America can hesitate a single moment respecting the propriety of complying with the just and honorable measures proposed. If their arguments do not produce conviction, I know of nothing that will have greater influence, especially when we recollect that the system referred to, being the result of the collected wisdom of the continent, must be esteemed, if not perfect, certainly the least objectionable of any that could be devised; and that, if it shall not be carried into immediate execution, a national bankruptcy, with all its deplorable consequences, will take place before any different plan can possibly be proposed and adopted, so pressing are the present circumstances! And such is the alternative now offered to the states!

The ability of the country to discharge the debts, which have been incurred in its defense, is not to be doubted; an inclination, I flatter myself, will not be wanting. The path of our duty is plain before us. Honesty will be found on every experiment to be the best and only true policy. Let us then, as a nation, be just—let us fulfill the public contracts which Congress had undoubtedly a right to make for the purpose of carrying on the war, with the same good faith we suppose ourselves bound to perform our private engagements. In the meantime let an attention to the cheerful performance of their proper business as individuals and as members of society be earnestly inculcated on the citizens of America. Then will they strengthen the hands of government and be happy under its protection; everyone will reap the fruit of his labors, everyone will enjoy his own acquisitions without molestation and without danger.

In this state of absolute freedom and perfect security, who will grudge to yield a very little of his property to support the common interests of society and ensure the protection of government? Who does not remember the frequent declarations at the commencement of the war that we should be completely satisfied, if at the expense of one half, we could defend the remainder of our possessions? Where is the man to be found, who wishes to remain indebted for the defense of his own person and property, to the exertions, the bravery, and the blood of others, without making one generous effort to repay the debt of honor and of gratitude? In what part of the continent shall we find any man, or body of men, who would not blush to stand up and propose measures purposely calculated to rob the soldier of his stipend and the public creditor of his due? And were it possible that such a flagrant instance of injustice could ever happen, would it not excite the general indignation and tend to bring down upon the authors of such measures the aggravated vengeance of Heaven?...

For my own part, conscious of having acted, while a servant of the public, in the manner I conceived best suited to promote the real interests of my country; having, in consequence of my fixed belief, in some measure, pledged myself to the army that their country would finally do them complete and ample justice; and not wishing to conceal any instance of my official conduct from the eyes of the world, I have thought proper to transmit to your excellency the enclosed collection of papers relative to the half-pay and commutation granted by Congress to the officers of the army. From these communications, my decided sentiment will be clearly comprehended, together with the conclusive reasons which induced me, at an early period, to recommend the adoption of this measure, in the most earnest and serious manner. As the proceedings of Congress, the army, and myself are open to all, and contain, in my opinion, sufficient information to remove the prejudices and errors, which may have been entertained by any, I think it unnecessary to say anything more, than just to observe, that the resolutions of Congress now alluded to, are undoubtedly as absolutely binding upon the United States, as the most solemn acts of confederation or legislation....

It is necessary to say but a few words on the third topic which was proposed and which regards particularly the defense of the republic—as there can be little doubt but Congress will recommend a proper peace establishment for the United States, in which a due attention will be paid to the importance of placing the militia of the Union upon a regular and respectable footing. If this should be the case, I would beg leave to urge the great advantage of it in the strongest terms. The militia of this country must be considered as the Palladium[1] of our security and the first effectual resort in case of hostility. It is essential, therefore, that the same system should pervade the whole—that the formation and discipline of the militia of the continent should be absolutely

---

[1] A safeguard; refers to a legendary statue of Pallas Athena, ca. 700 B.C., the preservation of which was believed to ensure the safety of Troy.

uniform and the same species of arms, accouterments, and military apparatus should be introduced in every part of the United States. No one, who has not learned it from experience, can conceive the difficulty, expense, and confusion, which result from a contrary system, or the vague arrangements which have hitherto prevailed.

If, in treating of political points, a greater latitude than usual has been taken in the course of this address, the importance of the crisis, and the magnitude of the objects in discussion, must be my apology. It is, however, neither my wish nor expectation, that the preceding observations should claim any regard, except so far as they shall appear to be dictated by a good intention, consonant to the immutable rules of justice, calculated to produce a liberal system of Policy and founded on what ever experience may have been acquired by a long and close attention to public business. Here I might speak with the more confidence, from my actual observations, and, if it would not swell this letter (already too prolix)[2] beyond the bounds I had prescribed myself, I could demonstrate to every mind open to conviction, that in less time and with much less expense than has been incurred, the war might have been brought to the same happy conclusion if the resources of the continent could have been properly drawn forth—that the distresses and disappointments, which have very often occurred, have in too many instances resulted more from a want of energy in the Continental government, than a deficiency of means in the particular states. That the inefficacy of measures, arising from the want of an adequate authority in the supreme power, from a partial compliance with the requisitions of Congress in some of the states and from a failure of punctuality in others, while it tended to damp the zeal of those which were more willing to exert themselves, served also to accumulate the expenses of the war and to frustrate the best concerted plans; and that the discouragement, occasioned by the complicated difficulties and embarrassments in which our affairs were by this means involved, would have long ago produced the dissolution of any army, less patient, less virtuous, and less persevering than that which I have had the honor to command....

I have thus freely disclosed, what I wished to make known, before I surrendered up my public trust to those who committed it to me. The task is now accomplished. I now bid adieu[3] to your excellency, as the chief magistrate of your state, at the same time I bid a last farewell to the cares of office and all the employments of public life.

---

[2] Wordy; long-winded.
[3] *French:* goodbye.

It remains then to be my final and only request, that your excellency will communicate these sentiments to your legislature at their next meeting and that they may be considered as the legacy of one who has ardently wished on all occasions to be useful to his country and who, even in the shade of retirement, will not fail to implore the divine benediction upon it.

I now make it my earnest prayer, that God would have you and the state over which you preside, in his holy protection; that he would incline the hearts of the citizens to cultivate a spirit of subordination and obedience to government; to entertain a brotherly affection and love for one another, for their fellow citizens of the United States at large, and particularly for their brethren who have served in the field; and finally, that he would most graciously be pleased to dispose us all to do justice, to love mercy, and to demean ourselves, with that charity, humility, and pacific temper of mind, which were the characteristics of the Divine Author of our blessed religion, and without a humble imitation of whose example in these things, we can never hope to be a happy nation....

DOCUMENT 42

# Treaty of Paris

*September 3, 1783*

News of Cornwallis's surrender at Yorktown reached London on November 25, 1781. When Lord North (1732–1792) received word from Lord George Germain (1716–1785), his secretary of state for America, he exclaimed, "Oh God! It is all over." Despite the prime minister's assessment, George III (1738–1820) remained unconvinced. After Parliament voted in favor of a resolution insisting that "the war in America be no longer pursued for the impractical purpose of reducing the inhabitants to obedience by force," Lord North had to talk the king out of abdicating the throne—and into acquiescing to his own resignation as prime minister. The new government, headed by the Marquess of Rockingham (1730–1782), stood ready to acknowledge American independence and turned its attention toward the pursuit of peace.

Official negotiations began in July 1782. Scottish merchant Richard Oswald (1705–1784) represented the British. Benjamin Franklin (1706–1790), ambassador to France, led a team of American negotiators that included Henry Laurens (1724–1792), John Adams (1735–1826), and John Jay (1745–1829). Although the Continental Congress instructed Franklin to work with France, which also needed to negotiate peace with Britain, Franklin understood that the interests of America's European allies diverged from its own. Spain, for example, would also be part of the settlement; it viewed the United States as a potential competitor in North America, and sought control of all British land west of the Appalachians and east of the Mississippi River.

Sensing that Britain feared a strong United States less than it did a strengthened France and Spain, Franklin worked directly with Oswald to reach an agreement so favorable to America that British criticism prompted Oswald to resign. He was replaced by David Hartley (1732–1813). In September 1783, when agreements had been readied between Britain and all the other belligerents, the Treaty of Paris was signed. The British had recognized the independence of the United States. Seemingly against all odds, Americans had won the Revolutionary War.

SOURCE: Richard Peters, et al., eds., *The Public Statutes at Large of the United States of America*, 17 vols. (Boston: Charles C. Little and James Brown, 1845–73), 8:80–83. https://archive.org/details/publicstatutesa04statgoog/page/n98

In the name of the Most Holy and Undivided Trinity.[1]

IT having pleased the Divine Providence to dispose the hearts of the most serene and most potent Prince GEORGE the Third, by the Grace of God King of Great Britain, France and Ireland, Defender of the Faith, Duke of Brunswick and Lüneburg, Arch-Treasurer and Prince Elector of the Holy Roman Empire, etc., and of the UNITED STATES OF AMERICA, to forget all past misunderstandings and differences that have unhappily interrupted the good correspondence and friendship which they mutually wish to restore; and to establish such a beneficial and satisfactory intercourse between the two countries, upon the ground of reciprocal advantages and mutual convenience, as may promote and secure to both perpetual peace and harmony; and having for this desirable end, already laid the foundation of peace and reconciliation, by the provisional articles, signed at Paris, on the thirtieth of November, one thousand seven hundred and eighty-two, by the commissioners empowered on each part, which articles were agreed to be inserted in, and to constitute the treaty of peace proposed to be concluded between the crown of Great-Britain and the said United States, but which treaty was not to be concluded until terms of peace should be agreed upon between Great Britain and France, and his Britannic Majesty should be ready to conclude such treaty accordingly; and the treaty between Great-Britain and France, having since been concluded, his Britannic Majesty and the United States of America, in order to carry into full effect the provisional articles abovementioned, according to the tenor thereof, have constituted and appointed, that is to say, His Britannic Majesty on his part, David Hartley, Esquire, Member of the Parliament of Great Britain; and the said United States of America at the Court of Versailles, late Delegate in Congress from the state of Massachusetts, and Chief Justice of the said state, and Minister Plenipotentiary of the said United States to their High Mightinesses, the States General of the United Netherlands; Benjamin Franklin, Esquire, late Delegate in Congress from the state of Pennsylvania, President of the Convention of the said state, and Minister Plenipotentiary from the United States of America at the Court of Versailles; John Jay, Esquire, late President of Congress, and Chief Justice of the state of New York, and Minister Plenipotentiary from the

---

[1] Trinity: in most Christian religions, the term used to refer to the three "persons" or natures of God—Father, Son, and Holy Spirit—who are distinct from one another and yet unified as the diety.

said United States at the Court of Madrid to be the plenipotentiaries for the concluding and signing the present definitive treaty; who after having reciprocally communicated their respective full powers, have agreed upon and confirmed the following articles.

## ARTICLE I.

His Britannic Majesty acknowledges the said United States—that is, New Hampshire, Massachusetts Bay, Rhode Island and Providence Plantations, Connecticut, New York, New Jersey, Pennsylvania, Delaware, Maryland, Virginia, North Carolina, South Carolina, and Georgia—to be free, sovereign, and independent States; that he treats with them as such; and for himself, his heirs, and successors, relinquishes all claims to the government, propriety, and territorial rights of the same, and every part thereof.

## ARTICLE II.

And that all disputes which might arise in [the] future, on the subject of the boundaries of the said United States may be prevented, it is hereby agreed and declared, that the following are, and shall be their boundaries: From the northwest angle of Nova-Scotia, that is, that angle which is formed by a line, drawn due north from the source of St. Croix River to the highlands; along the said highlands which divide those rivers, that empty themselves into the river St. Lawrence, from those which fall into the Atlantic ocean, to the northwesternmost head of Connecticut River, thence down along the middle of that river, to the forty-fifth degree of north latitude; from thence, by a line due west on said latitude, until it strikes the river Iroquois or Cataraqui; thence along the middle of said river into Lake Ontario, through the middle of said lake until it strikes the communication by water between that lake and Lake Erie; thence along the middle of said communication into Lake Erie, through the middle of said lake until it arrives at the water communication between that lake and Lake Huron; thence through the middle of said lake to the water communication between that lake and Lake Superior: thence through lake Superior northward of the isles Royal and Phelipeaux, to the Long Lake; thence through the middle of said Long Lake, and the water communication between it and the Lake of the Woods, to the said Lake of the Woods; thence through the said lake to the most northwestern point thereof, and from thence on a due west course to the river Mississippi; thence by a line to be drawn along the middle of the said river Mississippi; thence by a line to be drawn along the middle of the said river Mississippi until it shall intersect the northernmost part of the thirty-first degree of north latitude. South by a line to be drawn due east from the determination of the line last mentioned, in the latitude of thirty-one degrees north of the Equator, to the middle of the river Apalachicola or Chattahoochee; thence along the middle thereof to its junction with the Flint River; thence strait to the head of St. Mary's River; and thence down along the middle of St. Mary's River to the Atlantic Ocean. East by a line to be drawn along the middle of the river St. Croix, from its mouth in the Bay of Fundy to its source, and from its source directly north to the aforesaid highlands which divide the rivers that fall into the Atlantic Ocean, from those which fall into the river St. Lawrence; comprehending all islands within twenty leagues of any part of the shores of the United States, and lying between lines to be drawn due east from the points where the aforesaid boundaries between Nova Scotia on the one part, and East Florida on the other, shall respectively touch the Bay of Fundy and the Atlantic ocean; excepting such islands as now are, or heretofore have been within the limits of the said province of Nova Scotia.

## ARTICLE III.

It is agreed that the people of the United States shall continue to enjoy unmolested the right to take fish of every kind on the Grand Bank, and on all the other banks of Newfoundland; also in the Gulf of St. Lawrence, and at all other places in the sea, where the inhabitants of both countries used at any time heretofore to fish; and also that the inhabitants of the United States shall have liberty to take fish of every kind on such part of the coast of Newfoundland as British fishermen shall use (but not to dry or cure the same on that island); and also on the coasts, bays, and creeks of all other of his Britannic Majesty's dominions in America; and that the American fishermen shall have liberty to dry and cure fish in any of the unsettled bays, harbors, and creeks of Nova Scotia, Magdalen Islands, and Labrador, so long as the same shall remain unsettled; but so soon as the same or either of them shall be settled, it shall not be lawful for the said fishermen to dry or cure fish at such settlement, without a previous agreement for that purpose with the inhabitants, proprietors, or possessors of the ground.

## ARTICLE IV.

It is agreed that creditors on either side, shall meet with no lawful impediment to the recovery of the full value in sterling money, of all bona fide debts heretofore contracted.

## ARTICLE V.

It is agreed that the Congress shall earnestly recommend it to the legislatures of the respective states, to provide for the restitution of all estates, rights, and properties, which have been confiscated, belonging to real British subjects, and also of the estates, rights, and properties of persons resident in districts in the possession of his Majesty's arms, and who have not borne arms against the said United States. And that persons of any other description shall have free liberty to go to any part or parts of any of the thirteen United States, and therein to remain twelve months, unmolested in their endeavors, to obtain the restitution of such of their estates, rights, and properties, as may have been confiscated; and that Congress shall also earnestly recommend to the several states a reconsideration and revision of all acts or laws regarding the premises, so as to render the said laws or acts perfectly consistent, not only with justice and equity, but with that spirit of conciliation, which on the return of the blessings of peace should universally prevail. And that Congress shall also earnestly recommend to the several states, that the estates, rights, and properties of such last mentioned persons, shall be restored to them, they refunding to any persons who may be now in possession, the bona fide price (where any has been given) which such persons may have paid on purchasing any of the said lands, rights, or properties, since the confiscation. And it is agreed, that all persons who have any interest in confiscated lands, either by debts, marriage settlements, or otherwise, shall meet with no lawful impediment in the prosecution of their just rights.

## ARTICLE VI.

That there shall be no future confiscations made, nor any prosecutions commenced against any person or persons for... the part which he or they may have taken in the present war; and that no person shall, on that account, suffer any future loss or damage, either in his person, liberty, or property; and that those who may be in confinement on such charges, at the time of the ratification of the treaty in America, shall be immediately set at liberty, and the prosecutions so commenced be discontinued.

## ARTICLE VII.

There shall be a firm and perpetual peace between his Britannic Majesty and the said States, and between the subjects of the one and the citizens of the other, wherefore all hostilities, both by sea and land, shall from henceforth cease. All prisoners on both sides shall be set at liberty, and his Britannic Majesty shall, with all convenient speed, and without causing any destruction, or carrying away any Negroes or other property of the American inhabitants, withdraw all his armies, garrisons, and fleets from the said United States, and from every post, place, and harbor within the same; leaving in all fortifications the American artillery that may be therein; and shall also order and cause all archives, records, deeds, and papers, belonging to any of the said states, or their citizens, which in the course of the war may have fallen into the hands of his officers, to be forthwith restored and delivered to the proper states and persons to whom they belong.

## ARTICLE VIII.

The navigation of the river Mississippi, from its source to the ocean, shall forever remain free and open to the subjects of Great Britain and the citizens of the United States.

## ARTICLE IX.

In case it should so happen that any place or territory belonging to Great Britain or to the United States should have been conquered by the arms of either from the other, before the arrival of the said provisional articles in America, it is agreed, that the same shall be restored without difficulty, and without requiring any compensation.

## ARTICLE X.

The solemn ratifications of the present treaty, expedited in good and due form, shall be exchanged between the contracting parties, in the space of six months, or sooner if possible, to be computed from the day of the signature of the present treaty. In witness whereof, we the undersigned, their ministers plenipotentiary, have in their name and in virtue of our full powers, signed with our hands the present definitive treaty, and caused the seals of our arms to be affixed thereto.

Done at Paris, this third day of September, in the year of our Lord one thousand seven hundred and eighty-three.

D. HARTLEY (L. S.)[2]<br>
JOHN ADAMS (L. S.)<br>
B. FRANKLIN (L. S.)<br>
JOHN JAY (L. S.)

---

[2] L. S.: Abbreviation for *locus sigilli* (Latin), meaning "the place of the seal." Each of the four representatives signed his name above a wax seal.

DOCUMENT 43

# Petition of the Philadelphia Synagogue to the Council of Censors of Pennsylvania

Haym Salomon, et al.

*December 23, 1783*

Haym Salomon (ca. 1740–1785) sacrificed a great deal for the cause of independence—and risked much more. Born in Poland, he befriended leading members of the Sons of Liberty soon after his 1775 arrival in New York City. Arrested twice by the British for spying, he received a pardon the first time and a death sentence the second. His experience urging Hessians to desert and helping prisoners of the British to escape served him well when he ran away to Philadelphia. There he assisted Robert Morris (1734–1806), Congress's superintendent of finance, in arranging credit from foreign nations. When funds ran low, he helped keep the Revolutionary government afloat with his own donations and no-interest loans.

Yet the 1776 Pennsylvania constitution barred Salomon, who was Jewish, from service in his state's legislature. Its members had to take an oath affirming their belief "in the scriptures of the old and new testament." In this 1783 petition, Salomon as well as other members of Philadelphia's Mikveh Israel congregation, including Rabbi Gershom Seixas (1745–1816), called on the state's council of censors, a body empowered to call a convention to amend the constitution, to work toward the elimination of an oath that Jews could not in good conscience take. Although the council of censors tabled the petition, when Pennsylvania adopted a new constitution in 1790 the eligibility to hold office was extended to all who acknowledged "the being of a God and a future state of rewards and punishments."

The cause of religious freedom gained ground elsewhere, as well. In 1786, Virginia adopted the proposal of Thomas Jefferson (1743–1826) and James Madison (1751–1836) to separate church and state. The 1787 United States Constitution barred religious tests for office-holding, and the First Amendment, ratified in 1791, prohibited the federal government from establishing a national church or restricting the free exercise of religion. In 1790 President George Washington (1732–1799) wrote to the Jewish congregation in Newport, Rhode Island, that "the Government of the United States, which gives to bigotry no sanction, to persecution no *assistance, requires only that they who live under its protection should demean themselves as good citizens." The freedom to worship according to one's conscience, he affirmed, was among an individual's "inherent natural rights."*

SOURCE: "Petition of the Philadelphia Synagogue to the Council of Censors of Pennsylvania," *The Freeman's Journal or The North-American Intelligencer* (Philadelphia), January 21, 1784.

---

... By the tenth section of the frame of government of this commonwealth, it is ordered that each member of the general assembly of representatives of the freemen of Pennsylvania, before he takes his seat, shall make and subscribe a declaration, which ends in these words, "I do acknowledge the scriptures of the old and new testament to be given by divine inspiration," to which is added an assurance, that "no further or other religious test shall ever hereafter be required of any civil officer or magistrate in this state."

Your memorialists beg leave to observe, that this clause seems to limit the civil rights of your citizens to one very special article of the creed; whereas by the second paragraph of the declaration of the rights of the inhabitants, it is asserted without any other limitation than the professing the existence of God, in plain words, "that no man who acknowledges the being of a God can be justly deprived or abridged of any civil rights as a citizen on account of his religious sentiments." But certainly this religious test deprives the Jews of the most eminent rights of freemen, solemnly ascertained to all men who are not professed atheists.

May it please your honors: Although the Jews in Pennsylvania are but few in number, yet liberty of the people in one country, and the declaration of the government thereof, that these liberties are the rights of the people, may prove a powerful attractive to men, who live under restraints in another country. Holland and England have made valuable acquisitions of men, who for their religious sentiments, were distressed in their own countries.

And if Jews in Europe or elsewhere, should incline to transport themselves to America, and would, for reason of some certain advantage of the soil, climate, or the trade of Pennsylvania, rather become inhabitants thereof, than of any other state; yet the disability of Jews to take seat among the representatives of the people, as worded by the said religious test, might determine their free choice to go to New York, or to any other of the United States of America, where there is no such like restraint laid upon the nation and religion of the Jews, as in Pennsylvania.

Your memorialists cannot say that the Jews are particularly fond of being representatives of the people in assembly or civil officers and magistrates in the state; but with great submission they apprehend that a clause in the constitution, which disables them to be elected by their fellow citizens to represent them in assembly, is a stigma upon their nation and religion, and it is inconsonant with the second paragraph of the said bill of rights;[1] otherwise Jews are as fond of liberty as their religious societies can be, and it must create in them a displeasure, when they perceive that for their professed dissent to doctrine, which is inconsistent with their religious sentiments, they should be excluded from the most important and honorable part of the rights of a free citizen.

Your memorialists beg further leave to represent, that in the religious books of the Jews, which are or may be in every man's hands, there are no such doctrines or principles established as are inconsistent with the safety and happiness of the people of Pennsylvania, and that the conduct and behavior of the Jews in this and the neighboring states, has always tallied with the great design of the Revolution; that the Jews of Charlestown, New York, Newport, and other posts, occupied by the British troops, have distinguishedly suffered for their attachment to the Revolution principles; and their brethren at St. Eustatius, for the same cause, experienced the most severe resentments of the British commanders.

The Jews of Pennsylvania, in proportion to the number of their members, can count with any religious society whatsoever, the Whigs[2] among either of them; they have served some of them in the Continental army; some went out in the militia to fight the common enemy; all of them have cheerfully contributed to the support of the militia, and of the government of this state; they have no inconsiderable property in lands and tenements, but particularly in the way of trade, some more, some less, for which they pay taxes; they

---

[1] "That all men have a natural and unalienable right to worship Almighty God according to the dictates of their own consciences and understanding; and that no man ought or of right can be compelled to attend any religious worship, or erect or support any place of worship, or maintain any ministry, contrary to, or against, his own free will and consent; nor can any man, who acknowledges the being of a God, be justly deprived or abridged of any civil right as a citizen, on account of his religious sentiments or peculiar mode of religious worship: And that no authority can or ought to be vested in, or assumed by any power whatever, that shall in any case interfere with, or in any manner control, the right of conscience in the free exercise of religious worship."

[2] Patriots who supported independence.

have, upon every plan formed for public utility, been forward to contribute as much as their circumstances would admit of; and as a nation or a religious society, they stand unimpeached of any matter whatsoever, against the safety and happiness of the people.

And your memorialists humbly pray, that if your honors, from any consideration than the subject of this address, should think proper to call a convention for revising the constitution, you would be pleased to recommend this to the notice of that convention.

DOCUMENT 44

# Cincinnatus Reborn

George Washington
*December 23, 1783*

When news of the Treaty of Paris reached America in November 1783, much of the British army had already set sail from New York. Meanwhile, the Continental Army had been disbanding since June, when George Washington (1732–1799), to cut costs for the cash-strapped Confederation Congress, furloughed two-thirds of his troops. On November 25, as the last British regiments evacuated Manhattan, Washington and what remained of his army arrived in the city. On December 4 he said farewell to his officers during an emotional banquet at Fraunces Tavern, then walked past assembled infantrymen to a dock where a barge waited to ferry him across the Hudson. From New Jersey, he made his way south to Annapolis, Maryland, where Congress was in session.

Celebrations slowed his journey as communities through which he passed detained him for banquets and balls in his honor. On December 20, he arrived in Annapolis, sending a note to Thomas Mifflin (1744–1800), president of Congress, asking "in what manner it will be most proper to offer my resignation." Congressmen Thomas Jefferson (1743–1826) and Elbridge Gerry (1744–1814) prepared a document orchestrating Washington's appearance before Congress, which was set for noon on December 23. As scripted, after Washington was escorted into what is now the Old Senate Chamber of the Maryland State House, Mifflin informed the commander-in-chief that "Congress, sir, are prepared to receive your communications." When Washington rose to speak, he bowed to Congress; the members of Congress responded by removing their hats but not bowing—a demonstration of civilian control of the military.

Washington delivered his remarks with calm composure until he arrived at the passage in which he entrusted "the interests of our dearest country to the protection of Almighty God." Here, his voice cracked as he choked back tears. When Washington regained his composure and finished the speech, it was his audience that felt overcome with emotion. "The spectators all wept," remembered Maryland Congressman James McHenry (1753–1816), "and there was hardly a member of Congress who did not drop tears."

Washington's resignation caused many to compare him to Cincinnatus (ca.

519–ca. 430 B.C.), *the famed Roman statesman entrusted with nearly unlimited power during wartime who achieved swift victory and then returned to private life on his farm. Artist Benjamin West (1738–1820) later reported that King George III (1738–1820) said Washington's willingness to give up power made him "the most distinguished of any man living" and "the greatest character of the age."*

SOURCE: Washington's Address to Congress Resigning his Commission, [December 23, 1783,] *Founders Online,* National Archives, https://founders.archives.gov/documents/Jefferson/01-06-02-0319-0004.

---

The great events on which my resignation depended having at length taken place, I have now the honor of offering my sincere congratulations to Congress and of presenting myself before them to surrender into their hands the trust committed to me, and to claim the indulgence of retiring from the service of my country.

Happy in the confirmation of our independence and sovereignty, and pleased with the opportunity afforded the United States of becoming a respectable nation, I resign with satisfaction the appointment I accepted with diffidence[1]—a diffidence in my abilities to accomplish so arduous a task, which, however, was superseded by a confidence in the rectitude of our cause, the support of the supreme power of the Union, and the patronage of Heaven.

The successful termination of the war has verified the more sanguine expectations, and my gratitude, for the interposition of Providence, and the assistance I have received from my countrymen, increases with every review of the momentous contest.

While I repeat my obligations to the army in general, I should do injustice to my own feelings not to acknowledge in this place the peculiar services and distinguished merits of the gentlemen who have been attached to my person during the war. It was impossible the choice of confidential officers to compose my family should have been more fortunate. Permit me, sir,[2] to recommend in particular those, who have continued in service to the present moment, as worthy of the favorable notice and patronage of Congress.

I consider it an indispensable duty to close this last solemn act of my official life, by commending the interests of our dearest country to the

---

[1] Modesty; hesitancy.
[2] The "sir" to whom Washington addressed his remarks was Thomas Mifflin.

protection of Almighty God, and those who have the superintendence of them, to his holy keeping.

Having now finished the work assigned me, I retire from the great theater of action—and bidding an affectionate farewell to this august body under whose orders I have so long acted, I here offer my commission, and take my leave of all the employments of public life.

APPENDIX A

# Thematic Table of Contents

## Economics

4  "A Farmer" (John Dickinson), "Letters from a Farmer in Pennsylvania, No. 2" ................................................. 18
5  Charleston Nonimportation Agreement ................................. 22
8  "An Impartial Observer," An Account of the Boston Tea Party ........ 35
9  Gouverneur Morris, "We Shall be under the Domination of a Riotous Mob" ........................................................ 39
10 Thomas Jefferson, *A Summary View of the Rights of British America* .. 42
13 The Association Enacted by the First Continental Congress ........... 61
18 John Dickinson and Thomas Jefferson, Declaration of the Causes and Necessity of Taking Up Arms ..................................... 82
20 Thomas Paine, *Common Sense* ........................................ 90
22 Abigail and John Adams, "Remember the Ladies" ....................... 99
25 Thomas Jefferson, Draft of the Declaration of Independence ......... 117
32 Private Joseph Plumb Martin, Foraging for Valley Forge ............. 147
38 Thomas Jefferson, *Notes on the State of Virginia* ................. 175
41 George Washington, Circular Letter to the States ................... 187
42 Treaty of Paris .................................................... 195

## Individual Rights

1  James Otis, Speech Against *Writs of Assistance* ..................... 3
2  James Otis, "Rights of the British Colonies Asserted and Proved" ..... 8
7  Samuel Adams, "The Rights of the Colonists" ......................... 29
13 The Association Enacted by the First Continental Congress ........... 61
15 "Friend to America" (Alexander Hamilton), *The Farmer Refuted* ...... 70
18 John Dickinson and Thomas Jefferson, Declaration of the Causes and Necessity of Taking Up Arms ..................................... 82
19 Lancaster County Committee of Correspondence and Observation, Resolution Regarding Quaker Pacifists .................. 87
20 Thomas Paine, *Common Sense* ........................................ 90

22  Abigail and John Adams, "Remember the Ladies" .......................... 99
24  George Mason, Virginia Declaration of Rights ............................ 114
25  Thomas Jefferson, Draft of the Declaration of Independence .......... 117
28  Prince Hall, et. al., Massachusetts Antislavery Petition ................ 133
33  Lieutenant Colonel John Laurens, Envisioning an African
    American Regiment .................................................................. 154
42  Treaty of Paris ........................................................................ 195
43  Haym Salomon, et al., Petition of the Philadelphia Synagogue to
    the Council of Censors of Pennsylvania .................................... 202

## Divisions of Political Power

2   James Otis, "Rights of the British Colonies Asserted and Proved" ..... 8
3   Resolutions of the Stamp Act Congress ...................................... 15
4   "A Farmer" (John Dickinson), "Letters from a Farmer in
    Pennsylvania, No. 2" ................................................................ 18
10  Thomas Jefferson, *A Summary View of the Rights of British America* .. 42
12  Joseph Galloway, Plan of Union ................................................. 57
23  John Adams, *Thoughts on Government* ..................................... 106
24  George Mason, Virginia Declaration of Rights ............................ 114
25  Thomas Jefferson, Draft of the Declaration of Independence .......... 117
31  Articles of Confederation ......................................................... 143
39  George Washington, The Newburgh Address .............................. 179
40  Captain Samuel Shaw, An Officer's Account of Washington's
    Remarks ................................................................................ 184
41  George Washington, Circular Letter to the States ....................... 187
42  Treaty of Paris ........................................................................ 195
44  George Washington, Cincinnatus Reborn .................................. 206

## The Purpose of Government

2   James Otis, "Rights of the British Colonies Asserted and Proved" ..... 8
7   Samuel Adams, "The Rights of the Colonists" ............................. 29
10  Thomas Jefferson, *A Summary View of the Rights of British America* .. 42
18  John Dickinson and Thomas Jefferson, Declaration of the Causes
    and Necessity of Taking Up Arms ............................................... 82
20  Thomas Paine, *Common Sense* ................................................. 90
23  John Adams, *Thoughts on Government* ..................................... 106
24  George Mason, Virginia Declaration of Rights ............................ 114

25  Thomas Jefferson, Draft of the Declaration of Independence .......... 117

## The Process of Government

1   James Otis, Speech Against Writs of Assistance............................ 3
2   James Otis, "Rights of the British Colonies Asserted and Proved" ..... 8
3   Resolutions of the Stamp Act Congress ................................... 15
4   "A Farmer" (John Dickinson), "Letters from a Farmer in
    Pennsylvania, No. 2" ................................................... 18
10  Thomas Jefferson, *A Summary View of the Rights of British America* .. 42
12  Joseph Galloway, Plan of Union ......................................... 57
22  Abigail and John Adams, "Remember the Ladies"........................ 99
23  John Adams, *Thoughts on Government* .................................. 106
24  George Mason, Virginia Declaration of Rights.......................... 114
25  Thomas Jefferson, Draft of the Declaration of Independence .......... 117
31  Articles of Confederation ............................................. 143
38  Thomas Jefferson, *Notes on the State of Virginia*.................... 175
39  George Washington, The Newburgh Address ............................... 179
40  Captain Samuel Shaw, An Officer's Account of Washington's
    Remarks................................................................ 184
41  George Washington, Circular Letter to the States ..................... 187
43  Haym Salomon, et al., Petition of the Philadelphia Synagogue to
    the Council of Censors of Pennsylvania................................ 202
44  George Washington, Cincinnatus Reborn................................. 206

## "Created Equal"

5   Charleston Nonimportation Agreement................................... 22
10  Thomas Jefferson, *A Summary View of the Rights of British America* .. 42
13  The Association Enacted by the First Continental Congress ........... 61
21  Stratford, Connecticut's Thomas Gage—and Monmouth County,
    New Jersey's Dunmore .................................................. 97
22  Abigail and John Adams, "Remember the Ladies"........................ 99
25  Thomas Jefferson, Draft of the Declaration of Independence .......... 117
28  Prince Hall, et. al., Massachusetts Antislavery Petition ............ 133
30  Generals Gates and Burgoyne on the Murder of Jane McCrea ........ 138
33  Lieutenant Colonel John Laurens, Envisioning an African
    American Regiment...................................................... 154
32  Private Joseph Plumb Martin, Foraging for Valley Forge ............. 147

34 Franklin and Lafayette, List of Prints to Illustrate
   British Cruelties .................................................. 158
35 Eliza Wilkinson, Redcoats in South Carolina ............................ 163
38 Thomas Jefferson, *Notes on the State of Virginia* ..................... 175
42 Treaty of Paris ........................................................ 195
43 Haym Salomon, et al., Petition of the Philadelphia Synagogue to
   the Council of Censors of Pennsylvania ................................ 202

## Loyalists

12 Joseph Galloway, Plan of Union ......................................... 57
14 "A. W. Farmer" (Reverend Samuel Seabury), *A View of the
   Controversy Between Great-Britain and her Colonies* ................... 66
21 Stratford, Connecticut's Thomas Gage—and Monmouth County,
   New Jersey's Dunmore .................................................. 97
27 Thomas Paine, *The American Crisis* ................................... 128
29 Private Hugh McDonald, The Continentals Encounter Civilians .... 135
30 Generals Gates and Burgoyne on the Murder of Jane McCrea ........ 138
34 Franklin and Lafayette, List of Prints to Illustrate British
   Cruelties ............................................................ 158
36 "Plain Truth," "To the Traitor General Arnold" ........................ 167
42 Treaty of Paris ....................................................... 195

## Uniting Americans

5  Charleston Nonimportation Agreement .................................... 22
6  Deacon John Tudor, Account of the Boston Massacre ...................... 25
9  Gouverneur Morris, "We Shall be under the Domination of a
   Riotous Mob" .......................................................... 39
11 Philadelphia Welcomes the First Continental Congress
   (September 16, 1774) .................................................. 53
13 The Association Enacted by the First Continental Congress .......... 61
14 "A. W. Farmer" (Reverend Samuel Seabury), *A View of the
   Controversy Between Great-Britain and her Colonies* ................... 66
15 "Friend to America" (Alexander Hamilton), *The Farmer Refuted* ...... 70
18 John Dickinson and Thomas Jefferson, Declaration of the Causes
   and Necessity of Taking Up Arms ....................................... 82
19 Lancaster County Committee of Correspondence and
   Observation, Resolution Regarding Quaker Pacifists .................... 87

THEMATIC TABLE OF CONTENTS 213

20  Thomas Paine, *Common Sense* .................................................. 90
21  Stratford, Connecticut's Thomas Gage—and Monmouth County,
    New Jersey's Dunmore ......................................................... 97
25  Thomas Jefferson, Draft of the Declaration of Independence .......... 117
26  Celebrations of American Independence in Boston and
    Watertown, Massachusetts .................................................... 125
27  Thomas Paine, *The American Crisis* ........................................ 128
29  Private Hugh McDonald, The Continentals Encounter Civilians .... 135
30  Generals Gates and Burgoyne on the Murder of Jane McCrea ........ 138
34  Franklin and Lafayette, List of Prints to Illustrate British
    Cruelties ......................................................................... 158
36  "Plain Truth," "To the Traitor General Arnold" ........................... 167
41  George Washington, Circular Letter to the States ........................ 187

## War or Peace?

14  "A. W. Farmer" (Reverend Samuel Seabury), A View of the
    Controversy Between Great-Britain and her Colonies ................... 66
15  "Friend to America" (Alexander Hamilton), *The Farmer Refuted* ... 70
16  Patrick Henry, "Give me liberty or give me death!" ....................... 75
17  John Andrews, Account of the Battles of Lexington and Concord ..... 79
18  John Dickinson and Thomas Jefferson, Declaration of the Causes
    and Necessity of Taking Up Arms ............................................ 82
25  Thomas Jefferson, Draft of the Declaration of Independence .......... 117
42  Treaty of Paris ................................................................. 195

## Military Operations

17  John Andrews, Account of the Battles of Lexington and Concord ..... 79
18  John Dickinson and Thomas Jefferson, Declaration of the Causes
    and Necessity of Taking Up Arms ............................................ 82
27  Thomas Paine, *The American Crisis* ........................................ 128
29  Private Hugh McDonald, The Continentals Encounter Civilians .... 135
30  Generals Gates and Burgoyne on the Murder of Jane McCrea ........ 138
32  Private Joseph Plumb Martin, Foraging for Valley Forge ............... 147
33  Lieutenant Colonel John Laurens, Envisioning an African
    American Regiment ............................................................ 154
34  Franklin and Lafayette, List of Prints to Illustrate British
    Cruelties ......................................................................... 158

35 Eliza Wilkinson, Redcoats in South Carolina .............................. 163
36 "Plain Truth," "To the Traitor General Arnold"........................... 167
37 Dr. James Thacher, Account of the British Surrender at Yorktown ...170
39 George Washington, The Newburgh Address ...............................179
40 Captain Samuel Shaw, An Officer's Account of Washington's
    Remarks............................................................................. 184
41 George Washington, Circular Letter to the States.......................187
42 Treaty of Paris ..................................................................... 195
44 George Washington, Cincinnatus Reborn................................. 206

## "Reliance on Divine Providence"

2 James Otis, "Rights of the British Colonies Asserted and Proved"..... 8
16 Patrick Henry, "Give me liberty or give me death!" ....................... 75
19 Lancaster County Committee of Correspondence and
    Observation, Resolution Regarding Quaker Pacifists .................... 87
25 Thomas Jefferson, Draft of the Declaration of Independence .......... 117
27 Thomas Paine, *The American Crisis*..........................................128
28 Prince Hall, et. al., Massachusetts Antislavery Petition ................. 133
32 Private Joseph Plumb Martin, Foraging for Valley Forge .............. 147
41 George Washington, Circular Letter to the States.......................187
42 Treaty of Paris ..................................................................... 195
43 Haym Salomon, et al., Petition of the Philadelphia Synagogue to
    the Council of Censors of Pennsylvania.................................. 202
44 George Washington, Cincinnatus Reborn................................. 206

## The People Mobilize

6 Deacon John Tudor, Account of the Boston Massacre..................... 25
8 "An Impartial Observer," An Account of the Boston Tea Party ........ 35
9 Gouverneur Morris, "We Shall be under the Domination of a
    Riotous Mob"...................................................................... 39
11 Philadelphia Welcomes the First Continental Congress ................. 53
17 John Andrews, Account of the Battles of Lexington and Concord..... 79
21 Stratford, Connecticut's Thomas Gage—and Monmouth County,
    New Jersey's Dunmore .......................................................... 97
25 Thomas Jefferson, Draft of the Declaration of Independence .......... 117
26 Celebrations of American Independence in Boston and
    Watertown, Massachusetts.................................................... 125

32 Private Joseph Plumb Martin, Foraging for Valley Forge .............. 147
33 Lieutenant Colonel John Laurens, Envisioning an African American Regiment............................................................ 154
35 Eliza Wilkinson, Redcoats in South Carolina ........................... 163
38 Thomas Jefferson, *Notes on the State of Virginia*........................... 175

APPENDIX B

# Discussion Questions

For each of the Documents in this collection, we suggest below in section A questions relevant for that document alone and in Section B questions that require comparison with other documents.

## 1. James Otis, Speech Against Writs of Assistance (February 24, 1761)

A. Why did the principle that "a man's house is his castle" cause James Otis to oppose writs of assistance? Why was this principle important to the preservation of individual liberty? How did it limit the powers of government?

B. How were the principles for which Otis took a stand protected in the Constitution and Bill of Rights (Appendix)?

## 2. James Otis, "Rights of the British Colonies Asserted and Proved" (July 1764)

A. What is the basis of James Otis's assertion that taxation without representation is wrong?

B. In what ways were Otis's 1764 "Rights of the British Colonies" and his 1761 speech against writs of assistance similar? In what ways were they different? Compare and contrast the arguments and evidence these documents use to assert their points.

## 3. Resolutions of the Stamp Act Congress (October 19, 1765)

A. What were the Stamp Act Congress's practical objections to the Stamp Act? What important constitutional principle did the Congress believe the Stamp Act violated?

B. According to the arguments of James Otis (Documents 1 and 2) and the Stamp Act Congress, what were the principles that limited the authority of Parliament?

217

### 4. "A Farmer" (John Dickinson), "Letters from a Farmer in Pennsylvania, No. 2" (December 10, 1767)

A. What, according to Dickinson, limited Parliament's power—and why? What did Dickinson think would happen if colonists acquiesced to the Townshend Acts?

B. Compare Dickinson's argument here with his work in behalf of the Stamp Act Congress (Document 3). Which argument better undermined the authority of Parliament?

### 5. Charleston Nonimportation Agreement (July 22, 1769)

A. What was the stated purpose of this agreement? In what other ways might this agreement have worked to bolster Americans' resistance to Britain's imperial policies?

B. How does this agreement complement and complicate the assertion of James Otis (Document 1) that "a man's house is his castle"?

### 6. Deacon John Tudor, Account of the Boston Massacre (March 1770)

A. In what specific ways did John Tudor's account of the Boston Massacre differ from what appears to have actually happened? What might explain these differences? Did Tudor's understanding of the incident make the British soldiers seem more or less blameworthy?

B. Compare and contrast the roles of colonists in upholding nonimportation agreements (Document 5) with the role played by Americans in the Boston Massacre and its aftermath. To what extent was unity important in both situations, and in what ways was it encouraged?

### 7. Samuel Adams, "The Rights of the Colonists" (November 20, 1772)

A. How does Samuel Adams make clear the connection between his argument and the principles of John Locke's *Two Treatises of Government*, which explained the legitimacy of the reign of William and Mary? In what ways does highlighting this connection make Adams's assertions more convincing and less easily dismissed?

B. In what ways is the premise of Adams's argument similar to and different from James Otis's in his Speech against Writs of Assistance (Document 1)?

## 8. "An Impartial Observer," An Account of the Boston Tea Party (December 1773)

A. Just how impartial was the "Impartial Observer"? How did this writer describe the group of Massachusetts residents who met to discuss the situation at Griffin's Wharf? Why might this writer have considered it important to record this description?

B. The Boston Tea Party involved the destruction of about 90,000 pounds of tea—all of it privately owned. Should the actions of participants in the Tea Party be understood as a departure from a commitment to property rights (see Documents 1, 3, and 7), or somehow as an affirmation of them?

## 9. Gouverneur Morris, "We Shall be under the Domination of a Riotous Mob" (May 20, 1774)

A. Although opposed to British policies such as the Coercive Acts, Gouverneur Morris was also opposed to direct democracy. What did he seem to believe was a better means for securing individual liberty? What were the strengths and weaknesses of the alternative favored by Morris?

B. Morris dismissed common people who "roared out liberty, and property, and religion ... which everyone thought he understood, and was egregiously mistaken." In what ways does the account of the Boston Tea Party (Document 8) support Morris's assertion that regular people knew slogans but failed to comprehend the principles they were meant to convey? In what ways does the account contradict Morris's claim?

## 10. Thomas Jefferson, *A Summary View of the Rights of British America* (July 1774)

A. What was the basis for Jefferson's assertion that "the British Parliament has no right to exercise authority over us"? Was his argument compelling? Why or why not?

B. Like Jefferson's *Summary View*, Samuel Adams's "The Rights of the Colonists" (Document 7) based its argument, in part, on English history. Which moments in time attracted their attention? Given their somewhat different assertions and audiences, why did certain episodes in history attract Adams while others attracted Jefferson?

## 11. Philadelphia Welcomes the First Continental Congress (September 16, 1774)

A. When Philadelphians welcomed members of Congress on September 16, they were extending their hospitality. Did the festivities on that day serve any other purposes? What were they?

B. Compare and contrast this account with Gouverneur Morris's description (Document 9) of a Patriot meeting in New York City. In which location did the "spirit of the English Constitution" (as Morris referred to it) manifest itself most clearly? Why?

## 12. Joseph Galloway, Plan of Union (September 28, 1774)

A. Had Galloway's Plan of Union been adopted by the colonies and approved by the British, how effectively would it have protected colonists' rights and colonies' capacity for self-government?

B. Compare and contrast the constitutional visions of Galloway and Thomas Jefferson (Document 10). How did Galloway's understanding of the colonies' political relationship with Britain differ from Jefferson's?

## 13. The Association Enacted by the First Continental Congress (October 20, 1774)

A. In what ways did the Continental Association go beyond the halting of trade with the British empire to minimize distinctions between members of the resistance who were financially well off and those who were not?

B. Compare and contrast the Continental Association with Charleston's 1769 Nonimportation Agreement (Document 5). In terms of its means and ends, was the Continental Association more or less radical? How did the Association differ from Charleston's Nonimportation Agreement in its approach to the slave trade?

## 14. "A. W. Farmer" (Reverend Samuel Seabury), *A View of the Controversy between Great-Britain and her Colonies*, (December 24, 1774)

A. What did Samuel Seabury predict would happen if colonists allowed the Continental Congress to escalate their resistance to Great Britain? How sound were the reasons on which he based his prediction?

B. Why did Seabury consider the Continental Association's plan (Document 13) to cease the importation and consumption of British goods as well as American exports to Britain unfair and unwise?

## 15. "Friend to America" (Alexander Hamilton), *The Farmer Refuted* (February 23, 1775)

A. How and why did Alexander Hamilton's suggestion that Boston, and maybe all the colonies, had been plunged into a "state of nature" by the Coercive Acts undermine the legitimacy of British rule?

B. How effectively did Hamilton refute Samuel Seabury's argument (Document 14) that the Continental Congress lacked legitimacy?

## 16. Patrick Henry, "Give me liberty or give me death!" (March 23, 1775)

A. Why did Patrick Henry say that attempts to reconcile the colonies with Great Britain were pointless? Why did he think that "chains and slavery" were the only alternatives to war?

B. Compare Patrick Henry's argument to Alexander Hamilton's (Document 15), which was written only one month earlier. How do they differ in terms of reasoning and evidence? Which is more compelling? Which was more radical?

## 17. John Andrews, Account of the Battles of Lexington and Concord (April 20, 1775)

A. Military conflict is sometimes characterized as an attempt to use force to intimidate the enemy into submission. Other times the use of force is carefully calibrated to avoid alienating people and turning those who might be friends into enemies. Given Andrews's account, which of these strategies did the British employ on April 19? How well did the redcoats achieve their objective?

B. Compare and contrast the ways in which the people of Boston and nearby communities prepared and organized themselves during the 1770 Boston Massacre (Document 6), the 1773 Boston Tea Party (Document 8), and the 1775 Battles of Lexington and Concord. Which likely did more to influence the outcomes of these events: preparation and organization, or other factors that could not have been anticipated?

## 18. John Dickinson and Thomas Jefferson, Declaration of the Causes and Necessity of Taking Up Arms (July 6, 1775)

A. In what ways was this declaration by the Continental Congress less than, equal to, and more than a formal declaration of war against Great Britain? In which of these capacities did it serve the most valuable purpose?

B. Compare and contrast the arguments advanced by Dickinson and Jefferson with those employed by Patrick Henry (Document 16). How and why are these arguments in some ways similar? How and why are they in some ways different?

## 19. Lancaster Committee of Correspondence and Observation, Resolution Regarding Quaker Pacifists (July 11, 1775)

A. In what ways did the Lancaster County Committee of Correspondence and Observation balance the belief that all needed to do their part to resist British aggression with a recognition of Quakers' sincere pacifism? How well did it succeed?

B. The Lancaster County Committee of Correspondence and Observation sought to advance "the protection of *America* and this *colony*" while also respecting Quakers' religious freedom. Given colonists' principles and circumstances, did this group of Pennsylvanians do better or worse in its attempt to reconcile the good of the many with the rights of individuals than members of Congress who in 1774 approved the Continental Association (Document 13)?

## 20. Thomas Paine, *Common Sense* (January 1776)

A. What accounted for the popularity of *Common Sense*? Was it what Paine argued for, the way in which he conveyed his argument, or some combination of these factors?

B. Compare Paine's assertions about monarchy and the British monarch with the way in which Dickinson and Jefferson (Document 18) address the king. What accounts for the difference?

## 21. Stratford, Connecticut's Thomas Gage—and Monmouth County, New Jersey's Dunmore (May 30, 1776)

A. Why did the *New-England Chronicle*, a Patriot newspaper, decide to circulate news of Loyalists naming babies after Thomas Gage and Lord Dunmore? Were these accounts more likely to embolden Loyalists or solidify support for colonists resisting British rule?

B. Gouverneur Morris (Document 9) worried that resistance to British authority was unleashing mob rule and mob violence. Did the actions of Stratford's "petticoat army" confirm or contradict his fears?

## 22. Abigail and John Adams, "Remember the Ladies" (March 31–May 26, 1776)

A. On what different principles did Abigail and John Adams base their different assertions? Why were these principles in conflict? Must these principles always be in conflict, or only under certain circumstances?

B. As examples of increased assertiveness among women of the Revolutionary era, how were Stratford, Connecticut's petticoat army (Document 21) and Abigail Adams's belief that the Continental Congress should "remember the ladies" similar and different? What factors seem most likely to have contributed to this increased assertiveness?

## 23. John Adams, *Thoughts on Government* (April 1776)

A. In Adams's plan for a new government, to which extent did he adapt the political structure of most American colonies, and to what extent did he invent entirely new features? How did Adams seek to give voice to the will of the people while also minimizing the dangers posed to the common good by potentially self-interested citizens and their representatives?

B. Compare and contrast Adams's *Thoughts on Government* with Thomas Paine's *Common Sense* (Document 20). In 1776 Adams's pamphlet was printed in two editions while Paine's was reprinted 25 times. Why was Paine's work so much more popular than Adams's?

## 24. George Mason, Virginia Declaration of Rights (June 12, 1776)

A. According to the Virginia Declaration of Rights, what is the purpose of government?

B. After reading the Virginia Declaration, examine the Constitution and its first ten amendments, which are called the Bill of Rights (Appendix). Which specific components of the Constitution and Bill of Rights are similar to Mason's declaration?

## 25. Thomas Jefferson, Draft of the Declaration of Independence (July 2–4, 1776)

A. Examine the list of grievances that make up the bulk of the Declaration of Independence. How accurate a history of the imperial crisis (1760–1776) does this list present? One of the grievances listed in Jefferson's draft was the king's refusal to allow the colonies to end the slave trade. To what extent did the deletion of this grievance change the character of the Declaration?

B. How does the Declaration confirm, complement, complicate, and/or contradict the central arguments of Samuel Adams's "Rights of the Colonists" (Document 7) and Patrick Henry's "Give me liberty or give me death!" speech (Document 16)?

## 26. Celebrations of American Independence in Boston and Watertown, Massachusetts (July 18, 1776)

A. How were organized events that demonstrated support for the Continental Congress's decision to declare independence different from seemingly spontaneous ones? How did these different demonstrations work together to reassure Patriots that independence was the right decision? How did they encourage people opposed to or unsure about independence to change their minds?

B. Examine this newspaper account alongside the *Pennsylvania Packet*'s 1774 coverage of the convening of the first Continental Congress in Philadelphia (Document 12). How can you tell that these newspapers both supported American resistance to Great Britain?

## 27. "Common Sense" (Thomas Paine), *The American Crisis* (December 23, 1776)

A. Paine's *American Crisis* extended no kind words to Loyalists (he used the term "Tories"). How did he criticize them? Were his criticisms fair and factual?

B. Paine wrote this first installment of *American Crisis* about a year after *Common Sense* (Document 20). How are these two essays similar and how are they different? Are the differences best explained by changing circumstances, or did other factors prompt the differences?

## 28. Prince Hall, et. al., Massachusetts Antislavery Petition (January 13, 1777)

A. What was the central argument of this petition? What were its main supporting points? Who was its intended audience? How well did its authors craft this document to appeal to its audience?

B. How is this petition's argument similar to and different from Jefferson's draft of the Declaration of Independence (Document 25)?

## 29. Private Hugh McDonald, The Continentals Encounter Civilians (December 1776–April 1777)

A. In what ways did the army's leaders—even under imperfect circumstances—try to maintain good relations with civilians? To what extent did soldiers such as Private McDonald and his compatriots follow suit? Based on McDonald's anecdotes, did civilians fear the Continental army?

B. Compare and contrast the Continental army's handling of the Richmond Loyalist with the actions of Stratford, Connecticut's petticoat army (Document 21). In these two instances, to what extent did the Continental army and the petticoat army respect the lives, liberty, and property of dissenters? To what extent did the actions of the Continental army and the petticoat army seem calibrated to diminish Loyalism among the American people?

### 30. Generals Gates and Burgoyne on the Murder of Jane McCrea (September 2–6, 1777)

A. Compare and contrast General Gates's account of Jane McCrea's murder with General Burgoyne's. On which facts do they agree? Which elements of their statements are in dispute? How effective is Burgoyne's account as a vindication of the British army and its alliance with Native American warriors?

B. In what ways would the accounts of Gates and Burgoyne appear to confirm or complicate, in the minds of Patriots and Loyalists during the War for Independence, the portrayal of Great Britain's partnership with "merciless Indian savages" described in both the draft (Document 25) and final (Appendix) versions of the Declaration of Independence?

### 31. Articles of Confederation (proposed November 15, 1777; ratified March 1, 1781)

A. Which specific powers did the Articles of Confederation reserve for the government of the United States? How did this first constitution attempt to prevent the American government from threatening the powers of the thirteen states and the liberty of the American people?

B. To what extent does the framework for government prescribed by the Articles of Confederation accord with the precepts of John Adams's *Thoughts on Government* (Document 23)?

### 32. Private Joseph Plumb Martin, Foraging for Valley Forge (December 1777–April 1778)

A. In what ways does Private Martin's account suggest that serving in the Continental army deepened his identity as an American while diminishing his fealty to his native New England? What might explain this change?

B. Martin made clear that, even though his assignment was to confiscate civilians' property for the use of the Continental army, he enjoyed generally good relations with the Pennsylvanians he encountered. What might explain this? How did his interactions with civilians compare with those of Private Hugh McDonald (Document 29)? How did their treatment of civilians compare with those of British forces and their allies as depicted in the story of the death of Jane McCrea (Document 30)?

## 33. Lieutenant Colonel John Laurens, Envisioning an African American Regiment (February 2, 1778)

A. In what ways did Laurens's plan for raising an African American regiment reflect not only his hostility to slavery but also his desire to sacrifice his own self-interest in behalf of the Revolution?

B. What did Laurens mean when he wrote that "those who fall in battle will not lose much"? Compare his sentiments with those of Patrick Henry (Document 16) and the signers of the Massachusetts antislavery petition (Document 28). According to these documents, what was worse than death? Why?

## 34. Benjamin Franklin and the Marquis de Lafayette, List of Prints to Illustrate British Cruelties (ca. May 1779)

A. Given all its responsibilities, why would the Continental Congress ask Franklin—its ambassador to France, a man with his own heavy responsibilities—to take the lead in putting together a children's book about the British military's past misdeeds?

B. Compare the accounts of Hugh McDonald (Document 29) and Joseph Plumb Martin (Document 32) with the accounts of the murder of Jane McCrea (Document 30) and the items on this list. Assuming that these testimonials are accurate, why would Continental soldiers be more respectful, considerate, and kind to Americans than British soldiers? In what ways might respect, consideration, and kindness toward the civilian population both help and hinder the Continentals' war efforts?

## 35. Eliza Wilkinson, Redcoats in South Carolina (June 1779)

A. Examine Wilkinson's account and make a list of the malevolent acts committed by the particular British soldiers who entered her home. Did these redcoats' behavior seem motivated by a desire to reestablish British authority—or something else?

B. Compare Wilkinson's experience with the "British atrocities" listed by Franklin and Lafayette (Document 34). Would Wilkinson's encounter with Redcoats, which she described as the "day of terror," merit inclusion on the list of Franklin and Lafayette? Why or why not?

## 36. "Plain Truth," "To the Traitor General Arnold" (September 25, 1781)

A. Arnold might have argued that he was not a traitor—that instead, those who continued to fight for independence were the real traitors. What points does "Plain Truth" make that undermine such an assertion, exposing Arnold as especially worthy of scorn?

B. In what ways was the writer's response to Arnold's treason and subsequent actions similar to and different from the actions of the Connecticut petticoat army that paid a visit to the parents of baby "Thomas Gage" (Document 21)? What were the advantages and disadvantages of these efforts to express and reinforce anti-British opinion?

## 37. Dr. James Thacher, Account of the British Surrender at Yorktown (October 19, 1781)

A. According to Dr. Thacher, what attitudes regarding the Continental army did British soldiers display during their surrender? Did these attitudes likely do more to help or hurt the British war effort?

B. What do Dr. Thacher's account and the exchange of letters between Generals Gates and Burgoyne (Document 30) reveal about the rules of warfare followed by the British, American, and French militaries? What purposes do these rules of warfare seem to serve?

## 38. Thomas Jefferson, *Notes on the State of Virginia* (1781–1784)

A. It is obvious that slavery was bad for people who were enslaved. But why, exactly, did Thomas Jefferson believe that it was also bad for slave owners? How did the practice of slaveholding diminish the ability of white people to serve as good citizens in a republic?

B. In what ways was Jefferson's assertion that "those who labor in the earth are the chosen people of God" in agreement with John Adams's belief that voting rights should be awarded only to landowning heads of households (Document 22)? Why was a dependence on others considered a trait incompatible with the ability to participate fully and positively in the new American republic?

## 39. George Washington, The Newburgh Address (March 15, 1783)

A. What reasons did Washington give his officers to ignore calls to confront Congress and instead "give one more distinguished proof of unexampled patriotism and patient virtue"?

B. Compare and contrast the actions and motivations of Benedict Arnold (Document 36) with the contemplated actions and motivations of the Newburgh conspirators. Which actual or contemplated actions were more reprehensible? Whose motivations were more reprehensible?

## 40. Captain Samuel Shaw, An Officer's Account of Washington's Remarks (April 1783)

A. According to Shaw, what enabled Washington to restore his leadership of the army after appearing before its officers as a man "not at the head of his troops, but as it were in opposition to them"?

B. Both Washington (Document 40) and Shaw referenced "the last stage of perfection to which human nature is capable of attaining." What did they mean?

## 41. George Washington, Circular Letter to the States (June 8–21, 1783)

A. At several junctures, Washington apologized to the states' governors for opining about politics. Why did he consider these apologies necessary? Why did he seem to believe himself especially qualified him to offer his insights regarding Americans' central government? Would an official who had spent the Revolution serving a state's government see things differently? Why or why not?

B. To what extent did Washington, through this circular letter, keep the promises he had made to army officers in March 1783 at Newburgh (Documents 39 & 40)?

## 42. Treaty of Paris (September 3, 1783)

A. To what extent did the Treaty of Paris help to secure a durable peace between the United States and Great Britain? What did Britain gain by acknowledging the land between the Appalachian Mountains and the Mississippi River as part of the United States? What would be the long-term consequences, for America's Spanish allies and Britain's Indian allies, of a United States spanning the eastern half of the North American continent?

B. The Treaty of Paris began by invoking "the name of the Most Holy and Undivided Trinity," and, like the Declaration of Independence (Document 25), made reference to "Divine Providence." Why were references to God considered appropriate and necessary in documents such as the Treaty of Paris and the Declaration?

## 43. Haym Salomon, et al., Petition of the Philadelphia Synagogue to the Council of Censors of Pennsylvania (December 23, 1783)

A. On what points did Haym Salomon and the other members of Philadelphia's Jewish community base their arguments? What does the way in which they substantiated their arguments reveal about what they believed mattered to the leaders of Pennsylvania?

B. Compare this petition for the right of Jewish Pennsylvanians to hold office with the petition for the right of African Americans in Massachusetts to be free of slavery. What do the similarities and differences of this petition and the Massachusetts Antislavery Petition (Document 29) suggest about the beliefs and attitudes of Americans during the Revolution?

## 44. George Washington, Cincinnatus Reborn (December 23, 1783)

A. Examine Washington's speech tendering his resignation to the Continental Congress. What did it reveal about his views on being a good winner? What specific virtues did his statement exemplify?

B. Compare and contrast the ceremonial aspects of Washington's resignation with those on display at the British surrender at Yorktown (Document 37). What were the different values that these two ceremonies meant to emphasize?

APPENDIX C

# Declaration of Independence
*In CONGRESS, July 4, 1776*

The unanimous Declaration of the thirteen united States of America, When in the Course of human events, it becomes necessary for one people to dissolve the political bands which have connected them with another, and to assume among the powers of the earth, the separate and equal station to which the Laws of Nature and of Nature's God entitle them, a decent respect to the opinions of mankind requires that they should declare the causes which impel them to the separation.

We hold these truths to be self-evident, that all men are created equal, that they are endowed by their Creator with certain unalienable Rights, that among these are Life, Liberty and the pursuit of Happiness.—That to secure these rights, Governments are instituted among Men, deriving their just powers from the consent of the governed,—that whenever any Form of Government becomes destructive of these ends, it is the Right of the People to alter or to abolish it, and to institute new Government, laying its foundation on such principles and organizing its powers in such form, as to them shall seem most likely to effect their Safety and Happiness. Prudence, indeed, will dictate that Governments long established should not be changed for light and transient causes; and accordingly all experience hath shewn, that mankind are more disposed to suffer, while evils are sufferable, than to right themselves by abolishing the forms to which they are accustomed. But when a long train of abuses and usurpations, pursuing invariably the same Object evinces a design to reduce them under absolute Despotism, it is their right, it is their duty, to throw off such Government, and to provide new Guards for their future security.—Such has been the patient sufferance of these Colonies; and such is now the necessity which constrains them to alter their former Systems of Government. The history of the present King of Great Britain is a history of repeated injuries and usurpations, all having in direct object the establishment of an absolute Tyranny over these States. To prove this, let Facts be submitted to a candid world.

He has refused his Assent to Laws, the most wholesome and necessary for the public good.

He has forbidden his Governors to pass Laws of immediate and pressing importance, unless suspended in their operation till his Assent should be obtained; and when so suspended, he has utterly neglected to attend to them.

He has refused to pass other Laws for the accommodation of large districts of people, unless those people would relinquish the right of Representation in the Legislature, a right inestimable to them and formidable to tyrants only.

He has called together legislative bodies at places unusual, uncomfortable, and distant from the depository of their public Records, for the sole purpose of fatiguing them into compliance with his measures.

He has dissolved Representative Houses repeatedly, for opposing with manly firmness his invasions on the rights of the people.

He has refused for a long time, after such dissolutions, to cause others to be elected; whereby the Legislative powers, incapable of Annihilation, have returned to the People at large for their exercise; the State remaining in the mean time exposed to all the dangers of invasion from without, and convulsions within.

He has endeavoured to prevent the population of these States; for that purpose obstructing the Laws for Naturalization of Foreigners; refusing to pass others to encourage their migrations hither, and raising the conditions of new Appropriations of Lands.

He has obstructed the Administration of Justice, by refusing his Assent to Laws for establishing Judiciary powers.

He has made Judges dependent on his Will alone, for the tenure of their offices, and the amount and payment of their salaries.

He has erected a multitude of New Offices, and sent hither swarms of Officers to harrass our people, and eat out their substance.

He has kept among us, in times of peace, Standing Armies without the Consent of our legislatures.

He has affected to render the Military independent of and superior to the Civil power.

He has combined with others to subject us to a jurisdiction foreign to our constitution, and unacknowledged by our laws; giving his Assent to their Acts of pretended Legislation:

For Quartering large bodies of armed troops among us:

For protecting them, by a mock Trial, from punishment for any Murders which they should commit on the Inhabitants of these States:

For cutting off our Trade with all parts of the world:

For imposing Taxes on us without our Consent:

For depriving us in many cases, of the benefits of Trial by Jury:

For transporting us beyond Seas to be tried for pretended offences:

For abolishing the free System of English Laws in a neighbouring Province, establishing therein an Arbitrary government, and enlarging its Boundaries so as to render it at once an example and fit instrument for introducing the same absolute rule into these Colonies:

For taking away our Charters, abolishing our most valuable Laws, and altering fundamentally the Forms of our Governments:

For suspending our own Legislatures, and declaring themselves invested with power to legislate for us in all cases whatsoever.

He has abdicated Government here, by declaring us out of his Protection and waging War against us.

He has plundered our seas, ravaged our Coasts, burnt our towns, and destroyed the lives of our people.

He is at this time transporting large Armies of foreign Mercenaries to compleat the works of death, desolation and tyranny, already begun with circumstances of Cruelty & perfidy scarcely paralleled in the most barbarous ages, and totally unworthy the Head of a civilized nation.

He has constrained our fellow Citizens taken Captive on the high Seas to bear Arms against their Country, to become the executioners of their friends and Brethren, or to fall themselves by their Hands.

He has excited domestic insurrections amongst us, and has endeavoured to bring on the inhabitants of our frontiers, the merciless Indian Savages, whose known rule of warfare, is an undistinguished destruction of all ages, sexes and conditions.

In every stage of these Oppressions We have Petitioned for Redress in the most humble terms: Our repeated Petitions have been answered only by repeated injury. A Prince whose character is thus marked by every act which may define a Tyrant, is unfit to be the ruler of a free people.

Nor have We been wanting in attentions to our British brethren. We have warned them from time to time of attempts by their legislature to extend an unwarrantable jurisdiction over us. We have reminded them of the circumstances of our emigration and settlement here. We have appealed to their native justice and magnanimity, and we have conjured them by the ties of our common kindred to disavow these usurpations, which, would inevitably interrupt our connections and correspondence. They too have been deaf to the voice of justice and of consanguinity. We must, therefore, acquiesce in the necessity, which denounces our Separation, and hold them, as we hold the rest of mankind, Enemies in War, in Peace Friends.

We, THEREFORE, the Representatives of the UNITED STATES OF AMERICA, in General Congress, Assembled, appealing to the Supreme Judge of the world for the rectitude of our intentions, do, in the Name, and by Authority of the good People of these Colonies, solemnly publish and declare, That these United Colonies are, and of Right ought to be FREE AND INDEPENDENT STATES; that they are Absolved from all Allegiance to the British Crown, and that all political connection between them and the State of Great Britain, is and ought to be totally dissolved; and that as Free and Independent States, they have full Power to levy War, conclude Peace, contract Alliances, establish Commerce, and to do all other Acts and Things which Independent States may of right do. And for the support of this Declaration, with a firm reliance on the protection of divine Providence, we mutually pledge to each other our Lives, our Fortunes and our sacred Honor.

[Georgia:]
Button Gwinnett
Lyman Hall
George Walton

[North Carolina:]
William Hooper
Joseph Hewes
John Penn

[South Carolina:]
Edward Rutledge
Thomas Heyward, Jr.
Thomas Lynch, Jr.
Arthur Middleton

[Maryland:]
Samuel Chase
William Paca
Thomas Stone
Charles Carroll of Carrollton

[Virginia:]
George Wythe
Richard Henry Lee
Thomas Jefferson

Benjamin Harrison
Thomas Nelson, Jr.
Francis Lightfoot Lee
Carter Braxton

[Pennsylvania:]
Robert Morris
Benjamin Rush
Benjamin Franklin
John Morton
George Clymer
James Smith
George Taylor
James Wilson
George Ross

[Delaware:]
Caesar Rodney
George Read
Thomas McKean

[New York:]
William Floyd
Philip Livingston
Francis Lewis
Lewis Morris

[New Jersey:]
Richard Stockton
John Witherspoon
Francis Hopkinson
John Hart
Abraham Clark

[New Hampshire:]
Josiah Bartlett
William Whipple
Matthew Thornton

[Massachusetts:]
John Hancock

Samuel Adams
John Adams
Robert Treat Paine
Elbridge Gerry

[Rhode Island:]
Stephen Hopkins
William Ellery

[Connecticut:]
Roger Sherman
Samuel Huntington
William Williams
Oliver Wolcott

APPENDIX D

# Constitution of the United States of America
*September 17, 1787*

[Editors' note: Bracketed sections in the text of the Constitution have been superceded or modified by Constitutional amendments.]

**We the People** of the United States, in Order to form a more perfect Union, establish Justice, insure domestic Tranquility, provide for the common defence, promote the general Welfare, and secure the Blessings of Liberty to ourselves and our Posterity, do ordain and establish this Constitution for the United States of America.

## Article I

**Section 1.** All legislative Powers herein granted shall be vested in a Congress of the United States, which shall consist of a Senate and House of Representatives.

**Section 2.** The House of Representatives shall be composed of Members chosen every second Year by the People of the several States, and the Electors in each State shall have the Qualifications requisite for Electors of the most numerous Branch of the State Legislature.

No Person shall be a Representative who shall not have attained to the Age of twenty five Years, and been seven Years a Citizen of the United States, and who shall not, when elected, be an Inhabitant of that State in which he shall be chosen.

[Representatives and direct Taxes shall be apportioned among the several States which may be included within this Union, according to their respective Numbers, which shall be determined by adding to the whole Number of free Persons, including those bound to Service for a Term of Years, and excluding Indians not taxed, three fifths of all other Persons.][1]
The actual Enumeration shall be made within three Years after the first

---

[1] modified by Section 2 of the Fourteenth Amendment

Meeting of the Congress of the United States, and within every subsequent Term of ten Years, in such Manner as they shall by Law direct. The Number of Representatives shall not exceed one for every thirty Thousand, but each State shall have at Least one Representative; and until such enumeration shall be made, the State of New Hampshire shall be entitled to chuse three, Massachusetts eight, Rhode-Island and Providence Plantations one, Connecticut five, New-York six, New Jersey four, Pennsylvania eight, Delaware one, Maryland six, Virginia ten, North Carolina five, South Carolina five, and Georgia three.

When vacancies happen in the Representation from any State, the Executive Authority thereof shall issue Writs of Election to fill such Vacancies.

The House of Representatives shall chuse their Speaker and other Officers; and shall have the sole Power of Impeachment.

**Section 3.** The Senate of the United States shall be composed of two Senators from each State, [*chosen by the Legislature thereof,*][2] for six Years; and each Senator shall have one Vote.

Immediately after they shall be assembled in Consequence of the first Election, they shall be divided as equally as may be into three Classes. The Seats of the Senators of the first Class shall be vacated at the Expiration of the second Year, of the second Class at the Expiration of the fourth Year, and of the third Class at the Expiration of the sixth Year, so that one third may be chosen every second Year; [*and if Vacancies happen by Resignation, or otherwise, during the Recess of the Legislature of any State, the Executive thereof may make temporary Appointments until the next Meeting of the Legislature, which shall then fill such Vacancies.*][3]

No Person shall be a Senator who shall not have attained to the Age of thirty Years, and been nine Years a Citizen of the United States, and who shall not, when elected, be an Inhabitant of that State for which he shall be chosen.

The Vice President of the United States shall be President of the Senate, but shall have no Vote, unless they be equally divided.

The Senate shall chuse their other Officers, and also a President pro tempore, in the Absence of the Vice President, or when he shall exercise the Office of President of the United States.

The Senate shall have the sole Power to try all Impeachments. When sitting for that Purpose, they shall be on Oath or Affirmation. When the

---

[2] superseded by the Seventeenth Amendment
[3] modified by the Seventeenth Amendment

President of the United States is tried, the Chief Justice shall preside: And no Person shall be convicted without the Concurrence of two thirds of the Members present.

Judgment in Cases of Impeachment shall not extend further than to removal from Office, and disqualification to hold and enjoy any Office of honor, Trust or Profit under the United States: but the Party convicted shall nevertheless be liable and subject to Indictment, Trial, Judgment and Punishment, according to Law.

**Section 4.** The Times, Places and Manner of holding Elections for Senators and Representatives, shall be prescribed in each State by the Legislature thereof; but the Congress may at any time by Law make or alter such Regulations, except as to the Places of chusing Senators.

The Congress shall assemble at least once in every Year, and such Meeting shall be [on the first Monday in December,][4] unless they shall by Law appoint a different Day.

**Section 5.** Each House shall be the Judge of the Elections, Returns and Qualifications of its own Members, and a Majority of each shall constitute a Quorum to do Business; but a smaller Number may adjourn from day to day, and may be authorized to compel the Attendance of absent Members, in such Manner, and under such Penalties as each House may provide.

Each House may determine the Rules of its Proceedings, punish its Members for disorderly Behaviour, and, with the Concurrence of two thirds, expel a Member.

Each House shall keep a Journal of its Proceedings, and from time to time publish the same, excepting such Parts as may in their Judgment require Secrecy; and the Yeas and Nays of the Members of either House on any question shall, at the Desire of one fifth of those Present, be entered on the Journal.

Neither House, during the Session of Congress, shall, without the Consent of the other, adjourn for more than three days, nor to any other Place than that in which the two Houses shall be sitting.

**Section 6.** The Senators and Representatives shall receive a Compensation for their Services, to be ascertained by Law, and paid out of the Treasury of the United States. They shall in all Cases, except Treason, Felony and

---

[4] modified by Section 2 of the Twentieth Amendment

Breach of the Peace, be privileged from Arrest during their Attendance at the Session of their respective Houses, and in going to and returning from the same; and for any Speech or Debate in either House, they shall not be questioned in any other Place.

No Senator or Representative shall, during the Time for which he was elected, be appointed to any civil Office under the Authority of the United States, which shall have been created, or the Emoluments whereof shall have been encreased during such time; and no Person holding any Office under the United States, shall be a Member of either House during his Continuance in Office.

**Section 7.** All Bills for raising Revenue shall originate in the House of Representatives; but the Senate may propose or concur with Amendments as on other Bills.

Every Bill which shall have passed the House of Representatives and the Senate, shall, before it become a Law, be presented to the President of the United States; If he approve he shall sign it, but if not he shall return it, with his Objections to that House in which it shall have originated, who shall enter the Objections at large on their Journal, and proceed to reconsider it. If after such Reconsideration two thirds of that House shall agree to pass the Bill, it shall be sent, together with the Objections, to the other House, by which it shall likewise be reconsidered, and if approved by two thirds of that House, it shall become a Law. But in all such Cases the Votes of both Houses shall be determined by yeas and Nays, and the Names of the Persons voting for and against the Bill shall be entered on the Journal of each House respectively. If any Bill shall not be returned by the President within ten Days (Sundays excepted) after it shall have been presented to him, the Same shall be a Law, in like Manner as if he had signed it, unless the Congress by their Adjournment prevent its Return, in which Case it shall not be a Law.

Every Order, Resolution, or Vote to which the Concurrence of the Senate and House of Representatives may be necessary (except on a question of Adjournment) shall be presented to the President of the United States; and before the Same shall take Effect, shall be approved by him, or being disapproved by him, shall be repassed by two thirds of the Senate and House of Representatives, according to the Rules and Limitations prescribed in the Case of a Bill.

**Section 8.** The Congress shall have Power To lay and collect Taxes, Duties, Imposts and Excises, to pay the Debts and provide for the common Defence and general Welfare of the United States; but all Duties, Imposts and Excises shall be uniform throughout the United States;

To borrow Money on the credit of the United States;

To regulate Commerce with foreign Nations, and among the several States, and with the Indian Tribes;

To establish an uniform Rule of Naturalization, and uniform Laws on the subject of Bankruptcies throughout the United States;

To coin Money, regulate the Value thereof, and of foreign Coin, and fix the Standard of Weights and Measures;

To provide for the Punishment of counterfeiting the Securities and current Coin of the United States;

To establish Post Offices and post Roads;

To promote the Progress of Science and useful Arts, by securing for limited Times to Authors and Inventors the exclusive Right to their respective Writings and Discoveries;

To constitute Tribunals inferior to the supreme Court;

To define and punish Piracies and Felonies committed on the high Seas, and Offenses against the Law of Nations;

To declare War, grant Letters of Marque and Reprisal, and make Rules concerning Captures on Land and Water;

To raise and support Armies, but no Appropriation of Money to that Use shall be for a longer Term than two Years;

To provide and maintain a Navy;

To make Rules for the Government and Regulation of the land and naval Forces;

To provide for calling forth the Militia to execute the Laws of the Union, suppress Insurrections and repel Invasions;

To provide for organizing, arming, and disciplining, the Militia, and for governing such Part of them as may be employed in the Service of the United States, reserving to the States respectively, the Appointment of the Officers, and the Authority of training the Militia according to the discipline prescribed by Congress;

To exercise exclusive Legislation in all Cases whatsoever, over such District (not exceeding ten Miles square) as may, by Cession of particular States, and the Acceptance of Congress, become the Seat of the Government of the United States, and to exercise like Authority over all Places purchased by the Consent of the Legislature of the State in which the Same shall be, for the Erection of Forts, Magazines, Arsenals, dock-Yards, and other needful Buildings;—And

To make all Laws which shall be necessary and proper for carrying into Execution the foregoing Powers, and all other Powers vested by this Constitution in the Government of the United States, or in any Department or Officer thereof.

**Section 9.** The Migration or Importation of such Persons as any of the States now existing shall think proper to admit, shall not be prohibited by the Congress prior to the Year one thousand eight hundred and eight, but a Tax or duty may be imposed on such Importation, not exceeding ten dollars for each Person.

The Privilege of the Writ of Habeas Corpus shall not be suspended, unless when in Cases of Rebellion or Invasion the public Safety may require it.

No Bill of Attainder or ex post facto Law shall be passed.

No Capitation, or other direct, Tax shall be laid, unless in Proportion to the Census or Enumeration herein before directed to be taken.[5]

No Tax or Duty shall be laid on Articles exported from any State.

No Preference shall be given by any Regulation of Commerce or Revenue to the Ports of one State over those of another: nor shall Vessels bound to, or from, one State, be obliged to enter, clear, or pay Duties in another.

No Money shall be drawn from the Treasury, but in Consequence of Appropriations made by Law; and a regular Statement and Account of the Receipts and Expenditures of all public Money shall be published from time to time.

No Title of Nobility shall be granted by the United States: And no Person holding any Office of Profit or Trust under them, shall, without the Consent of the Congress, accept of any present, Emolument, Office, or Title, of any kind whatever, from any King, Prince, or foreign State.

**Section 10.** No State shall enter into any Treaty, Alliance, or Confederation; grant Letters of Marque and Reprisal; coin Money; emit Bills of Credit; make any Thing but gold and silver Coin a Tender in Payment of Debts; pass any Bill of Attainder, ex post facto Law, or Law impairing the Obligation of Contracts, or grant any Title of Nobility.

No State shall, without the Consent of the Congress, lay any Imposts or Duties on Imports or Exports, except what may be absolutely necessary for executing it's inspection Laws: and the net Produce of all Duties and Imposts,

---

[5] modified by the Sixteenth Amendment

laid by any State on Imports or Exports, shall be for the Use of the Treasury of the United States; and all such Laws shall be subject to the Revision and Controul of the Congress.

No State shall, without the Consent of Congress, lay any Duty of Tonnage, keep Troops, or Ships of War in time of Peace, enter into any Agreement or Compact with another State, or with a foreign Power, or engage in War, unless actually invaded, or in such imminent Danger as will not admit of delay.

## Article II

**Section 1.** The executive Power shall be vested in a President of the United States of America. He shall hold his Office during the Term of four Years, and, together with the Vice President, chosen for the same Term, be elected, as follows:

Each State shall appoint, in such Manner as the Legislature thereof may direct, a Number of Electors, equal to the whole Number of Senators and Representatives to which the State may be entitled in the Congress: but no Senator or Representative, or Person holding an Office of Trust or Profit under the United States, shall be appointed an Elector.

[The Electors shall meet in their respective States, and vote by Ballot for two Persons, of whom one at least shall not be an Inhabitant of the same State with themselves. And they shall make a List of all the Persons voted for, and of the Number of Votes for each; which List they shall sign and certify, and transmit sealed to the Seat of the Government of the United States, directed to the President of the Senate. The President of the Senate shall, in the Presence of the Senate and House of Representatives, open all the Certificates, and the Votes shall then be counted. The Person having the greatest Number of Votes shall be the President, if such Number be a Majority of the whole Number of Electors appointed; and if there be more than one who have such Majority, and have an equal Number of Votes, then the House of Representatives shall immediately chuse by Ballot one of them for President; and if no Person have a Majority, then from the five highest on the List the said House shall in like Manner chuse the President. But in chusing the President, the Votes shall be taken by States, the Representation from each State having one Vote; A quorum for this purpose shall consist of a Member or Members from two thirds of the States, and a Majority of all the States shall be necessary to a Choice. In every Case, after the Choice of the President, the Person having the greatest Number of Votes of the Electors shall be the Vice President. But if there should remain two or more who have equal Votes, the Senate shall chuse from them by Ballot the Vice President.][6]

The Congress may determine the Time of chusing the Electors, and the Day on which they shall give their Votes; which Day shall be the same throughout the United States.

No Persons except a natural born Citizen, or a Citizen of the United States, at the time of the Adoption of this Constitution, shall be eligible to the Office of President; neither shall any Person be eligible to that Office who shall not have attained to the Age of thirty five Years, and been fourteen Years a Resident within the United States.

[In Case of the Removal of the President from Office, or of his Death, Resignation, or Inability to discharge the Powers and Duties of the said Office, the Same shall devolve on the Vice President, and the Congress may by Law provide for the Case of Removal, Death, Resignation or Inability, both of the President and Vice President, declaring what Officer shall then act as President, and such Officer shall act accordingly, until the Disability be removed, or a President shall be elected.][7]

The President shall, at stated Times, receive for his Services, a Compensation, which shall neither be increased nor diminished during the Period for which he shall have been elected, and he shall not receive within that Period any other Emolument from the United States, or any of them.

Before he enter on the Execution of his Office, he shall take the following Oath or Affirmation:—"I do solemnly swear (or affirm) that I will faithfully execute the Office of President of the United States, and will to the best of my Ability, preserve, protect and defend the Constitution of the United States."

**Section 2.** The President shall be Commander in Chief of the Army and Navy of the United States, and of the Militia of the several States, when called into the actual Service of the United States; he may require the Opinion, in writing, of the principal Officer in each of the executive Departments, upon any Subject relating to the Duties of their respective Offices, and he shall have Power to grant Reprieves and Pardons for Offences against the United States, except in Cases of Impeachment.

He shall have Power, by and with the Advice and Consent of the Senate,

---

[6] modifed by the Twelfth Amendment
[7] modified by the Twenty-Fifth Amendment

to make Treaties, provided two thirds of the Senators present concur; and he shall nominate, and by and with the Advice and Consent of the Senate, shall appoint Ambassadors, other public Ministers and Consuls, Judges of the supreme Court, and all other Officers of the United States, whose Appointments are not herein otherwise provided for, and which shall be established by Law: but the Congress may by Law vest the Appointment of such inferior Officers, as they think proper, in the President alone, in the Courts of Law, or in the Heads of Departments.

The President shall have Power to fill up all Vacancies that may happen during the Recess of the Senate, by granting Commissions which shall expire at the End of their next Session.

**Section 3.** He shall from time to time give to the Congress Information of the State of the Union, and recommend to their Consideration such Measures as he shall judge necessary and expedient; he may, on extraordinary Occasions, convene both Houses, or either of them, and in Case of Disagreement between them, with Respect to the Time of Adjournment, he may adjourn them to such Time as he shall think proper; he shall receive Ambassadors and other public Ministers; he shall take Care that the Laws be faithfully executed, and shall Commission all the Officers of the United States.

**Section 4.** The President, Vice President and all civil Officers of the United States, shall be removed from Office on Impeachment for, and Conviction of, Treason, Bribery, or other high Crimes and Misdemeanors.

# Article III

**Section 1.** The judicial Power of the United States, shall be vested in one supreme Court, and in such inferior Courts as the Congress may from time to time ordain and establish. The Judges, both of the supreme and inferior Courts, shall hold their Offices during good Behaviour, and shall, at stated Times, receive for their Services, a Compensation, which shall not be diminished during their Continuance in Office.

**Section 2.** The judicial Power shall extend to all Cases, in Law and Equity, arising under this Constitution, the Laws of the United States, and Treaties made, or which shall be made, under their Authority;—to all Cases affecting Ambassadors, other public Ministers and Consuls;—to all Cases of admiralty and maritime Jurisdiction;—to Controversies to which the United States shall be a Party;—to Controversies between two or more States;—[*between a State and Citizens of another State;—*]⁸ between Citizens of different States;—between Citizens of the same State claiming Lands under Grants of different States, [*and between a State, or the Citizens thereof, and foreign States, Citizens or Subjects.*]⁹

In all Cases affecting Ambassadors, other public Ministers and Consuls, and those in which a State shall be Party, the supreme Court shall have original Jurisdiction. In all the other Cases before mentioned, the supreme Court shall have appellate Jurisdiction, both as to Law and Fact, with such Exceptions, and under such Regulations as the Congress shall make.

The Trial of all Crimes, except in Cases of Impeachment, shall be by Jury; and such Trial shall be held in the State where the said Crimes shall have been committed; but when not committed within any State, the Trial shall be at such Place or Places as the Congress may by Law have directed.

**Section 3.** Treason against the United States, shall consist only in levying War against them, or in adhering to their Enemies, giving them Aid and Comfort. No Person shall be convicted of Treason unless on the Testimony of two Witnesses to the same overt Act, or on Confession in open Court.

The Congress shall have Power to declare the Punishment of Treason, but no Attainder of Treason shall work Corruption of Blood, or Forfeiture except during the Life of the Person attained.

## Article IV

**Section 1.** Full Faith and Credit shall be given in each State to the public Acts, Records, and judicial Proceedings of every other State. And the Congress may by general Laws prescribe the Manner in which such Acts, Records and Proceedings shall be proved, and the Effect thereof.

**Section 2.** The Citizens of each State shall be entitled to all Privileges and Immunities of Citizens in the several States.

A Person charged in any State with Treason, Felony, or other Crime, who shall flee from Justice, and be found in another State, shall on Demand of

---

⁸ superseded by the Eleventh Amendment
⁹ superseded by the Eleventh Amendment

the executive Authority of the State from which he fled, be delivered up, to be removed to the State having Jurisdiction of the Crime.

[No Person held to Service or Labour in one State, under the Laws thereof, escaping into another, shall, in Consequence of any Law or Regulation therein, be discharged from such Service or Labour, but shall be delivered up on Claim of the Party to whom such Service or Labour may be due.][10]

**Section 3.** New States may be admitted by the Congress into this Union; but no new State shall be formed or erected within the Jurisdiction of any other State; nor any State be formed by the Junction of two or more States, or Parts of States, without the Consent of the Legislatures of the States concerned as well as of the Congress.

The Congress shall have Power to dispose of and make all needful Rules and Regulations respecting the Territory or other Property belonging to the United States; and nothing in this Constitution shall be so construed as to Prejudice any Claims of the United States, or of any particular State.

**Section 4.** The United States shall guarantee to every State in this Union a Republican Form of Government, and shall protect each of them against Invasion; and on Application of the Legislature, or of the Executive (when the Legislature cannot be convened) against domestic Violence.

## Article V

The Congress, whenever two thirds of both Houses shall deem it necessary, shall propose Amendments to this Constitution, or, on the Application of the Legislatures of two thirds of the several States, shall call a Convention for proposing Amendments, which, in either Case, shall be valid to all Intents and Purposes, as Part of this Constitution, when ratified by the Legislatures of three fourths of the several States, or by Conventions in three fourths thereof, as the one or the other Mode of Ratification may be proposed by the Congress; Provided that no Amendment which may be made prior to the Year One thousand eight hundred and eight shall in any Manner affect the first and fourth Clauses in the Ninth Section of the first Article; and that no State, without its Consent, shall be deprived of its equal Suffrage in the Senate.

---

[10] superseded by the Thirteenth Amendment

## Article VI

All Debts contracted and Engagements entered into, before the Adoption of this Constitution, shall be as valid against the United States under this Constitution, as under the Confederation.

This Constitution, and the Laws of the United States which shall be made in Pursuance thereof; and all Treaties made, or which shall be made, under the Authority of the United States, shall be the supreme Law of the Land; and the Judges in every State shall be bound thereby, any Thing in the Constitution or Laws of any State to the Contrary notwithstanding.

The Senators and Representatives before mentioned, and the Members of the several State Legislatures, and all executive and judicial Officers, both of the United States and of the several States, shall be bound by Oath or Affirmation, to support this Constitution; but no religious Test shall ever be required as a Qualification to any Office or public Trust under the United States.

## Article VII

The Ratification of the Conventions of nine States, shall be sufficient for the Establishment of this Constitution between the States so ratifying the Same.

Done in Convention by the Unanimous Consent of the States present the Seventeenth Day of September in the Year of our Lord one thousand seven hundred and Eighty seven and of the Independence of the United States of America the Twelfth In Witness whereof We have hereunto subscribed our Names,

Go. Washington—
Presidt. and deputy from Virginia

**New Hampshire**
John Langdon
Nicholas Gilman

**Massachusetts**
Nathaniel Gorham
Rufus King

**Connecticut**
Wm. Saml. Johnson
Roger Sherman

**New York**
Alexander Hamilton

**New Jersey**
Wil: Livingston
David Brearley
Wm. Paterson
Jona: Dayton

**Pennsylvania**
B Franklin

Thomas Mifflin
Robt. Morris
Geo. Clymer
Thos. FitzSimons
Jared Ingersoll
James Wilson
Gouv Morris

**Delaware**
Geo: Read
Gunning Bedford jun
John Dickinson
Richard Bassett
Jaco: Broom

**Maryland**
James McHenry
Dan of St Thos. Jenifer
Danl. Carroll

**Virginia**
John Blair—
James Madison Jr.

**North Carolina**
Wm. Blount
Richd. Dobbs Spaight
Hu Williamson

**South Carolina**
J. Rutledge
Charles Cotesworth Pinckney
Charles Pinckney
Pierce Butler

**Georgia**
William Few
Abr Baldwin

Attest William Jackson Secretary

## AMENDMENTS TO THE CONSTITUTION OF THE UNITED STATES OF AMERICA

### Amendment I

*Ratified December 15, 1791*

Congress shall make no law respecting an establishment of religion, or prohibiting the free exercise thereof; or abridging the freedom of speech, or of the press; or the right of the people peaceably to assemble, and to petition the Government for a redress of grievances.

### Amendment II

*Ratified December 15, 1791*

A well regulated Militia, being necessary to the security of a free State, the right of the people to keep and bear Arms, shall not be infringed.

## Amendment III

*Ratified December 15, 1791*

No Soldier shall, in time of peace be quartered in any house, without the consent of the Owner, nor in time of war, but in a manner to be prescribed by law.

## Amendment IV

*Ratified December 15, 1791*

The right of the people to be secure in their persons, houses, papers, and effects, against unreasonable searches and seizures, shall not be violated, and no Warrants shall issue, but upon probable cause, supported by Oath or affirmation, and particularly describing the place to be searched, and the persons or things to be seized.

## Amendment V

*Ratified December 15, 1791*

No person shall be held to answer for a capital, or otherwise infamous crime, unless on a presentment or indictment of a Grand Jury, except in cases arising in the land or naval forces, or in the Militia, when in actual service in time of War or public danger; nor shall any person be subject for the same offence to be twice put in jeopardy of life or limb, nor shall be compelled in any criminal case to be a witness against himself, nor be deprived of life, liberty, or property, without due process of law; nor shall private property be taken for public use, without just compensation.

## Amendment VI

*Ratified December 15, 1791*

In all criminal prosecutions, the accused shall enjoy the right to a speedy and public trial, by an impartial jury of the State and district wherein the crime shall have been committed, which district shall have been previously ascertained by law, and to be informed of the nature and cause of the accusation; to be confronted with the witnesses against him; to have compulsory process for obtaining witnesses in his favor, and to have the assistance of counsel for his defence.

## Amendment VII

*Ratified December 15, 1791*

In Suits at common law, where the value in controversy shall exceed twenty dollars, the right of trial by jury shall be preserved, and no fact tried by a jury, shall be otherwise reexamined in any Court of the United States, than according to the rules of the common law.

## Amendment VIII

*Ratified December 15, 1791*

Excessive bail shall not be required, nor excessive fines imposed, nor cruel and unusual punishments inflicted.

## Amendment IX

*Ratified December 15, 1791*

The enumeration in the Constitution, of certain rights, shall not be construed to deny or disparage others retained by the people.

## Amendment X

*Ratified December 15, 1791*

The powers not delegated to the United States by the Constitution, nor prohibited by it to the States, are reserved to the States respectively, or to the people.

APPENDIX E

# Suggestions for Further Reading

Bernard Bailyn, *The Ideological Origins of the American Revolution* (Cambridge, Mass.: Harvard University Press, 1967).

T. H. Breen, *The Marketplace of Revolution: How Consumer Politics Shaped American Independence* (New York: Oxford University Press, 2004).

Benjamin L. Carp, *Defiance of the Patriots: The Boston Tea Party and the Making of America* (New Haven, Conn.: Yale University Press, 2010).

Don Higginbotham, *The War of American Independence: Military Attitudes, Policies, and Practice, 1763–1789* (New York: Macmillan, 1971).

Maya Jasanoff, *Liberty's Exiles: American Loyalists in the Revolutionary World* (New York: Alfred A. Knopf, 2011).

Pauline Maier, *From Resistance to Revolution: Colonial Radicals and the Development of American Opposition to Britain, 1765–1776* (New York: Alfred A. Knopf, 1972).

Robert Middlekauff, *The Glorious Cause: The American Revolution, 1763–1789* (New York: Oxford University Press, 1982).

Edmund S. Morgan, *American Slavery, American Freedom: The Ordeal of Colonial Virginia* (New York: W. W. Norton, 1975).

Barbara B. Oberg, ed., *Women in the American Revolution: Gender, Politics, and the Domestic World* (Charlottesville, Va.: University of Virginia Press, 2019).

Robert G. Parkinson, *The Common Cause: Creating Race and Nation in the American Revolution* (Chapel Hill, N.C.: University of North Carolina Press, 2016).

Charles Royster, *A Revolutionary People at War: The Continental Army and American Character, 1775–1783* (Chapel Hill, N.C.: University of North Carolina Press, 1979).

John A. Ruddiman, *Becoming Men of Some Consequence: Youth and Military Service in the Revolutionary War* (Charlottesville, Va.: University of Virginia Press, 2014).

Seanegan P. Sculley, *Contest for Liberty: Military Leadership in the Continental Army, 1775–1783* (Yardley, Penn.: Westholme, 2019).

Craig Bruce Smith, *American Honor: The Creation of the Nation's Ideals during the Revolutionary Era* (Chapel Hill, N.C.: University of North Carolina Press, 2018).

Judith L. Van Buskirk, *Standing in Their Own Light: African American Patriots in the American Revolution* (Norman, Okla.: University of Oklahoma Press, 2017).

David Waldstreicher, *In the Midst of Perpetual Fetes: The Making of American Nationalism, 1776–1820* (Chapel Hill, N.C.: University of North Carolina Press, 1997).

Gordon S. Wood, *The Creation of the American Republic, 1776–1787* (Chapel Hill, N.C.: University of North Carolina Press, 1969).

Gordon S. Wood, *The Radicalism of the American Revolution* (New York: Alfred A. Knopf, 1992).